The Career Is Dead—
Long Live the Career

The Career Is Dead— Long Live the Career

A Relational Approach to Careers

Douglas T. Hall and Associates

Jossey-Bass Publishers • San Francisco

Figure 1. Career states (learning versus age). The new model: learning stages. From "Psychological Success and the Boundaryless Career" by Philip H. Mirvis and Douglas T. Hall in *Journal of Organizational Behavior,* Vol. 15, 365–380 (1994), p. 371. Copyright © 1994 by John Wiley & Sons, Ltd. Reprinted by permission.

Substantial discounts on bulk quantities of Jossey-Bass books are available to corporations, professional associations, and other organizations. For details and discount information, contact the special sales department at Jossey-Bass Inc., Publishers (415) 433–1740; Fax (800) 605–2665.

For sales outside the United States, please contact your local Simon & Schuster International Office.

 Manufactured in the United States of America on Lyons Falls Pathfinder Tradebook. This paper is acid-free and 100 percent totally chlorine-free.

Library of Congress Cataloging-in-Publication Data

Hall, Douglas T., date.
    The career is dead—long live the career : a relational approach
to careers / Douglas T. Hall and associates.—1st ed.
        p. cm.—(The Jossey-Bass business and management series)
    Includes bibliographical references and index.
    ISBN 0-7879-0233-0
    1. Career development.   I. Title.   II. Series.
HF5381.H1316   1996
650.14—dc20   96-11293

FIRST EDITION
HB Printing 10 9 8 7 6 5 4 3 2 1

The Jossey-Bass
Business & Management Series

Contents

Preface

Twenty years ago, I wrote a book called *Careers in Organizations*. Near the end of that book, I speculated that there would be a new form of career emerging, the *protean career,* which means a career that is driven more by the individual than the organization. This career would call for frequent change and self-invention and would be propelled by the desire for psychological success rather than by externally determined measures of success.

Then ten years ago, I edited another book, *Career Development in Organizations,* in which my colleagues and I delved into those factors in the organizational work environment that drive career development. This work was very much rooted in the culture of the 1980s, a time when organizations were beginning to restructure and were calling on career professionals to develop "strategic human resource management" to create programs for effective selection, utilization, and development of employees in their careers.

Looking back, it appears that the 1980s were the heyday of the organizational career. At that point, careers appeared to be anything but protean. In the resource-constrained world of that time, those people who were fortunate enough to still have jobs were more concerned with meeting corporate expectations and surviving than they were with finding their own path.

Fortunately (for me), at that point not many people thought much about my 1976 ideas on the protean career. A lucky few careerists were making a killing on Wall Street, in law firms, and in corporate life, but most were barely holding on. Even those who were doing well financially were not doing so well personally, putting in grueling hours, with high stress, low security, constant travel, and gnawing doubts about the intrinsic value of the work they were doing.

So here we are in 1996, and here is another book on careers . . . and lo and behold, the protean career is here. Although resources are still tight, organizational and social cultures have changed enough so that people no longer expect—or, in many cases, want—a long-term career within a particular organization; more likely, they think, If I can't get to the top or make a big financial killing, I might as well do what I really want to do. Furthermore, those who did do well financially or organizationally have seen that the rewards from those achievements were not completely satisfying and that there is more to life.

As we approach the twenty-first century, then, our career focus has shifted inward. The driving questions are now more about meaning than money, purpose than power, identity than ego, and learning than attainments. When no one was looking, the protean career snuck up on us!

Let's check in again in 2006.

Purpose and Audience

This book, then, is about these changes in our work and career environments. It is aimed at career practitioners, those professionals who help individuals and organizations improve their development practices. There is a need for new theoretical inputs to the field of career practice, and we see this volume as a sort of reference manual for the informed professional.

Although we hope this book will be useful for individuals who are developing their own careers, our primary audience is the person who coaches, counsels, and consults with individuals and organizations regarding career matters (programs, policies, decisions, crises). We want to provide practical help, not just new theoretical or research perspectives. (However, we also hope that it will be helpful at times to provide new perspectives.)

Examples of career professionals might be career consultants, counselors, staff members in school career centers, human resource development professionals, therapists, outplacement consultants, executive search consultants, management consultants, and students and faculty who teach about and study careers.

Although the other chapter authors and I attempt to provide practical recommendations, the fact is that we are speaking from our own particular experience base, which for most of us is academic. Indeed, a career professional reading this book probably has a better sense of the practical implications of these ideas than we ever could. So this is not a "how-to" book but rather a "think-about-how-to" book!

Our hope is that this volume will be useful for new insights on vexing problems and for an advance look at emerging issues (for example, *single adults without dependent children*). Because the field of organizational career development has changed so fundamentally in recent years, we think there is a need to provide the career practitioner with new ways of understanding the current landscape.

In this spirit, we welcome feedback from you who are career professionals: how do these ideas relate to your own practice, and how can we modify our ideas based on your experiences? (Please send feedback to us care of The Business & Management Series, Jossey-Bass Inc., Publishers.)

Who Are We?

Although the authors of this volume work in quite different areas of research, we have come to realize that we all share a deep interest in certain perspectives: meaning, values, connection and community, development over time, and the value of linking theory and practice. We are all connected in some way to the Organizational Behavior Department and a related research center, the Executive Development Roundtable, both at Boston University (we are all either current or former faculty, students, roundtable members, or collaborators).

In our department at Boston University, we have a tradition of inquiry into what we call *transforming ideas,* ideas and theories that fundamentally affect practice and in turn are informed by action. I think this orientation is especially useful in the study and practice of careers. My request to my colleagues was to "think careers" as they wrote about their most recent research on individuals' experiences in work settings. As Mike Arthur, Barbara Lawrence, and I have said earlier, career theory is badly in need of new perspectives. We tried to provide some in *Handbook of Career Theory,* and it is my hope that the reader will find some here as well.

Acknowledgments

Like the field we are describing in this book, the book itself is a relational product. In addition to the gratitude expressed by the individual authors in their respective chapters, I would like to offer thanks for the many sources of support for this project.

First, I would like to thank the School of Management and the Department of Organizational Behavior at Boston University for providing such fertile ground for relevant research. In particular, thanks to Dean Lou Lataif and our department chair, Leonard Johnson. Also, our crack department office staff, headed by Betty Pereira, has always been there when needed.

We are also blessed in the Organizational Behavior Department to have such an outstanding doctoral program, whose members stimulate us all; five of those members contributed chapters to this book: Barbara Altman, Joyce Fletcher, Vicky Parker, Mary Young, and Kent Seibert. All of their chapters break important new ground, and I am proud to have them appear in this volume.

Another important source of learning for many of us faculty and students in the Boston University School of Management is our research centers, which represent true partnerships between industry and academe. In particular, the Executive Development Roundtable has supported a program of research on executive development and learning, which informs many of the chapters in this book. The opportunity to work with the thirty corporate members represents a field laboratory in which we in the university learn about new ideas by observing them in action. (In management, new ideas often start in practice rather than in a university laboratory.) I have been privileged to be able to serve as director of the roundtable, and a major part of that privilege has been the opportunity to work closely with our assistant director, Cindy Newson, who has shepherded this book project through all of its phases with speed, ease, and grace.

Two other research centers at the university have been important learning environments for me: the Human Resources Policy Institute and the Center for Research on Work and Family. Many thanks to colleagues Fred Foulkes, director of HRPI, and to Brad Googins, director, and Ellen Bankert, assistant director, of the Work/Family Center. I am particularly grateful for a grant from the Human Resources Policy Institute, which provided part of my sabbatical salary during the year this book was produced.

For me, an important relational source of development has been a group of male colleagues known variously as the Brookline Circle, the Mystic Knights of Marginality, and simply the Boys' Group. We are a support group of itinerant organizational behavior and organizational development educators and consultants that meet every month to discuss problems in our personal lives—and to save the world! Members include Lee Bolman, Dave Brown, Todd Jick, Bill Kahn, Phil Mirvis, and Barry Oshry. As an only child, I now know how good it feels to have brothers—without all the dysfunctional family dynamics!

At Jossey-Bass, my colleagues and I are all extremely grateful to our first editor, Sarah Polster, who helped us frame the project and identify our audience. She was a marvelous consultant to us, and we hope she is pleased with the final product. We wish her great success (psychologically and otherwise) with her new religion series for Jossey-Bass. More recently, we have been most fortunate to have the gifts of editors Cedric Crocker, Byron Schneider, and Lasell Whipple on this project. Their wise counsel in the review, revision, and production process was most helpful, as was their general enthusiasm for the project.

Most importantly, I want to thank two members of my family who have provided the ground for this work. Marcy Crary, my soulmate, wife, confidant, and partner in love, homebuilding, and parenting, is the most generous person I have ever known. Her love and support have been a secure base for me, and I have learned much from her about families, interpersonal dynamics, difference, humor, and the importance of being on time.

My father, Robert E. Hall, taught me about the protean career and psychological success. He has always pursued his own path and aspired to psychological success for himself and his family. He is my "career hero." The goals and qualities that I value (unconditional love, autonomy, finding meaning, psychological success) I learned from him. This one's for you, Dad!

West Newton, Massachusetts   DOUGLAS T. HALL
February 1996

To Robert E. Hall

The Authors

DOUGLAS T. (TIM) HALL is a professor of organizational behavior in the School of Management at Boston University, where he has served as acting dean and associate dean of faculty development and faculty director for the master's programs. He is also the director of the Executive Development Roundtable and a core faculty member of the Human Resources Policy Institute. He received his B.S. degree from Yale University and his M.S. and Ph.D. degrees from the Sloan School of Management at Massachusetts Institute of Technology. He has held faculty positions at Yale, York, Michigan State, and Northwestern Universities as well as visiting positions at Columbia and the U.S. Military Academy at West Point.

The author of many books on career issues and the recipient of the American Psychological Association's Ghiselli Award, Hall is a fellow of the American Psychological Association and of the Academy of Management. He has been a member of the board of governors of the Center for Creative Leadership, and he has served on the editorial boards of seven scholarly journals. His research—as well as his consulting activities with such organizations as Sears, AT&T, and Eli Lilly—have dealt with career development, women's careers, career plateauing, work-family balance, and executive succession.

Barbara W. Altman is an advanced doctoral candidate at Boston University's School of Management. Her research interests include business-society relations, organizational change, environmental management, and executive development. At Boston University she has played a major role in four research projects: The Changing Purpose of the American Corporation, Environmental Challenges for American Manufacturing, Organizational Learning and Corporate Environmentalism, and Creating the Learning Organization. She has published findings from these studies in the *Academy of Management Executive*, the *Journal of Organizational Change*

Management, and *Research in Corporate Social Performance and Policy.* Altman's research, teaching, and consulting is enlightened by her previous career in municipal management, where she gained expertise in environmental and community affairs, public-private partnerships, public financial management, and organizational restructuring. Her dissertation investigates the influences of managerial values and corporate strategy on the current practice of corporate community relations.

Joyce K. Fletcher is an associate professor of cooperative education at Northeastern University's College of Business Administration and currently holds a two-year appointment as the Asa S. Knowles Research Fellow at Northeastern's newly established Institute for Learning, Work and the Workplace. She teaches in the field of experiential learning and consults to organizations in areas related to organizational learning, gender equity, and work and family integration. Her research interest lies in applying feminist theory to organizational issues related to learning, equity, and adult development.

Jane L. Hodgetts is president of Hodgetts Associates, a Newton, Massachusetts-based firm specializing in coaching and consulting to individuals and groups for career and life transition issues. She has lectured at Boston University and led workshops in many organizations. Hodgetts has worked in the career development field for thirteen years in the public and private sectors as a consultant, trainer, counselor, and manager. She holds an M.B.A. degree from Harvard Business School and a B.S. degree in human development and psychology from Cornell University.

William H. Hodgetts is a director of management and organizational development at Fidelity Investments. His primary responsibilities include executive development, individual coaching, and facilitating organizational learning across business units. He has worked as an internal organizational development consultant at Fidelity for over thirteen years. Hodgetts holds a Ph.D. degree in human development and psychology from Harvard University, where he specialized in adult development and organizational behavior. His dissertation research involved studying the impact of gender and ego stage (levels of psychological maturity) on managerial authority styles and transitions at midlife.

William A. Kahn is an associate professor of organizational behavior at Boston University. He received his Ph.D. degree in psychology at Yale University in 1987. His research and consulting focus is on the creation of meaningful attachments among organization members to facilitate individual and organizational effectiveness. He is particularly interested in action research with caregiving organizations that focuses on creating conditions in which organization members feel securely attached to one another. His articles on the nature of work attachments have appeared in *Administrative Science Quarterly, Human Relations, Academy of Management Journal,* and the *Journal of Applied Behavioral Science.*

Kathy E. Kram is an associate professor in the Department of Organizational Behavior at the Boston University School of Management. Her primary interests are in the areas of adult development and career dynamics, values and ethics in corporate decision making, diversity issues in executive development, gender and leadership, and organizational change processes. In addition to her book, *Mentoring at Work,* she has published in a wide range of journals including *Organizational Dynamics, Academy of Management Journal, Academy of Management Review, Business Horizons, Qualitative Sociology, Mentoring International, Journal of Management Development, Organizational Behavior and Human Performance,* and *Psychology of Women Quarterly.* Kram teaches courses in global management, leadership, team dynamics, and organizational change and consults with private and public sector organizations on a variety of human resource management concerns. She received her B.S. and M.S. degrees from the M.I.T. Sloan School of Management and her Ph.D. degree from Yale University.

Meryl Reis Louis is an associate professor of organizational behavior at the School of Management at Boston University where she was also a senior research associate at the Center for Applied Social Science for five years. Before returning to the University of California, Los Angeles, where she earned her Ph.D. degree in the organizational sciences, she served on the consulting staff of

Arthur Andersen & Co. and worked as a paraprofessional counselor at a community mental health center. Her substantive research has focused on career transitions and organizational socialization, workplace cultures, and cognitive processes in organizational settings. Most recently, her interests have led her to examine life in post-bureaucratic organizations.

Philip H. Mirvis is an organizational psychologist whose research and private practice concerns large-scale organizational change and the character of the workforce and workplace. A regular contributor to academic and professional journals, he has authored six books, including *Failures in Organizational Development and Change, Managing the Merger,* the highly acclaimed study of national attitudes, *The Cynical Americans,* and most recently, a survey of corporate human resource strategies, *Building the Competitive Workforce.* He has led seminars all over the United States, addressed many university facilities and professional groups, and lectured throughout Europe and in China, India, Japan, Latvia, and Russia. Among Mirvis's corporate clients are Ben & Jerry's and Hewlett-Packard; his government and nonprofit clients include Blue Cross/Blue Shield, National Association of Meal Providers, and the National Council on Aging. He is a member of the board of directors of the Foundation for Community Encouragement.

Mirvis received his B.A. degree from Yale University and his Ph.D. degree in organizational psychology from the University of Michigan. He has been a professor in the School of Management at Boston University and has held research positions at Boston University's Center for Applied Social Science and at the University of Michigan's Institute for Social Research.

Victoria A. Parker is currently doing dissertation fieldwork in the department of Organizational Behavior at the Boston University School of Management, examining the linkages between organizational context and the quality of interpersonal relationships formed between care providers and their clients. Parker received her A.B. degree (1981) in biology/health and society from Brown University and her Ed.M. degree (1988) from the Harvard Graduate School of Education and has taught in the undergraduate management program at Boston University. Prior to pursuing her graduate education, she worked in both commercial banking and higher education administration. Her research interests include work and home linkages, adult and career development, group dynamics, care-giving work, and gender relations in organizations.

James E. Post is professor of management at Boston University. He holds graduate degrees in law and management and teaches in the areas of strategic management, business-government relations, and public affairs management. Post is also a senior research fellow at The Conference Board, where he previously served as director of the business and society research program. The author of more than a hundred publications on public affairs and the role of business in society, he is coauthor (with William C. Frederick, Anne T. Lawrence, and James Weber) of *Business and Society: Corporate Strategy, Public Policy, and Ethics*, recently published in its eighth edition. His recent research has focused on long-term trends in corporate economic and social performance.

Kent W. Seibert is assistant professor of business and economics at Wheaton College in Illinois. He recently received a Best Paper Award from the Eastern Academy of Management for "The Reflective Manager: Oxymoron or Imperative?" Seibert received his A.B. degree (1979) in psychology from Kenyon College and two M.A. degrees (1982 and 1983) in industrial psychology and industrial relations from the University of Minnesota. He is currently in the final stages of doctoral studies in organizational behavior at Boston University. His current research interest is in the area of naturally occurring learning in the workplace.

Barbara A. Walker is the key architect of Valuing Differences, a diversity model widely used in the corporate world to help people deal with the complex issues created by all kinds of differences. In 1983, she became Digital Equipment Corporation's, as well as the country's, first valuing differences manager. At Digital, Walker led the design and implementation of a company-wide network of ongoing Dialogue groups as the primary instrument of the Valuing Differences work. Prior to joining Digital in 1979, she spent seventeen years in legal and management positions in the U.S. Federal Government in Washington, D.C., including deputy assistant general counsel and national training director for the Office for Civil Rights. Since leaving Digital, she has worked as vice president of human resources and diversity at the University of Cincinnati and as director of diversity at a small high-tech company in Silicon Valley in California. She is an attorney with degrees from Howard University and Georgetown Law School.

Mary Young is currently completing her D.B.A. degree in organizational behavior from Boston University. Her research interests include organizational communication, careers, the role of business in society, and the interface between work and personal life. Her dissertation examines the relationship between employees' life status, their work time, and other outcomes. She is particularly interested in career issues for single adults without dependent children. With Douglas T. Hall, she is also studying the career impacts of computer-mediated communication. She contributed a chapter to *A Fatal Embrace? Assessment Holistic Trends in Human Resources Programs* (Heuberger and Nash, 1994) and has published articles in the *Journal of Management Education* and *Organizational Dynamics*. She teaches organizational behavior and management communication in Boston University's M.B.A. program.

The Career Is Dead—
Long Live the Career

Long Live the Career
A Relational Approach
Douglas T. Hall

The career is dead—long live the career: A relational approach to careers. What does the strange title of this book mean?

The career as we once knew it—as a series of upward moves, with steadily increasing income, power, status, and security—has died. Nevertheless, people will always have work lives that unfold over time, offering challenge, growth, and learning. So if we think of the career as a series of lifelong work-related experiences and personal learnings (Hall, 1976), it will never die.

Our title also means that not only has the career itself changed but also our understanding of the influences on the career has changed. Whereas in the past we tended to look more at the external career, the actual jobs or positions that a person holds over the course of the career, what seems to be more important now is the internal career, the person's perceptions and self-constructions of career phenomena. As we will argue, this shift from outside to inside as the place where the career lives is happening both in people's actual experience as well as in scholars' inquiry into career matters.

Still another meaning of our title is that many of the traditional theoretical models for explaining career phenomena seem less valid today than they did twenty or thirty years ago. Models based on notions of organizations as pyramids and careers as regular progressions through ladder-like job sequences seem as outdated as the organizational forms on which they were based. Instead, we can better understand the career experience by separating it into its component elements: work, people, identity and subidentities, difference, community, meaning, learning processes, aging, development, and organizations. As careers have changed, so have the conceptual perspectives necessary to understand them (Arthur, Hall, and Lawrence, 1989; Arthur, Claman, and DeFillippi, 1995).

A Relational Approach

What does our subtitle, "A relational approach to careers," mean?

This book is an exploration of the subjective career as it is played out in relation to today's work environment—work challenges, relationships, and a multitude of experiences. Although many organizational resources are vanishing, the primary resources for career development—work challenges and relationships with other people (Hall and Associates, 1986; McCall, Lombardo, and Morrison, 1988)—have never been so plentiful. Indeed, the more turbulent and difficult conditions become in today's work settings, the more naturally occurring work challenges there are (Hall and Richter, 1990) and the more motivated people are to give and receive help (Kram and Hall, 1991; in press) because most people realize that banding together is the best bet for survival.

In contrast to the traditional view of development, which is based on individual mastery and the development of autonomy, the relational approach, as described in Chapter Four of this volume, points out that the earliest forms of child development take place in a context of connection and mutual influence and benefit. In this relational view, development is a mutual process rather than one in which one person is the "agent" of growth (the parent, the teacher, the mentor) and the other party is the "learner" (the child, the student, the protégé). In fact, in the current organizational world, career development and mentoring is necessarily a process of *colearning* (Kram and Hall, in press) because change is occurring so rapidly and junior parties to a relationship often are more expert in certain areas (such as technology) than are their seniors.

The object of growth in the relational model is not individual mastery and independence but rather interdependence. In today's complex, chaotic world, achieving understanding of how things work is beyond the ken of one person and instead demands pooled or social intelligence (Wheatley, 1994).

In addition to mutuality and interdependence, the relational approach to development also entails reciprocity, the expectation that both parties to a developmental relationship will possess the skills to function as interdependent colearners and that they will be motivated to use these skills (Arthur, 1994; Chapter Four, this volume). Thus either party could be the "teacher" or the "learner" in any given situation, with both roles equally valued. In fact, one might even question making a distinction between teaching and learning, as it is becoming clear that the best ways to learn are through teaching and co-inquiry. *Learner* appears to be the superordinate term, and we would argue that the most powerful form of development in the contemporary work setting is continuous mutual learning.

In this book, you will find varying degrees of explicit use of the dimensions of relational learning. Some, such as Chapter Six on the "secure base" for learning or Chapter Seven on extra-organizational relationships or Chapters Four and Five on relational theory, are very explicit in their use of relational concepts. Others, such as Chapter Two on the new social contract or Chapter Eight's introduction of the notion of "SAWDCs" (single adults without dependent children), use relational concepts in a background sense, as part of the social environment in which contemporary career issues are being played out.

All of the writers, however, share the view that the relational environment of the present and future work world is a primary influence on career development. Indeed, this is the silver lining in the cloud of turbulence and corporate anorexia that we are seeing in today's downsized organizations: while most resources are declining rapidly, relational resources (connections to others around work tasks) have never been greater than they are in this era of teams, projects, and information networks.

Development

The value of the relational perspective is that it sheds light on new ways to think about and promote development. Since we are always living and working in a relationship-rich environment, this approach has tremendous implications for the work of career practitioners.

Growth happens when a person becomes more competent in interacting with his or her environment and experiences a more competent and confident self-identity as a result (White, 1959). A person's identity does not occur in a vacuum. It is a social product, the result of repeated exchanges with others significant in one's world. It is through relationships (and feedback and help and caring) that we discover who we are, what we do best, and how to be better. Thus, in the new career, notions of caregiving, mentoring, caring and respect, connection, and colearning (that is, learning through relationship with others), especially colearning with others whom one regards as different, provide the clues to growth and success. For example, Arthur, Claman, and DeFillippi (1995) describe "knowing whom" as one of three key competencies in the "intelligent career," along with "knowing how" and "knowing why." While many people might not associate these relational experiences with a term such as *career*, it is in these areas that we hope this volume will contribute to new career understandings.

This book, then, is about how people *develop* in their work and careers. We want to provide practical ideas for how people can grow in their career work and lead more meaningful, psychologically successful lives. We do not focus on static issues such as the fit between people and their work or organizations but rather on how these fits and other career experiences are constantly shifting around over the course of an individual lifetime.

The New Career Contract

Although we know that careers are shaped by relationships (Hall, 1976; Hall and Associates, 1986), this book represents the first effort to apply the relational model of development to careers.

It is our view that in this "age of unreason," as Charles Handy describes it (1989), people are experiencing turbulence, anxiety, and dis-ease. The old sense of security achieved through educational and career attainments and long-term organizational memberships is lost and mourned (and in fact may never have been as great as we now imagine). The "psychological contract" between the employee and the organization has shrunk to what Jack Welch, CEO of General Electric, has called a one-day contract, in which all that counts is the current value that each party contributes to the relationship.

Purpose and Learning

Like the career, the psychological contract and the major promoters of development (work challenges and relationships) are drastically changed. We see the new contract as one in which the individual contributes strong performance in response to customer needs, continuously learning in relation to others, with adaptability in developing new competencies as the business environment changes. The organization, on the other hand, can offer meaning and purpose, developmental relationships, space for learning, and good rewards and benefits, based on the employee's performance, flexibility, motivation, and ability to grow.

The "glue" that can hold this new relational contract together is business success, clarity of purpose and direction (for organization and individual), and healthy levels of mutual connection, respect, and trust. Now more than ever, people are seeking to base their careers on doing work that has meaning and produces value for the world and to do it in an organization whose purpose and values they can respect. This sense of meaning and purpose, along with good opportunities for continuous learning and development, has become the new corporate contribution to the contract, replacing job security. These ideas are developed in detail in Chapters One and Two.

Psychological Success

For the individual, the lack of security in the current organizational environment means that safety must now be generated internally, including developing the ability to marshal outside resources such as developmental relationships and stretching tasks. This means not only having solid skills and the ability to learn new ones quickly (not to mention being able to know what and when to learn)—it also means being able to learn about oneself, often with the help of friends (as well as to adapt and "reinvent" oneself from time to time). More than "knowing yourself" and "taking charge," you must know how to assess yourself, how to engage in self-inquiry and self-reflection, and how to ask for help in doing so.

The ability to be a continuous learner and to redirect one's life and career is what I call the *protean career* (Hall, 1976). In fact, it is precisely the excitement that comes from this continuous learning that is the major source of motivation in today's workplace, and it is the quest for psychological success—the fulfillment of one's own personal values and purpose and goals—that is driving the worker. Indeed, fewer people are pursuing that external "carrot" (be it power, money, or security) because in today's flatter organization and lower-paying wage structure, it simply does not exist. In the traditional career, the important goal was keeping up with the Joneses; now the individual is thinking, I've got my own life to lead!

The Dark Side of the New Contract

Although we believe that protean careers are self-invented, self-managed, and relational—or at least that they can be—we need to acknowledge that there is a dark side to this new career contract. Not everyone has the skills, relational help, self-esteem, past experience of psychological success, personal optimism, health, or other resources to be a continuous learner, which is required to make effective protean life changes. People who lack a basic education will find the world of the new contract very difficult. People who are not comfortable with technology will be at a disadvantage. People who are loners, uncomfortable being interdependent in novel situations, will be equally at a loss. In addition, many older workers will encounter prejudices and stereotypes that will make it difficult for them to show their protean sides. To compound these problems, the fact that many employees are and will continue to be working in contingent positions (as independent contractors, not as regular employees) means that the security of basic health care, pension, and other employee benefits will not be available to them.

Our emphasis in this book is on how workers can make the most of the opportunities afforded by the new work arrangements—how to take advantage of autonomy to develop continuous mutual learning, to build needed new skills, and to develop connections. Of course, we cannot claim that all who try will be successful. Our hope is that the book contains enough different approaches so that something will work.

Holistic Reframing of Career and Personal Life

What is needed in career theory and practice is a more holistic view of the individual, one that encompasses all spheres of activity and all corresponding facets of personal identity. When we look at career and occupational experiences later in the individual's life, we need to see these experiences in the context of that individual's total life, encompassing all other important current roles and sub-identities as well as hopes and dreams for the future. We need to look at the individual's overall quest for meaning and purpose as she or he pursues what Shepard (1984) calls "the path with a heart." (We know that these concerns are especially important for people at midlife and beyond [Levinson, 1986].) This requires the use of concepts and research methods that will let us probe the individual's sense of direction in the search for work that has personal meaning.

Viewing the career as a personal quest also implies finding influences on development that are uniquely equipped to promote personal development. As we will attempt to show in these chapters, relational influences are powerful methods for this task. More than formal education methods, more than the career self-help instrument, and even more than on-the-job learning, learning in the context of a caring relationship can create the conditions of openness, trust, vulnerability, and experimentation that can lead to the creation of new parts of the self.

In Part One, we look at the current environment in which careers are being played out. We discuss the driving forces behind the demands for new career competencies and attitudes. Then, in Part Two, we turn to those factors in the current environment that have the potential to help people grow in their careers. We conclude in Part Three with an examination of some new, hopeful methods of utilizing these relational influences in everyday work environments.

Overview of This Book

In Chapter One, Hall and Mirvis describe the "new career"—one that is protean or self-invented and striving for psychological success. This chapter suggests that we need to reframe the way we have been thinking of concepts such as career, family, personal, and so forth; each concept represents a part of an overall identity, and each part may contain subidentities. The chapter also describes how careers evolve: not as one single, lifelong set of career stages, as this writer earlier postulated (Hall, 1976), but as a series of career learning cycles with each cycle containing a set of ministages (exploration, trial, mastery).

Chapter Two by Altman and Post turns from the new career to the new "social contract": the new set of mutual employee-employer expectations that govern the career within an organization. Their survey of senior executives confirms the idea that the career is indeed the individual's responsibility (that is, protean), although the goal of maintaining employability is shared by employer and employee.

As Altman and Post spell out the ramifications of their findings, it is clear that there are some ominous signals here, as well as much potential for individual freedom and fulfillment. Chapter Three, by Mirvis and Hall, picks up on these specific implications of the new organization for career development. In particular, the authors look at the new forms of flexibility in the workplace and the concomitant flexibility they create—and indeed demand—in the new worker.

Rather than focus on specific job design characteristics such as "flexibility," we should look at the larger issue of how well the person's overall set of needs is being met by these work arrangements. This gets us into the issue of looking more deeply into the process of development, its relational nature and what nurtures it—the domain of Part Two. Fletcher, in Chapter Four, introduces in detail the theory of the relational model of growth-in-connection and its relevance to the protean career. This chapter breaks important new ground in career theory by showing how our traditional models of career development have been based on striving for autonomy and mastery and how we can now achieve higher levels of personal development by looking at careers from the perspective of relationships.

Kathy Kram, in Chapter Five, picks up this idea of other people as a prime source of development. She takes another look at the models of development that underlie most of our traditional work on careers and shows how powerful the relational elements are in the process of career growth as well as how to use relationships more effectively.

A more relational, holistic view could also mean focusing on restructuring work environments to make them less stressful and more secure. Chapter Six by William Kahn discusses attachment theory, the need of the growing person to have a secure base to provide the foundation for exploration, along with opportunities to explore and stretch. Caregiving and psychological availability of other people (peers, superiors, subordinates) in the work world are key ingredients in this mix of safety and challenge.

We are also asserting here that relationships are not bounded by the work environment, and all kinds of personal relationships have powerful effects on the person's development. In Chapter Seven, Victoria Parker discusses the different life settings and life-structure arrangements in which relationships are played out and the ways that they affect careers and growth. She also describes conditions under which the impacts of extra-organizational relationships are strengthened or weakened as well as ways to harness these connections in the service of career growth.

Mary Young (Chapter Eight) focuses on single adults without dependent children (SAWDCs). She describes the significance of this demographic group in contemporary society and how issues such as equity and work load arise between SAWDCs and other groups, such as employed parents of small children. Young shows how the issues of SAWDCs are issues that apply to *all* adults.

After identifying a number of new ways of viewing the relational influences on development, we turn to specific ideas for career-enhancing action. For organizational leaders in the new, competitive, high-stress workplace described in Part One, the implication of Part Two is that it will take conscious effort to create good conditions for personal career development. In particular, it is important to provide a sense of community—one that supports development, as Meryl Reis Louis argues in Chapter Nine. Such a developmental community is one in which all members at all levels can experience the sense of meaning and the psychological success that come from being part of a highly effective team or organization pursuing a valued purpose. Louis provides conceptual and concrete personal detail to show how "safe havens" can be created for reflection, for centering, and for marshaling resources.

The following chapter by Kent Seibert picks up on one kind of safe haven activity, the process of reflection. Seibert describes path-breaking research on the many ways managers reflect on and use experience in the service of growth. While many people believe that managers are too busy to reflect, Seibert's work shows that this is simply a myth. He discusses the different ways of thinking about reflection and presents his own model of how to describe and improve this process.

Barbara Walker (Chapter Eleven) picks up the issues of personal reflections on relationships in a safe environment and shows how relational learning is even more powerful when working with people whom one sees as different from oneself. Walker's work on valuing differences gives a new and much needed perspective for addressing issues of fairness and equal treatment, such as the glass ceiling.

At some point, if we are fortunate, we will all be older workers. Mirvis and Hall (Chapter Twelve) discuss the issues of aging in the career and how the concept of the protean career may look far less rosy to the over-fifty-five worker than to a twenty-four-year-old. By considering the effects of many years of work and the various ways in which the work experience is viewed by the worker and by others in the organization and outside, we reach a fuller understanding of the older person's current challenges.

One specific way to structure reflection, learning relationships, and other ways of learning in real time is the developmental sanctuary, as described in Chapter Thirteen by Jane and William Hodgetts. This concept, which has previously been applied to more clinical settings, is a powerful way of thinking through the kinds of conditions that can be created, with minimal expense, by arranging space and time for social reflection and support. The Hodgetts also identify key issues and dilemmas for career practitioners as well as frequently asked questions about developmental support groups.

The final two chapters, by this writer, consider what organizations and career practitioners are doing today—and what they might do in the future. It seems clear that we are just beginning to scratch the surface of what might be done with more conscious use of these natural and "free" career resources, such as relationships, work challenges, and reflection, in the service of a life worth living.

A Final Thought

Let us be mindful that there is much wisdom on this topic that may have become, for some of us, lost in familiar places. Remember the words attributed to Ralph Waldo Emerson on success:

> To laugh often and much; to win the respect of intelligent people and the affection of children; to earn the appreciation of honest critics and endure the betrayal of false friends; to appreciate beauty, to find the best in others; to leave the world a bit better, whether by a healthy child, a garden patch or a redeemed social condition; to know even one life has breathed easier because you lived. This is to have succeeded.

References

Arthur, M. B. (1994). The boundaryless career: A new perspective for organizational inquiry. *Journal of Organizational Behavior, 15,* 295–306.

Arthur, M. B., Claman, P. H., & DeFillippi, R. J. (1995). Intelligent enterprise, intelligent careers. *Academy of Management Executive, 9*(4), 1–15.

Arthur, M. B., Hall, D. T., & Lawrence, B. S. (Eds.). (1989). *The handbook of career theory.* New York: Cambridge University Press.

Hall, D. T. (1976). *Careers in organizations.* Glenview, IL: Scott, Foresman.

Hall, D. T., & Associates. (1986). *Career development in organizations.* San Francisco: Jossey-Bass.

Hall, D. T., & Richter, J. (1990). Baby-boomers hit the wall: Career gridlock? *Academy of Management Executive, 4*(3), 7–22.

Handy, C. (1989). *The age of unreason.* Boston: Harvard Business School Press.

Kram, K. E., & Hall, D. T. (1991). Mentoring as an antidote to stress during corporate trauma. *Human Resource Management, 28*(4), 493–510.

Kram, K. E., & Hall, D. T. (in press). Mentoring in a context of diversity and turbulence. In S. Lobel & E. E. Kossek (Eds.), *Human resource strategies for managing diversity.* London, England: Blackwell.

Levinson, D. J. (1986). A conception of adult development. *American Psychologist, 41,* 3–13.

McCall, M. W., Lombardo, M. M., & Morrison, A. M. (1988). *The lessons of experience.* Lexington, MA: Lexington Books.

Shepard, H. A. (1984). On the realization of human potential: A path with a heart. In Arthur, M. B., Bailyn, L., Levinson, D. J., & Shepard,

H. A. (Eds.), *Working with careers.* New York: Center for Research on Careers, Graduate School of Business, Columbia University.

Wheatley, M. J. (1994). *Leadership and the new science: Learning about organization from an orderly universe.* San Francisco: Berrett-Koehler.

White, R. W. (1959). Motivation reconsidered: The concept of competence. *Psychological Review, 66,* 297–323.

Part One

What's Happening in the New Organization?

"A funny thing happened on the way to the future."

This is the way Warren Bennis described contemporary organizations in the light of his futuristic predictions in the late 1960s and early 1970s. Bennis and others (such as Alvin Toffler and Philip Slater) predicted a "temporary society," a world of small, decentralized, fast-moving, project-oriented organizations, operating in a world of "ad-hocracy." Along with these ideas about new structures came rosy predictions about the personal liberation associated with this greater freedom and responsibility in the work setting.

Although the basic prediction of free, fast, and flexible structures proved prophetic ("AT&T will split into 3 companies: Efficiency, economy key to breakup," said the *Boston Globe* on September 21, 1995, p. 1), there have been many unforeseen personal consequences that are not so positive: the career effects have been profound.

How can we help people make sense of a strange new world? The first step is to help them understand the nature of that world. Making sense of the new world of careers is the scope of Part One.

In particular, we will show how the nature of careers has changed fundamentally, and we will explore the factors that contribute to career development. As the Introduction and Chapter One will show, careers are now driven by relational and personal influences, not organizational influences. There is much personal freedom, along with commensurate personal responsibility and demands for continuous learning.

With this shift in the career terrain, there has also been a basic change in the "career contract," the set of mutual expectations governing the relationship between employer and employee. Chapters One and Two discuss how this contract has shifted toward a more protean, shorter-term, transaction-based understanding, with the employee acting as a free agent. The new "glue," when the contract succeeds, is psychological success.

In Chapter Three, we look in more detail at the new organization and the changed workplace. By considering the kinds of flexibility demanded of the new organization, we can see how these translate into the new competencies required of employees. In the new workplace, people who can adapt quickly, learn continuously, and change their work identities over time will be fortunate enough to chart their own paths.

Chapter One

The New Protean Career

Psychological Success and the Path with a Heart

Douglas T. Hall
Philip H. Mirvis

> *Just remember: Even if you win the rat race . . . you're still a rat.*
> THE REV. WILLIAM SLOANE COFFIN, ADDRESSING THE
> YALE FRESHMAN CLASS, 1958

> *Oh, no! I just realized I let a twenty-year-old choose my husband and my career!*
> KAREN LOPEZ, A FORTY-TWO-YEAR-OLD RESEARCH
> MANAGER WORKING ON A CAREER SELF-ASSESSMENT, 1984

Karen Lopez and Bill Coffin are looking at the same period in career history—the 1970s and 1980s—from two perspectives. Mr. Coffin is looking ahead from the vantage point of his early civil rights and social change work; his duty, as our college chaplain, was to care for our souls. He knew that these students (all male at that time) were headed right toward that rat race. For many of them, that would mean moving away from their true selves and from work with personal meaning. Ms. Lopez, a woman of the same generation as those students, looking back, suddenly realized that she, too, had followed that same soulless path.

Ironically, there is now a long-distance road race through the business district of Toronto in which all runners have to wear business suits and carry a brief case!

This chapter is about emerging changes in this pattern of people moving away from themselves. It is about caring for the self and caring for others and how to find one's own path and meaning in life and career. We will consider how a person's identity evolves through relationships and work and examine how today's role and information overload can produce unmanageable stress. We will also discuss a new type of career, the *protean career,* in which the person, not the organization, is the "driver," and we will talk a lot about the "new success," *psychological success.* Finally, we will see what lessons about the rat race we can learn from cormorants.

In this discussion, the concept of the changing career contract will be used to understand the gap between theory and reality (Hall, 1993). We will argue that the new environment places developmental demands on the individual for two key competencies, called *meta-competencies* (Hall, 1986a, 1986b) because they are the skills of learning how to learn: *identity growth* (more complexity, more self-reflection and self-learning) and increased *adaptability.* However, as Robert Kegan (1994) suggests, the majority of workers may not have developed these competencies; therefore, many of us are in over our heads.

We will look at how people get stuck in the same career routines, and we will see how people can get out of such ruts by developing these meta-skills through a process of *midcareer routine busting.* We will also posit a new model of career stages, which describes protean change processes throughout the career. We believe that work life and home life are integrated (connected but not necessarily balanced), like it or not, especially for the midlife and older worker, who is likely to have more complex subidentities than the younger worker. Finally, we will call for a more holistic approach to the study of the person, work life, and private life.

The New Career Contract

There has been a great deal of recent interest in the psychological contract between employer and employee and in the ways that the contract is changing (Hall and Mirvis, 1995a; Kotter, 1995; "The revolving door at Rubbermaid," 1995; Rousseau, 1990; DeMeuse and Tornow, 1990). Popular magazines such as *The Atlantic Monthly* and *Fortune* have run cover stories with headlines proclaiming "the end of jobs" (Barnet, 1993; Bridges, 1994).

A psychological career contract is of course not a legal document but rather a description of the relationship between employer and employee. As identified originally in contract terms by Harry Levinson (1962) and later by Schein (1965), as well as in the inducements-contributions theory of Barnard (1940) and Simon (1947), the psychological contract is a set of mutual expectations, often implicit, held by both parties to the employment relationship. As long as each party's expectations are met by the "contributions" (for example, the employee's performance output, the employer's pay and benefits) of the other, the relationship is a fair exchange and will continue.

Later, MacNeill (1980, 1985) identified two forms of the contract. The first is *relational*, based on a long-term mutual commitment to the relationship and on a trust that over time any temporary imbalances in inducements or contributions would even themselves out. (We would hasten to add that this is a more narrow use of the term *relational* than we are using when we talk about a "relational approach to development"; MacNeill is talking only about the person's relationship to an organization, whereas we mean a reciprocal, mutually beneficial, interdependent connection with another person.)

A contrasting form of psychological contract identified by MacNeill is *transactional*, which is based on a shorter-term exchange of benefits and services. Value is in the utility of the entities exchanged rather than in the relationship itself.

One view of the current situation is that the contract has shifted from relational to transactional relationship, meaning it is short term and performance based. As Jack Welch is reputed to have described it to his managers at General Electric, it is now a "one-day contract." This means that managers should expect employees to be loyal only as long as today's expectations are being met, and the firm does not deserve any more loyalty than that. Likewise, the company's commitment to the employee extends only to the current need for that person's skills and performance.

Whither the Old Contract?

Many of the jobs that have been eliminated through restructuring and reengineering have been cut permanently as part of the move toward Handy's "shamrock" organization, which we describe in detail in Chapter Three. (In a "shamrock" firm, one group of workers—one "leaf"—consists of core, full-time employees; a second consists of part-time workers; and a third consists of contract or contingent workers.) One observer has noted that the fastest-growing segments of the U.S. population are the prison population and the contingent workforce (the third leaf in Handy's shamrock).

Pick up any newspaper's business section on any given day, and you will probably find an article about some firm that has just announced a reduction of several thousand jobs. Between 1989 and 1993, even though the economy was recovering from a recession, the United States lost 1.6 million jobs in the manufacturing sector, and the losses are expected to continue (Mirvis, 1993). During the decade of the 1980s, 3.4 million jobs were eliminated from Fortune 500 firms, with many more removed from smaller and medium-sized companies (Barnet, 1993). One study of more than four hundred employers found that over 80 percent had downsized between 1986 and 1991, cutting their workforces by an average of 12.4 percent (Mirvis, 1993). Similar restructuring has taken place in the other industrialized countries as well, most recently in Japan (Sasseen, 1994).

The impact of these cuts ripples through a workforce and a society. In the United States, workers are spending more hours at work and taking home less pay than they were a decade earlier (Schor, 1991). Whereas the phenomenon of the two-career, two-earner couple was fueled in part by the need of some fortunate women to enter the workforce for personal satisfaction (Hall and Hall, 1979), now it has become an essential matter of economic survival. If it had not been for the existence of so many two-earner families in the United States, the last recession, with all of its job cuts, would have been a depression.

With these structural changes has come a corresponding drop in the career aspirations of those who work in corporations. Job insecurity has soared, and any thoughts of long-term careers in one firm have been shattered (Mirvis, 1992). Most American firms have cut back on health care benefits, and many have reduced pensions and health care coverage for retirees. Many in fact have simply eliminated retiree health benefits. The bottom line: job mobility and retirement look less attractive as career options to employees—exactly the opposite of what employers need to create flexibility in the workforce!

Not surprisingly, we are also seeing a rise in cynicism as the quality of the workplace deteriorates (Kanter and Mirvis, 1989). Over half of the American public believes that the leaders of big business care more about their own power and rewards than they do about the well-being of their companies or their employees. Nearly as many doubt the truth of what they are told by their own managers (Kanter and Mirvis, 1992). As a result, the workforce is less loyal than in years past, and employees are acting like "free agents" as they job hop in order to survive ("Downward Mobility," 1992; Hirsch, 1987).

In our opinion, American workers' sense of personal economic insecurity has contributed to the success of politicians opposed to affirmative action, social benefits for undocumented immigrants, and various forms of public support for low-income and unemployed people. The voters appear to be sending this message: "I have to work two or three jobs to survive, and I could be fired at any time, so why should my hard-earned tax money go to support someone who doesn't work or is here illegally? Why does everyone seem so concerned about 'them' and not about 'us'?"

The traditional career contract has been dead since the 1980s, although we have only faced reality and tolled the death knell in the last few years. We have gone from the yuppies of the 1980s to the dumpies (downwardly mobile professionals) of the 1990s. Furthermore, the current generation entering the workforce in the United States will be the first in history to fail to exceed the economic success of their parents. Exhibit 1.1 recently made its way to the bulletin board of a firm experiencing widespread layoffs.

From Organizational to Protean Careers

From the perspective of the individual, we are seeing a shift from the organizational career to the protean career (Hall, 1976, 1986a). This means decoupling the concept of career from a connection to any one organization (or to an organization, period) and even from its exclusive association with paid employment. Thus the new career is boundaryless in much the same way as Mr. Welch's company (Arthur, 1994; DeFillippi and Arthur, 1994.) (See O'Connell, 1995, for specific company examples.)

Exhibit 1.1. What Companies Promise Workers Today.

- We can't promise you how long we'll be in business
- We can't promise you that we won't be acquired
- We can't promise that there'll be room for promotion
- We can't promise that your job will exist when you reach retirement age
- We can't promise that the money will be available for your pension
- We can't expect your undying loyalty, and we aren't sure we want it

---

The term *protean* is taken from the name of the Greek god Proteus, who could change shape at will, from wild boar to fire to tree and so on. Here is a definition:

> The protean career is a process which the person, not the organization, is managing. It consists of all the person's varied experiences in education, training, work in several organizations, changes in occupational field, etc. The protean career is *not* what happens to the person in any one organization. The protean person's own personal career choices and search for self-fulfillment are the unifying or integrative elements in his or her life. The criterion of success is internal (psychological success), not external.

> In short, the protean career is shaped more by the individual than by the organization and may be redirected from time to time to meet the needs of the person [Hall, 1976, p. 201].

Thus, whereas in the past the contract was with the organization, in the protean career the contract is with the self.

Three Forms of Protean Flexibility

As Mirvis and Hall (1994) have discussed, there are several advantages of flexibility and autonomy in the protean career concept, related to the current work environment. First, it provides new ways to think about time over the course of the career. Instead of more traditional concepts of the career as a linear progression of upward moves or as a fairly predictable series of discrete stages (for example, Dalton, Thompson, and Price, 1977) or even as a regular pattern that might be unique to each individual (Driver, 1994), the protean concept encompasses any kind of flexible, idiosyncratic career course, with peaks and valleys, left turns, moves from one line of work to another, and so forth. Rather than focusing outward on some ideal generalized career "path," the protean career is unique to each person—a sort of career fingerprint.

A second kind of flexibility it provides is the enlargement of career space. The literature on careers has tended to associate careers with paid work and with what goes on within the boundaries of a formal organization. In the discussion of work-and-family issues, there is an assumption of a clear boundary between those two domains (Hall and Richter, 1988; Lobel and Kossek, in press). In contrast, "A more elastic concept, however, acknowledges that work and nonwork roles overlap and shape jointly a person's identity and sense of self. In practical terms, an enlarged definition of career space enables people to consider seriously taking time off to spend with growing children or to care for aging parents under the rubric of attaining psychological success" (Mirvis and Hall, 1994, p. 369).

Another example of space flexibility is the option of working at home, done by many people either informally or as part of a formal home work program. Here, not only does work spill over into home life but also home can in turn spill back into work time, as one might occasionally engage in home tasks (paying an overdue bill, letting in a repair person, dealing with a family emergency).

Perhaps most fundamentally, the protean concept provides a different way of thinking about the relationship between the organization and the employee. Whereas most of our previous literature on the organizational career has had the organization as the figural element with the individual as background, in the protean career, the person is figure, and the organization is ground. Organizations provide a context, a medium in which individuals pursue their personal aspirations. This model is analogous to the free agent in sports or the arts. The person can go where the rewards they are seeking are the greatest, be they work opportunities, coworkers, family, geography, or simply a change of scene. Both parties have freedom to end the relationship, but it may work out that the relationship becomes a long-term, highly valued one. This is something other than simply a relational or a transactional contract. It is the free person pursuing her or his own "path with a heart," as Herbert Shepard (1984) describes it.

Are You a Cormorant?

Let us say you have avoided the rat race. Unfortunately, it is very easy to let others—the organization, family, superiors, peers—determine one's path. What are some of the pitfalls to watch out for?

Herb Shepard quotes Ralph Sui's tale of the cormorant. Sui describes how cormorants are used for fishing in China. A man with a rowboat has five or six cormorants, held by a line and with rings around their necks. As a bird spots a fish, it dives into the water and always catches the fish. It tries to swallow the fish, but the larger fish are held in the throat by the ring. The fisherman then pulls the bird out of the water and squeezes the fish out through the bird's throat. The bird then dives for another fish, and the cycle is repeated.

Sui says, "Observe the cormorant. . . . Why is it that of all the different vertebrates the cormorant has been chosen to slave away day and night for the fisherman? Were the bird not greedy for fish, or not efficient in catching it, or not readily trained, would society have created an industry to exploit the bird? Would the ingenious device of a ring around its neck, and the simple procedure of squeezing the bird's neck to force it to regurgitate the fish have been devised? Of course not" (Shepard, 1984, p. 176).

We too are prime candidates to be exploited to serve someone else's ends if we are talented, have the ability to learn . . . and are greedy. Ironically, these are precisely the qualities that our schools, professions, and employers strive to instill in us. Without self-awareness and a clear sense of self-identity, these same qualities will gradually but surely put us on the path to becoming a cormorant, not the path with a heart.

One of the authors of this chapter saw many examples of this process on a recent trip to Japan. (Although other countries have much to learn from business practices in Japan, we hope they do not try to emulate the Japanese approach to the balance between work and life.) When one Japanese executive was asked when he usually gets home at night, considering his late hours at the office and after-hours drinking with colleagues, he replied proudly, "I'm usually home before midnight."

The Downside of the Protean Life

The noncormorant protean career, with its freedom from the organization, can have its downside, however. In a world where personal identities are generally tied to formal organizational work roles, there can be problems of self-definition and possible normlessness when one is working independently. Research on telecommuting shows that people who are not working within the spatial boundaries of an organization (but who may be organizational employees) need to find ways to meet their social needs and needs for identification (Hall, 1989; Christensen, 1988, 1995), and we would expect these issues to be even stronger for protean careerists.

For the worker at midcareer and beyond, the prospect of being forced to pursue a more protean career may be even more daunting (Hall and Mirvis, 1995b; American Association of Retired Persons, 1989). Having spent twenty or more years developing a work identity tied to an organization and a group of co-workers, workers who are suddenly on their own, totally responsible for themselves, can be frightened, as we know from research on job loss (Kaufman, 1982; Brockner, 1988). After years of psychological success based on a certain set of job skills, to be told that new skills must be developed is a tremendous blow to a worker's self-esteem and confidence, calling for major identity development work (Hall, 1986a).

Add the prospect of having to move from the shamrock's core leaf to the contract or contingent leaves, with no benefits and a very short-term commitment, at a time in life when one's financial needs may be at their peak, the protean career looks like a cruel betrayal of trust in the old relational contract (Commonwealth Fund, 1993).

New Developmental Demands on the Employee

The adaptable employee will have to possess a depth and variety of skills to match the needs of the business of the organization (Wheatly, 1992). This need for complexity is one reason why diversity in one's work can promote personal development (Cox, 1993; Jackson and Associates, 1992; Walker and Hanson, 1992; also Chapter Eleven, this volume).

This need for complexity and diversity suggests a concomitant need for varied work experience, flexibility, and a clear sense of self-direction to permit workers to self-design much of their personal and career development (Mirvis and Hall, 1994). Kenneth Gergen (1991, p. 7) argues that the complex roles and demands on individuals produce social saturation, which pulls people "in myriad directions, inviting us to play such a variety of roles that the very concept of an 'authentic self' with knowable characteristics recedes from view."

Indeed, to make the new organizational structures work, even the champions of reengineering have come to see that development of employees and the "human systems" of the firm are necessary for restructuring to be successful. To make this new organizational decentralization work effectively, employees and managers need to be delegated authority (in other words, empowered) to recognize problems or opportunities and to figure out their own creative responses in order to create corporate and psychological success. As James Champy (1995), coauthor of the bible on reengineering, points out, reengineering is in trouble precisely because much of this restructuring did not attend to the development of experienced managers, employees, and human systems (leadership, teamwork, empowerment, and culture change).

Thus learning how to learn and continuous learning have become core career competencies. Also, it is increasingly necessary to have skills in self-assessment and identity exploration in order to have a "personal compass" to give direction to one's life as one navigates the white water. Unfortunately, as we will show later, these self-learning skills are not only different from those that most people have needed in the past, they also require a higher level of cognitive development than most people currently possess, and thus adaptation requires personal transformation. This is not an easy form of personal change. Let us be more specific.

Robert Kegan (1994) presents data on average levels of cognitive development for several samples of employed adults in the United States, based on his model of five stages of adult development (Kegan, 1982). He argues that the new work environment requires people to operate at level 4, which he calls institutional. This level requires that the individual have a clear sense of self-identity, autonomy, and personal direction while at the same time maintain awareness of the whole system in which she or he is functioning. Unfortunately, Kegan finds that fewer than half of the people in the research studies he cites have reached that level of functioning, and the majority are at stage 3 (interpersonal), where the person is embedded in mutually reciprocal, one-to-one relationships (read: old relational career contract).

Let us look in more detail at the nature of the developmental identity work that a person must do to become more protean. Are there new rules for the "development game"?

Career and Life Boundaries

Career Identity, Subidentities, and Psychological Success

A clear sense of career identity is a necessary condition for pursuing a self-directed protean career. The main entity in the person's "self-system," the identity is the person's image of her- or himself in relation to the environment (Hall, 1971). The term *identity* is used here synonymously with related terms such as *self-concept, self-image,* and *sense of self.* The distinction between identity and self-esteem is that identity is descriptive, indicating perceptions of one's personal qualities, while self-esteem is evaluative, indicating the value one attaches to one's personal qualities.

One's sense of identity is made up of multiple *subidentities.* Each subidentity is the view of self in a particular social role (such as worker, mother, father, community member). The role represents the expectations held by significant others in the role set, while the subidentity represents self-perceptions as one responds to these role expectations (Hall, 1972, 1976).

Career development and involvement occur as the career subidentity becomes larger and more differentiated (that is, as it comes to incorporate perceptions of more skills, knowledge, abilities, values, experiences, and motivations). Thus career development is literally the creation of new aspects of the self in relation to the career. In this way, career growth is one type of self-actualization or self-fulfillment. To illustrate these concepts, sample subidentities of two hypothetical people, with high and low career involvement, are shown in Figure 1.1.

Career development occurs in a self-reinforcing spiral of success experiences (Hall and Foster, 1975; Hall, 1976, 1986a). It starts when the person begins to work toward a goal or objective. If the task goal is one that the person values to some extent, and if the person is responsible for independent achievement of that goal (so that any success is experienced as one's own), and if the goal is attained, then the person will experience psychological success as a result of that achievement. Psychological success is the feeling of pride and personal accomplishment that comes from knowing that one has done one's "personal best."

The result of achieving psychological success on a career task is that one experiences increased self-esteem and a more competent career subidentity. Because these are such rewarding experiences, one's career involvement is increased, and one is motivated to choose a more challenging goal for the future. Thus the cycle is repeated, and success breeds success. In this way, self-esteem is both an outcome of psychological success and a cause or motivator of future career task activity (Hall, 1971, 1976). Extensive longitudinal research at AT&T, starting in the 1950s, has shown the operation of this career success cycle in the early career development of managers (Berlew and Hall, 1966; Hall and Nougaim, 1968; Bray, Campbell, and Grant, 1974; and Howard and Bray, 1988).

Gender and Development

Another way of viewing identity and its development is through a *relational* lens. As the work of Jean Baker Miller (1991) suggests, the model of psychological success just presented may be a better reflection of the development of men than women. Baker argues that the self cannot be separated from dynamic interaction, and that the "interacting sense of self" is present for both males and females as infants. However, the effects of culture and the nature of gender-based interactions leads girls and women to develop "a sense of one's self as a person who attends to and responds to what is going on in the relationships between two or more people" (1991, p. 14).

This relational view of the self suggests, then, that the basis of self-esteem and psychological success is also different for girls and

Figure 1.1. Sample Subidentities of Two Hypothetical People.

Low Career-Involved Person

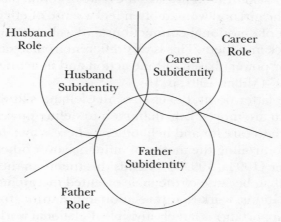

High Career-Involved Person

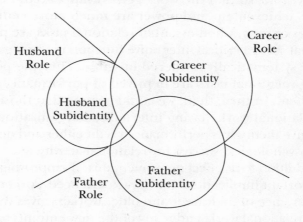

Source: Hall, 1976, p. 30.

women: "The girl's sense of self-esteem is based in feeling that she is a part of relationships and is taking care of those relationships . . . Another ramification involves the issue of competence or effectiveness. The girl and woman often feel a sense of effectiveness as arising out of emotional connections and as bound up with and feeding back into them. This is very different from a sense of effectiveness (or power) based in lone action and in acting against or over others" (Miller, 1991, p. 16).

On the latter point, Baker cites McClelland's finding (1979) that women are more likely than men to define power as having the strength to care for and help others, whereas men tend to view power as controlling the means of influence over others.

Fletcher (1994a, 1994b) extends this theory to the workplace and finds that, because of the male-oriented hierarchical cultures in organizations, work that is relational in nature (for example, helping, supporting) is largely invisible. Relational work is less central to the identities of men than it is to women's. In fact, Fletcher argues that there is an active process at work to make relational work invisible, so that the work gets "disappeared." Therefore, because achievement and power are much more central to the identities of men, when essential relational tasks are performed (tasks that serve a critical integrative function in the organization), they are systematically rendered invisible. Thus the people performing relational tasks are deprived of performance credit for doing them. In turn, then, we could assume that those who perform relational work, having internalized organizational norms, do not give themselves performance credit either and do not experience psychological success for relational activity.

In addition to its effect on women, this "disappearing" problem has important implications for the experienced worker. First, the life experience of midcareer and older workers gives them strong skills in relational work, and many of the new entrants to the workforce are older women (Auerbach and Welsh, 1994). Furthermore, one way some organizations can attack the glass ceiling for women (as well as for other underrepresented groups) is by extending organizational "timetables" so that people are considered for promotions at later ages than was formerly allowed under traditional age norms (Lawrence, 1987; Sekaran and Hall, 1989). But if the relational work they do gets disappeared in the way Fletcher's research suggests, this effect could contribute to a lack of appreciation for the full contributions of these older workers.

Thus it is important to widen the organizational culture's definition of what constitutes "real work" (Fletcher, 1994a). With the current need for improved teamwork and team-based learning as a means of enhancing organizational adaptability, there is in fact a large component of relational work and connected development taking place in effective teams. The more this work is rendered visible and rewarded and seen as a critical element of leadership, the more likely it is that it will enter into the psychological success cycle.

Artificiality of the Work-Life Distinction

Fuzzy Identity Boundaries

Miller's and Fletcher's ideas also apply to the ways work-and-life issues are viewed. Since relational work is undervalued in contemporary U.S. culture, much of the work related to home and family tasks is also undervalued. By extension, this includes those activities that are part of an employee's private life. The public or organizational work parts of the person's identity are seen as more important than the private (home, family, personal) subidentities (Hall and Hall, 1979). When work and family come into conflict, work usually wins out.

The fact is, however, that the private sphere is much more difficult to manage than the public for most people (Hall and Hall, 1979; Sekaran and Hall, 1989). We would also argue that for most people there is less of a psychological boundary between work and personal life than prevailing theory (Greenhaus and Beutell, 1985) would suggest. There is certainly a physical boundary to be crossed as the person moves from one role to the other (even for people who work in the home), but Hall and Richter (1988) have found that people move back and forth psychologically quite often and easily during the course of the work day. Because in the personal sphere there is less structure in roles, less acceptance of authority, and less psychological distance than in the public or work sphere, this puts more stress on the individual's personal skills to resolve conflicts and solve problems. So it could be argued that tasks in the personal arena are often more difficult than in a formal organizational work setting. Thus home work would seem to have at least as much claim to be "real work" as that performed in the place of employment.

To make matters even more complex, we should not equate roles in the family sphere with "family." It is becoming clear that the work-and-life issues of single adults without dependent children (SAWDCs) require just as much real work as the issues of employed parents (Young, 1994; also Chapter Eight, this volume). The sole responsibility for a home, possessions, and a set of personal relationships, along with, in many cases, responsibility for the well-being of parents or other family members or friends, creates the same sort of stress and overload that has traditionally been seen as unique to employed parents.

Thus it would appear that the term *work-family* as a boundary between different subidentities is deficient in multiple ways. First, the implication that the employment role represents "real work" whereas the subidentities of one's private life are somehow different from real work is not valid. Second, the existence of a boundary between the occupational role and the person's private life is often the figment of the imagination of those in the upper echelons of the employing organization's hierarchy. Third, for single, child-free employees, the term *family* as it is typically used to mean a partner and/or dependent children is inappropriate.

Thus the real issue to be addressed here is the basic nature of the relationship between the employee and the employing organization. The matters of stress and conflict and fit that are at the heart of the employee's satisfaction and effectiveness reflect how well integrated her or his personal needs are with the job requirements and rewards of the organization. So we are right back to one of the earliest dilemmas in organizational behavior: how to integrate the needs of healthy individuals and the task requirements of effective organizations (McGregor, 1961; Argyris, 1957). This is why the nature of the changing psychological contract is so salient today.

When Work Is Play

The concept of work versus life may be erroneous in yet another way. Many people obtain deep intrinsic satisfaction from their work, and for them work has many of the qualities we associate with play. These people choose to be overinvolved. Yet any job, no matter how exciting, that spills over into one's personal life and takes up seventy to eighty hours each week can drive out other fulfilling aspects of life such as family, friends, community, personal interests, and church.

But as long as work can be kept in perspective, it can be integrated into life better when it has the qualities of play—that is, when it is intrinsically rewarding, when it challenges and stretches the worker, and when it is under the worker's control. Thus a good job can have the same experiential qualities as a good puzzle or a good computer activity. It can be highly involving and absorbing, it can be terribly frustrating when solutions are not forthcoming, when the task at hand is interrupted by something else, or when the necessary resources are unavailable (for example, when the computer's memory capacity is reached, and the system suddenly crashes, and the work has not been saved), and it can lead to an exhilarating feeling of success and pride when the problem is finally solved.

As organizations pursue their work of restructuring, we need to learn more about how to reengineer in such a way that the resulting work—as well as the organization itself—is redesigned. As one practitioner put it, "We need to distinguish between real reengineering of work and mindless downsizing, such as across-the-board 10 percent job reductions." Also, we know from experience that it is possible to rearrange work, especially with new technology, so that it is divided into activities that stretch the employee to use more of his or her potential and also to produce more of a whole, visible product or service. In this way, not only is the resulting organization more competitive but also the employee feels more psychologically successful.

Stages of Lifelong Learning for the New Career Contract

One of the keys to understanding the new contract is the fact that the employee's needs and career concerns change over the course of the career in a much more dynamic way than in the past. Lifelong learning is required for continued success. We would argue that career stages do not operate the way they did in a more stable organizational environment, as described by Hall (1976) and Super (1992).

Career stages represent the *resultant,* to use a term from physics, of forces arising from stages of adult development and from forces in the career environment. Although adult development processes probably have not changed much over the last twenty years, the career environment certainly has, as we have said earlier, and with it, so has the need for lifelong learning. On the adult development side, then, the stages and transitions for men, as identified by Levinson (Levinson, Darrow, Klein, Levinson, and McKee, 1978; Levinson, 1986), and for women, as identified by Bardwick (1980) and Levinson (1996), still include an early tentative life structure (in the twenties) followed by an initial reexamination in the early thirties and then a midlife transition in the forties. The fifties can be a fairly stable midlife period for men (Levinson, Darrow, Klein, Levinson, and McKee, 1978) as they strive for balance by incorporating more personal and family involvements into their identities and lives, whereas for women this may be a time for renewed or continuing achievement in the world outside of the home (Bardwick, 1980).

Identity and Adaptability

An issue for women and men in midlife is how to learn continuously and be adaptable after establishing an initial life structure that seems to work and yield psychological success. Elsewhere (Hall, 1986a), we have discussed how early adult success can reinforce a stable routine of behavior and life-style, which can put the person at risk of being closed to necessary learning. In short, while success breeds success (Hall, 1971; Hall and Foster, 1975) over a period of, say, five years, over the longer run success may lead to failure—if it is unexamined and unchanged.

The keys to midcareer success are *identity* and *adaptability* (Hall, 1986a, 1986b; Howard and Bray, 1988; London, 1983; London and Mone, 1987). If a person has the ability to self-reflect, to continue assessing and learning about her- or himself, and to change behaviors and attitudes, the chances are much greater of making a successful midcareer transition and achieving a good fit with a new work environment (Hall and Mirvis, 1995b; Arthur, Claman, and DeFillippi, 1995).

Changing Career Routines

An earlier study (Hall, 1986a) described how a midcareer routine can be busted by various triggers in the person and in the environment, leading to conscious exploration of alternative ways of being and cycles of learning. If this exploration leads to experimental changes in behavior that in turn lead to success, these changes are likely to be integrated into the identity and may encourage future explorations and adaptations. External conditions, such as autonomy, feedback, and support, can greatly facilitate this midcareer identity change process.

Because of the greatly increased variety in the work environment (Duncan, 1971; Handy, 1989, 1994), based on the concept of equifinality, there is an equally great potential variety in the range of individual responses to changes in this environment. We would argue that what we are seeing now, instead of one set of career stages during a life span (as the Super model posits), is a series of many shorter learning cycles over the span of a person's work life (see Figure 1.2). Careers will be increasingly driven by the core competencies of the fields in which a person works (Quinn, 1992). Because the life cycle of technologies and products is so shortened (Handy, 1989), so too are personal mastery cycles. As a result, people's careers increasingly will become a succession of "ministages" (or short-cycle learning stages) of exploration-trial-mastery-exit, as they move in and out of various product areas, technologies, functions, organizations, and other work environments. The key issue determining a learning stage will not be chronological age (in which the forties and fifties were "midcareer") but career age, where perhaps five years in a given specialty may be "midlife" for that area. Thus the half-life of a career stage would be driven by the half-life of the competency field of that career work.

This model of career learning ministages provides a more specific view of what we mean by the protean career. A person's protean qualities do not usually produce random or capricious changes. These qualities are not negative, and proteanism is not career indecision (Fuqua and Hartman, 1983); it is a process of exploring and developing identity. Robert J. Lifton (1993)

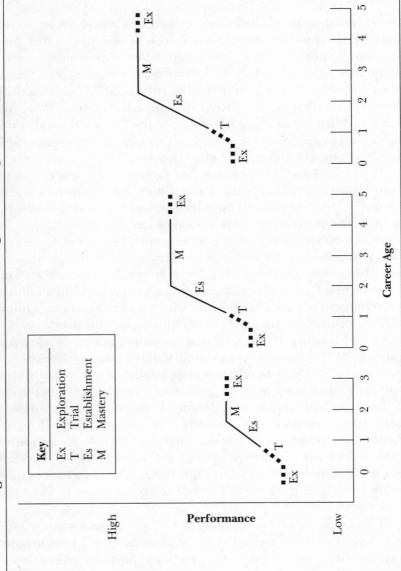

Figure 1.2. The New Model of Career Stages (Learning Versus Age).

Source: Hall, 1993, p. 15.

describes this growth process as follows: "Proteanism involves a quest for authenticity and meaning, a form-seeking assertion of self. The recognition of complexity and ambiguity may well represent a certain maturation in our concept of self. The protean self seeks to be both fluid and grounded, however tenuous that combination" (p. 9).

Interestingly, the more we come to view constant learning as part of the new career contract and not just as a particular career pattern for a certain type of person (such as the "spiral" or "transitory" people in Driver's typology [1994] of career concepts), the more we move toward valuing a form of development that includes both female and male patterns. The protean form involves horizontal growth, expanding one's range of competencies and ways of connecting to work and other people, as opposed to the more traditional vertical model of success (upward mobility). In the protean form of growth, the goal is learning, psychological success, and expansion of the identity. In the more traditional vertical form, the goal was advancement, success and esteem in the eyes of others, and power. Thus the protean form can embrace both mastery and relational growth, or "male" and "female" ways of developing (Miller, 1991).

Lifton's research (1993) on protean life changes confirms that this form of development encompasses the experiences of both sexes:

> [T]here is virtually no manifestation of the protean self that either sex cannot express. Men are given more opportunity by society, especially in connection with occupation, to experiment with forms and combinations. Women, on the other hand, perform (at least in American society) a special form of protean juggling in combining commitments to home, childbirth, and nurturing, with occupational and intellectual pursuits. At the same time, women in our study were more focused on grounding, more concerned with sustaining intimate relationships and relationships in general. That overall emphasis upon connection can discourage protean exploration in some women. But in others it contributes to that exploration either by providing elements of structure that free one for bold protean forays, or by suggesting an ideal model (of, say, significant work or an authentic relationship) for what one constantly seeks [Lifton, 1993, p. 9].

Why This Is Tough Work

The work involved in promoting the new protean career is difficult for individuals and for organizations precisely because this career represents such a fundamental change in a person's identity. We are not talking simply about new skills or competencies required for the new workplace. We are talking about a totally new way of relating to the world, as the work of Robert Kegan (1994) suggests. Such a change requires important personal development work, as we have been discussing.

It is also tough because if the employee is to become more autonomous and more oriented toward his or her own path with a heart, the employee's valued and loved others must change too. You can't change one side of a relationship without affecting the other.

If it is tough for an individual to find and pursue his or her own path, it is even more difficult for leaders in organizations to figure out what is the appropriate role of the organization in promoting the protean careers of its members while it also promotes its own success. Should an organization be in the career management business at all? Should it provide good stretching assignments, promote developmental relationships, provide financial resources for formal training and development activities, and leave it to the individual to manage her or his own development? Should it create organization-wide career management systems to facilitate and keep track of the development of employees? If the new contract is strictly a personal affair, what then is the role of the organization? This is very much an open question.

Implications for Organizations and Career Professionals

What might an organization look like if it had a more holistic, caring view of employees and their careers? That organization could be a Beth Israel Hospital, noted for world-class patient care, medical innovation, and strong employee involvement, a Johnson & Johnson, noted for its values-driven management process, or a San Francisco 49ers football team, who in 1995 won a record fifth Super Bowl championship.

Consider for a moment how life in the 49ers feels to linebacker Gary Plummer: "You come here and you see the difference with the 49ers, being treated like a king. You sign a contract, and the next day there's a bouquet the size of a table for your wife welcoming her to this organization. That was really something special for my family" (Ryan, 1995, p. 39).

According to defensive end Charles Mann, "It's like if you have a horse, and you want this horse to win the Kentucky Derby. You're going to feed it good. . . . You're going to take good care of it, so that when the time comes it's going to run for you. Well, it's the same thing with us. Mr. DeBartolo [the team's owner] does it. If I owned a team in professional sports, I'd be very much like him. There are owners in this league that really don't like the players, and it's just a way to make money. . . . Eddie DeBartolo and the 49er organization care about their players" (Ryan, 1995, p. 37).

As sports journalist Bob Ryan explains, this organizational philosophy of taking care of employees makes sense in economic as well as human terms in view of today's fierce competition for exceptional talent: "Now that luring players from one organization to another has less to do with money and far more to do with employment opportunity and the general quality of football life, the world champion 49ers are in better shape than ever before. Unless a player has an earthquake thing, why wouldn't he wish to play for the 49ers, especially if he consults with recent satisfied employees. . . ?" (Ryan, 1995, p. 39).

Take out the references to football, and the above comments about this San Francisco team could apply to any kind of organization. Respecting and taking care of employees pays off not only for those employees but also for owners and customers—and for the rest of the world, for whom it sets a good example!

Another implication, from this 49er example, is that the "new contract" between employee and employer can have a heart. It combines both a transactional and a relational quality, along with a respect for the employee's protean ("free agent") career. There is mutual loyalty here, but it is based on performance, not on the old contract's terms, length of service. What this example shows is that the best way to attract high-quality self-directed careerists is to provide not only a "good deal" in the transactional sense but also the opportunity to experience psychological success and to receive respect as a mature and whole person. An organization designed to tap the unique potential of its members can achieve that elusive goal: integration of the needs of healthy individuals and the success of the organization. As Bob Ryan says, "The 49ers are football as designed by football players, or at least intelligent football players committed to the singular goal of winning the championship. Immature, selfish people certainly need not apply" (Ryan, 1995, p. 39).

Getting back to the admonition of the Rev. William Sloane Coffin in the opening of this chapter, you can be a winner, but the event does not have to be a rat race. Nor do you have to be the only winner; it can be, and in fact increasingly has to be, a team enterprise. Also, the new career consists of many events, not just one, so that there is plenty of time and room for Karen Lopez to put her career under the control of her forty-year-old self.

Put together, all of these ideas reflect a sense that the new career contract between employee and employer, described earlier in this chapter, is alive and well in some parts of the work world, especially for more mature workers and for well-managed organizations. The career concerns reflected in the new contract are not just work-life issues, and they are not just career issues. They get to the core of what makes a life worth living (Shepard, 1984). We need to understand more about how to provide work environments that not only develop people (a key element of the new contract) but also provide caring for people (Kahn, 1994) throughout the career. Organizations that provide a valued mission and challenging, meaningful work, combined with an environment of fairness, good pay and benefits, support, and caring for employees, will not only meet the needs of the whole person; they will also engage that person (Kahn, 1990) and thus profit from a vast supply of untapped human potential.

Recommendations to the Reader

1. Do some reflecting on your psychological contract with your employer. What is it and how has it changed in recent years?
2. Use this reflection exercise with your clients.
3. Identify the life roles and corresponding subidentities that are most important to you. Draw a picture of them. (See Figure 1.1 for an example.) What conflicts do you experience in relation to various subidentities and roles? How do you cope with them? How do you maintain boundaries between various subidenti-

ties? How do you attempt to integrate certain subidentities? Use this exercise with your clients.

4. Assess the developmental culture of a client organization using the "Twenty Questions" in Exhibit 1.2. Better yet, ask individual clients to do their own assessment with this instrument, and use their responses to initiate a developmental dialogue in the organization.

5. Use "Twenty Questions" to help individual clients assess their degree of fit with their current organization. Alternative: use this instrument to help clients assess their degree of fit with an organization they are considering joining.

Exhibit 1.2. Twenty Questions: A Career Development Culture Index.

(An assessment of your culture for career development)

INSTRUCTIONS: If your answer is yes to a question, make a check mark in the space to the left of the number of that item. See scoring instructions at the end of the exercise.

_____ 1. Does senior management use work assignments and work relationships to develop employees?

_____ 2. Do they do it consciously or intentionally for developing people (as opposed to doing it only for business purposes)?

_____ 3. Are these career development activities part of the business plan for the employee's unit?

_____ 4. Is the organization's purpose expressed in human terms with which employees can identify?

_____ 5. Does top management value employee development?

_____ 6. Is career development owned by senior line management (as opposed to being seen as owned by HR)?

_____ 7. Is diversity actively promoted by senior line management?

_____ 8. Is employee development done by senior line management for the explicit purpose of supporting the business strategy?

_____ 9. Are new forms of employee mobility being used (such as cross-functional, cross-business)?

_____ 10. Is personal development or self-knowledge (for example, 360-degree feedback) promoted?

____ 11. Is career development part of the overall corporate strategy?

____ 12. Is there a strong succession planning process, which puts emphasis on development as well as identification?

____ 13. Do employees have significant input to plans for their future development and assignments?

____ 14. Does career development include opportunities for risk and learning (adaptability)?

____ 15. Does career development include personal (identity) learning as well as task learning?

____ 16. Do most people here believe that career development should also take family and personal balance needs into account?

____ 17. Is there general agreement in management about whether your historical career development approaches are appropriate for the future?

____ 18. Is it relatively easy for employees to access information about other job opportunities in the company?

____ 19. Are employees encouraged to be empowered and self-directed in their careers?

____ 20. (The acid test:) Are individual employees aware of your organization's career development activities?

____ = Total number
    of checks.   Key: 17 or more............Outstanding
                                  10 – 16....................Good
                                  6 – 9......................Fair
                                  < 5..........................Work needed!

Source: Developed by Douglas T. Hall with support from the Executive Development Roundtable.

References

American Association of Retired Persons. (1989). *Business and older workers: Current perceptions and new directions for the 1990s.* Washington, DC: Author.

Argyris, C. (1957). *Personality and organization.* New York: HarperCollins.

Arthur, M. B. (1994). The boundaryless career: A new perspective for organizational inquiry. *Journal of Organizational Behavior, 15,* 295–306.

Arthur, M. B., Claman, P. H., & DeFillippi, R. J. (1995). Intelligent enterprise, intelligent careers. *Academy of Management Executive, 9*(4), 1–15.

Auerbach, J. A., & Welsh, J. C. (Eds.). (1994). *Aging and competition: Rebuilding the U.S. workforce.* Washington, DC: National Council on the Aging and the National Planning Association.

Bardwick, J. (1980). The seasons of a woman's life. In D. G. McGuigan (Ed.), *Women's lives: New theory, research and policy* (pp. 35–55). Ann Arbor, MI: Center for Continuing Education of Women, University of Michigan.

Barnard, C. I. (1940). *The functions of the executive.* Cambridge, MA: Harvard University Press.

Barnet, R. J. (1993, September). The end of jobs: Employment is one thing the global economy is *not* creating. *Harper's Magazine,* 47–52.

Berlew, D. E., & Hall, D. T. (1966). The socialization of managers: Effects of expectations on performance. *Administrative Science Quarterly, 11,* 207–223.

Bray, D. W., Campbell, R. J., & Grant, D. L. (1974). *Formative years in business.* New York: Wiley.

Bridges, W. (1994, September 19). The end of the job. *Fortune,* 62–74.

Brockner, J. (1988). *Self-esteem at work: Research, theory, and practice.* Lexington, MA: Lexington Books.

Champy, J. (1995). *Reengineering management: The mandate for new leadership.* New York: HarperCollins.

Christensen, K. (1988). *Women and home-based work: The unspoken contract.* Troy, MO: Holt, Rinehart & Winston.

Christensen, K. (1995). *Contingent work arrangements in family-sensitive corporations* (Policy Paper Series R95.03). Boston: Boston University Center on Work and Family.

Commonwealth Fund. (1993, November). *The untapped resource: The final report of the Americans Over 55 At Work Program.* New York: Author.

Cox, T. (1993). *Cultural diversity in organizations: Theory, research and practice.* San Francisco: Berrett-Koehler.

Dalton, G. W., Thompson, P. H., & Price, R. L. (1977). The four stages of professional careers—A new look at performance. *Organizational Dynamics, 6,* 19–42.

DeFillippi, R. J., & Arthur, M. B. (1994). The boundaryless career: A competency-based approach. *Journal of Organizational Behavior, 15,* 307–324.

DeMeuse, K. P., & Tornow, W. W. (1990). The tie that binds—has become very, very frayed! *Human Resource Planning, 13,* 203–213.

Downward mobility. (1992, March 23). *Business Week,* 56–63.

Driver, M. J. (1994). Workforce personality and the new information age workplace. In J. A. Auerbach & J. C. Welsh (Eds.), *Aging and competition: Rebuilding the U.S. workforce* (pp. 185–204). Washington, DC: National Council on the Aging and the National Planning Association.

Duncan, R. B. (1971). Characteristics of organizational environments and perceived environmental uncertainty. *Administrative Science Quarterly, 17,* 313–327.

Fletcher, J. (1994a). *Toward a theory of relational practice in organizations: A feminist reconstruction of "real" work.* Unpublished doctoral dissertation, Boston University.

Fletcher, J. (1994b). Castrating the female advantage: Feminist standpoint research and management science. *Journal of Management Inquiry, 3,* 74–82.

Fuqua, D. R., & Hartman, B. W. (1983). Differential diagnosis and treatment of career indecision. *Personnel and Guidance Journal, 62,* 27–29.

Gergen, K. (1991). *The saturated self: Dilemmas of identity in contemporary life.* New York: Basic Books.

Greenhaus, J. H., & Beutell, N. J. (1985). Sources of conflict between work and family roles. *Academy of Management Review, 10,* 76–88.

Hall, D. T. (1971). A theoretical model of career subidentity development in organizational settings. *Organizational Behavior and Human Performance, 6,* 50–76.

Hall, D. T. (1972). A model of coping with role conflict: The role behavior of college educated women. *Administrative Science Quarterly, 17,* 471–486.

Hall, D. T. (1976). *Careers in organizations.* Glenview, IL: Scott, Foresman.

Hall, D. T. (1986a). Breaking career routines: Midcareer choice and identity development. In D. T. Hall & Associates, *Career development in organizations* (pp. 120–159). San Francisco: Jossey-Bass.

Hall, D. T. (1986b). Dilemmas in linking succession planning to individual executive learning. *Human Resource Management, 25,* 235–265.

Hall, D. T. (1989). Telecommuting and the management of work-home boundaries. In J. Abramson, A. Basu, A. Gupta, D. T. Hall, R. Hinckley, R. Solomon, & L. Waks, *Annual review of communications and soci-*

ety, 1989. Queenstown, MD: Institute for Information Studies, 177–208.

Hall, D. T. (1993). The new "career contract": Wrong on both counts. Technical Report, Executive Development Roundtable, School of Management, Boston University.

Hall, D. T., & Foster, L. W. (1975). A psychological success cycle and goal setting: Goals, performance, and attitudes. *Academy of Management Journal, 20,* 282–290.

Hall, D. T., & Mirvis, P. H. (1995a). Careers as lifelong learning. In A. Howard (Ed.), *The changing nature of work* (pp. 323–361). San Francisco: Jossey-Bass.

Hall, D. T., & Mirvis, P. H. (1995b). The new career contract: Developing the whole person at midlife and beyond. *Journal of Vocational Behavior, 47,* 269–289.

Hall, D. T., & Nougaim, K. E. (1968). An examination of Maslow's need hierarchy in an organizational setting. *Organizational Behavior and Human Performance, 3,* 12–35.

Hall, D. T., & Richter, J. (1988). Balancing work life and home life: What can organizations do to help? *Academy of Management Executive, 2,* 213–233.

Hall, F. S., & Hall, D. T. (1979). *The two-career couple.* Reading, MA: Addison-Wesley.

Handy, C. (1989). *The age of unreason.* Boston: Harvard Business School Press.

Handy, C. (1994). *The age of paradox.* Boston: Harvard Business School Press.

Hirsch, P. (1987). *Pack your own parachute.* Reading, MA: Addison-Wesley.

Howard, A., & Bray, D. W. (1988). *Managerial lives in transition: Advancing age and changing times.* New York: Guilford Press.

Jackson, S. E., & Associates. (1992). *Working through diversity: Human resources initiatives.* New York: Guilford Press.

Kahn, W. A. (1990). The psychological conditions of personal engagement and disengagement at work. *Academy of Management Journal, 33,* 692–724.

Kahn, W. A. (1994). Caring for the caregivers: Patterns of organizational caregiving. *Administrative Science Quarterly, 38,* 539–563.

Kanter, D. L., & Mirvis, P. H. (1989). *The cynical Americans.* San Francisco: Jossey-Bass.

Kaufman, H. G. (1982). *Professionals in search of work: Coping with the stress of job loss and underemployment.* New York: Wiley.

Kegan, R. (1982). *The evolving self: Problem and process in human development.* Cambridge, MA: Harvard University Press.

Kegan, R. (1994). *In over our heads: The mental demands of modern life.* Cambridge, MA: Harvard University Press.

Kotter, J. P. (1995). *The new rules: How to succeed in today's post-corporate world.* New York: Free Press.

Lawrence, B. S. (1987). An organizational theory of age effects. In S. Bacharach & N. DiTomaso (Eds.), *Research in the sociology of organizations.* Greenwich, CT: JAI Press, 37–71.

Levinson, D. J. (1986). A conception of adult development. *American Psychologist, 41,* 3–13.

Levinson, D. J. (1996). *Seasons of a woman's life.* New York: Knopf.

Levinson, D. J., with Darrow, C. N., Klein, E. B., Levinson, M. H., and McKee, B. (1978). *The seasons of a man's life.* New York: Knopf.

Levinson, H. (1962). *Men, management, and mental health.* Cambridge, MA: Harvard University Press.

Lifton, R. J. (1993). *The protean self: Human resilience in an age of fragmentation.* New York: Basic Books.

Lobel, S., & Kossek, E. E. (Eds.). (in press). *Human resource strategies for managing diversity.* London, England: Blackwell.

London, M. (1983). Toward a theory of career motivation. *Academy of Management Review, 8,* 620–630.

London, M., & Mone, E. M. (1987). *Career management and survival in the workplace.* San Francisco: Jossey-Bass.

McClelland, D. (1979). *Power: The inner experience.* New York: Irvington.

McGregor, D. (1961). *The human side of enterprise.* New York: Wiley.

MacNeill, I. R. (1980). *The new social contract.* New Haven, CT: Yale University Press.

MacNeill, I. R. (1985). Relational contracts: What we do and do not know. *Wisconsin Law Review,* 483–525.

Miller, J. B. (1991). The development of women's sense of self. In J. V. Jordan, A. G. Kaplan, J. B. Miller, I. P. Stiver, & J. L. Surrey (Eds.), *Women's growth in connection.* New York: Guilford Press, 11–27.

Mirvis, P. H. (1992). Job security: Current trends. In L. K. Jones (Ed.), *The encyclopedia of career change and work issues.* Phoenix: Oryx Press, 148–150.

Mirvis, P. H. (Ed.). (1993). *Building a competitive workforce: Investing in human capital for corporate success.* New York: Wiley.

Mirvis, P. H., & Hall, D. T. (1994). Psychological success and the boundaryless career. *Journal of Organizational Behavior, 15,* 365–380.

O'Connell, D. (1995). *The changing psychological contract: Spring meeting summary.* Boston: Executive Development Roundtable, Boston University School of Management.

Quinn, J. B. (1992). *Intelligent enterprise: A knowledge and service based paradigm for industry.* New York: Free Press.

The revolving door at Rubbermaid. (1995, September 18). *Business Week,* 80–83.

Rousseau, D. M. (1990). New hire perceptions of their own and their employer's obligations: A study of psychological contracts. *Journal of Organizational Behavior, 11,* 389–400.

Ryan, B. (1995, January 31). With win, DeBartolo receives the bouquets. *Boston Globe,* pp. 37, 39.

Sasseen, J. A. (1994, October 17). The winds of change blow everywhere: A more efficient workforce may mean a wider gap between haves and have-nots. *Business Week,* 92–93.

Schein, E. H. (1965). *Organizational psychology* (1st ed.). Englewood Cliffs, NJ: Prentice Hall.

Schor, J. B. (1991). *The overworked American.* New York: Basic Books.

Sekaran, U., & Hall, D. T. (1989). Asynchronism in dual-career and family linkages. In M. B. Arthur, D. T. Hall, & B. S. Lawrence (Eds.), *Handbook of career theory* (pp. 159–180). Cambridge, England: Cambridge University Press.

Shepard, H. A. (1984). On the realization of human potential: A path with a heart. In M. B. Arthur, L. Bailyn, D. J. Levinson, & H. A. Shepherd (Eds.), *Working with careers.* New York: Center for Research on Careers, Graduate School of Business, Columbia University, 25–46.

Simon, H. A. (1947). *Administrative behavior.* New York: Macmillan.

Super, D. E. (1992). Toward a comprehensive theory of career development. In D. H. Montross & C. J. Shinkman (Eds.), *Career development: Theory and practice* (pp. 35–64). Springfield, IL: Thomas.

Walker, B. A., & Hanson, W. C. (1992). Valuing differences at Digital Equipment Corporation. In S. E. Jackson & Associates, *Working through diversity: Human resources initiatives* (pp. 119–137). New York: Guilford Press.

Wheatley, M. J. (1992). *Leadership and the new science: Learning about organization from an orderly universe.* San Francisco: Berrett-Koehler.

Young, M. (1994). *Life status, work time, and the perceived fairness of who works when: Impacts on individuals and organizations.* Dissertation proposal, School of Management, Boston University.

Chapter Two

Beyond the "Social Contract"

An Analysis of the Executive View at Twenty-Five Large Companies

Barbara W. Altman
James E. Post

Harry had been the human resources director for his corporation for six years now, after working his way up through the department. He sat in his office pondering his most recent challenge—yet another set of layoffs. The first round had hit hard, and they compensated employees well; as a matter of fact, the generous severance packages allowed some employees to accomplish their dreams of opening up their own businesses or retiring early. Now, on their third round of major layoffs, the company could no longer afford such packages, and many let go would be in precarious positions. And what about the people left? Harry knew he could not continue to deal with them from one layoff to another, the "survivors'" levels of anxiety were negatively influencing morale and productivity. The corporation needed to clarify its responsibilities toward these employees. But what did that mean? He thought the company had always been a good corporate citizen, not just with the employees but in the local community too. Harry felt very unsettled trying to provide leadership on this

Note: The authors wish to acknowledge the support of the Alfred P. Sloan Foundation and the cooperation of members of Boston University School of Management's Human Resources Policy Institute.

issue—how could they continue to be good corporate citizens with *all* their stakeholders given the competitive pressures the company was facing?

American business continues to downsize and restructure at record rates, and the challenge facing Harry is shared widely among modern managers. *Business Week* noted that despite the economic recovery, American corporations laid off 615,186 employees in 1993, a record annual number (Byrne, 1994). Data from 1994 and 1995 suggest similar layoff levels, albeit in an economy that is producing more new jobs and record corporate profits. The long-term societal and business impacts of this era of massive downsizing are just beginning to be explored in the management literature; this volume represents a major step forward in that analysis. This chapter contributes by reporting on empirical research on the shifting social contract at both the corporate and corporate/society levels of analysis. The broader institutional framework is a crucial but sometimes overlooked perspective given the day-to-day crisis management mode that today's managers face.

Introduction

Prior to the current era of reduced corporate employment, many large corporations had created a climate of security for employees that integrated both social and economic responsibilities. The unwritten promise of lifelong employment and career advancement within a firm was pervasive. Throughout the 1980s, for example, *Fortune*'s list of most admired companies featured corporations whose economic success was supported by secure employment and progressive social policies.

The downsizing era of the 1990s has produced conditions that are the antithesis of a secure environment. Employees who are laid off feel betrayed; those who remain are apprehensive about their future. The "psychological" or "social" contract that once existed between corporations and employees is in a period of flux, as is discussed in other chapters of this book. Managing through and after downsizing presents a difficult paradox. Maintaining good relations with employees is extremely important, yet the cuts that accompany downsizing, restructuring, and reengineering undermine trust, loyalty, and commitment. The socioeconomic balance that previously helped maintain a satisfied and productive workforce has been shattered in many companies, contributing to what Robert Reich, U.S. Secretary of Labor in the Clinton administration, has called the "Age of Anxiety." In this chapter, we explore transformations in the social contract between corporation and employee and its implications for historical trends in corporate socioeconomic roles and responsibilities.

To understand how managers view these conditions and the challenges of establishing a new socioeconomic balance, we conducted interviews with senior executives at twenty-five Fortune 500 companies. The "Survey Results" section presents these executives' views on the shifting social contract with employees—its background, tenets of the old contract, new tenets, implications and undercurrents. Quotations from the interviews highlight the magnitude of these changes, the emotional intensity with which executives view them, and their perceived impacts on the organization. In the "Analysis" section, the experiences of these executives are discussed in the context of three questions:

1. What do executives on the "front lines" see as the ramifications of the current "contract" between employers and their employees?
2. Does this 1990s social contract represent a fundamental shift in American businesses' conceptualization of their economic and social responsibilities?
3. What is seen as the appropriate balance of corporate economic and social roles and responsibilities?

Our discussion then focuses on the "new balance" between social and economic roles and responsibilities that appears to be emerging in many companies. In the conclusion, this evolution in the socialization of the modern corporation is linked to broader societal trends, and future managerial issues are identified. Overall, the findings of this study provide insights to the challenges managers recognize in managing both the economic and social bottom line.

Survey Results

This group of executives identified global competition, deregulation, and rapid technological change as the driving forces behind downsizing. They identified shifts in stakeholder prioritization as having a more direct impact on relations with employees. Of the constituencies to which corporate managers are accountable, the perception is that shareholder demands now override employee welfare. Executives describe an environment where the emphasis has switched to short-term profits based on pressure from shareholders. Cost cutting is done via employees, both in terms of jobs and benefits. Two executives described how these trade-offs evolved:

> The company has been much sterner when it comes to financial performance; this is driven by shareholders. The fastest way to meet financial goals is through the hides of the employees. The shift has been to emphasize shareholders' concern over employees' concerns. The first biggest expense in the company is payroll and the second is benefits . . . the fastest way to impact the bottom line is through [cutting] these.

> If you look to other constituencies, the shift has been to place less value on employees, more on shareholders. The value to shareholder has always been there but now [it] is more difficult to balance constituencies.

Viewing the employee-corporation relationship historically, executives describe an environment where from the 1950s until the 1980s employees were treated benevolently. Job security, wages, benefits, and upward mobility were on the rise and became common practice. Employees could anticipate a satisfying lifelong career with one firm as long as they performed at least moderately well and made no serious mistakes. However, the situation began to change radically in the mid 1980s.

Demise of the Old Social Contract

During the first waves of corporate belt tightening, corporations tried to manage their social responsibilities toward negatively affected employees compassionately. Many of these first layoffs were voluntary and were accompanied by generous severance packages. Therefore, while they were painful, every attempt was made to minimize the trauma. Lessening the discomfort became increasingly difficult as crisis economic circumstances and more layoffs ensued. Human resources and other executives began to recognize that severance packages ameliorated neither the bad morale of the survivors left in the company nor the problems facing those laid off. One executive described a situation where employees were physically but not mentally on the job, resulting in a "loss of alignment," or a disconnect between employee commitment and corporate goals, and greatly reduced productivity.

As downsizing continued and executives began to think more systematically of restructuring and reengineering, they realized that they would have to deal differently with the two groups, those being laid off *and* those being retained. The result has been a rewritten employee "social contract." There are rich data from this set of executive interviews to support a hypothesis that the social contract between corporations and employees, as it existed in the past, is dead. Many different terms were used to describe the demise: the contract has been *shattered, broken,* or *eroded,* and the *fabric of the employee-employer relationship has been cut out.*

Even though the long-standing employer-employee relationship was rarely a written contract, it was commonly understood by all parties. The survey data highlight the following tenets of the old contract:

- A paternalistic system where employees are taken care of; employees felt like a member of a family.
- Long-term employment security with the firm was assured.
- Employees felt entitled to their jobs as long as they performed at an adequate level and did nothing wrong.
- The entitlement mentality spread beyond the job to include benefits, career development, and advancement.

The 1990s Social Contract

The transition from this old contract to a new one is currently playing itself out. The executives interviewed in this study described what some consider a paradigm shift:

- From an expectation of long term to a transitory relationship
- From perception of entitlement to shared responsibility
- From employees being part of an organization to being a factor in production
- From corporations taking a patriarch's role to employees bearing more of the responsibility

The following statements illustrate the challenges these executives see companies facing in this era of transition:

> People used to think of [our] company in terms of long-term security. They see the social contract shifting right under their feet. We are becoming more market driven, customer driven. But we also want to hold on to the old paternalistic atmosphere.

> We are still early in the continuum of how this will play out. Employees are skeptical, and this is intensified in a poor economy. This impacts productivity; people spend time talking about how bad they feel. We are entering a new paradigm with employees. We need to change expectations. The company isn't callous, it is doing what it feels needs to be done.

There was agreement from this group of executives that while many aspects of the new social contract are still evolving, several seem quite clear. These include the following: (1) an employment relationship that is exchange based; (2) a shift in responsibilities from employer to employee; and (3) a redefinition of a career within one firm to the idea of "employability" with many firms.

The following sections outline each of these new tenets as they were described by the executives interviewed.

An Exchange Relationship

The conditions for the new employee-corporation relationship involve a fair exchange that is situationally determined. The exchange continues as long as it is beneficial to both parties, as opposed to there being a long-term expectation. This employment relationship can stop at any time, based on termination by either the corporation or the employee. From the corporate perspective, continued employment is based on performance, rather than seniority. In addition, there must be a match of skills based on current business needs. In some circumstances, employees are offered retraining or relocation as a condition of continued employment. One executive describes the nature of this new relationship:

> In the past, there was a strong objective of providing job security. We began to change the language of this five years ago and we made a big deal in telling people about the change. The language became "employment security based upon performance." There has been a heavy emphasis on explaining to employees what that means. It doesn't mean security in one job: you must engage in life-long learning, must upgrade your skills, must make lateral shifts as the business shifts.

The corporate sentiment toward employees was described by another executive:

> We now say to employees, we'll invest in you while you are here, both in terms of training and pay. But even if you are a great performer, we can't guarantee you a job. It depends—we may cease being in this business, we don't know. It is a mutually beneficial relationship, but when it stops being so, that's it.

Employees have adopted a new attitude, based on the new relationship:

> The mentality now is, I'm the customer, this is a fair exchange, I am going to do what is best for my family and my economic circumstances.

Executives noted the new element of employee self-interest that did not exist under the previous long-term employment relationship:

> In the past ten years, corporate attitudes toward employees have changed and in turn, employee attitudes toward the corporation have changed. Employees are not loyal anymore. If there is a conflict between the corporation's interests and the employee's, the employee goes with his own; they have gotten much more self-interested.

Employees Bear the Burden

The burden of responsibility is shifting from the corporation to the employee. The corporation does not take care of employees any longer; employees must look out for their own futures. Two frequently cited examples of this emerging notion of shared responsibility are medical and retirement benefits, where employees are taking on a greater share of the financial burden. A more subtle but significant trend of shifting responsibility involves employees assuming responsibility for their developmental needs:

> Employees are expected to look after their own self-improvement. This is compared to several years ago when the manager was more responsible for the development of his employees. Now, it is a mutual role with more emphasis on the employee.

"Employability" Is the Career Goal

The notion of "employability" is the third component of the new social contract described by these executives. (See Chapter Twelve on older employees for an additional perspective on employability.) Corporations recognize that employees may lose their job at any time and accept responsibility for enhancing employees' abilities to get a job elsewhere:

> We now as a company see the change that Lynn Martin [U.S. Secretary of Labor during the Bush administration] portrayed as moving from job security to employability. We have a responsibility to train employees, help them be marketable so if they don't have a job here, they will be employable elsewhere.

This means continuing training and development opportunities and broadening employees' abilities to be flexible and adaptive:

> The shift is to keeping people employable—we put more burden on the employee for more flexibility. The commitment is not necessarily to do a job but continuing to be productive. Four or five years ago, we introduced an employee job transition effort as a result of rightsizing. It even used outside agency assistance. It put more burden on the employees to be responsible for their future. We began to realize that change and flexibility were the name of the game.

Table 2.1 summarizes elements of the social contract as it existed through the 1980s and shows the evolving 1990s version described above.

Implications of the 1990s Contract

The evolving social contract described in the previous section is a radical change in corporation-employee relations. The ramifications of this new arrangement are wide ranging, with many features yet to be understood. In the interviews, executives were asked their thoughts on the implications on this changing contract. The following section presents a summary of respondents' views on how the new social contract is affecting the work environment and the workforce.

Implications for the Work Environment

Many of the executives interviewed in this study used the metaphor of a pendulum to describe what is happening in their companies and in the business community. Some saw the pendulum swinging between a humanized and a dehumanized work environment; others saw it swinging between economic forces and social forces affecting the workplace.

Nearly all of the executives said that many of the elements of the new employee contract translate to a work environment that is harsher and not as people oriented:

Table 2.1. Elements of the Employee-Corporation Social Contract.

1950s to 1980s	1990s
Corporation as patriarch—relationship built on family loyalty	"Exchange" relationship—mutually beneficial, greater self-interest on both corporations' and employees' parts
Long-term security with the same firm	Employees bear the burden—responsibility shifting to employee, must look after own future
Entitlement mentality—included job, benefits, and career development	"Employability" as career goal—corporations recognize their role in enhancing employees' abilities to get jobs elsewhere if necessary

> What I would like to see is a long-term view of the social contract. . . .
> There are continuing reverberations of layoffs: you lay off fifty peo-
> ple but two hundred stop working because they are so worried about
> losing their jobs. This is a crude way of running the business; it is like
> cutting off your leg if you have gangrene before you see if there is
> another way to stop the infection.

This harsher environment has managerial consequences
including poor morale, more employee self-interest, and employee
mistrust of the corporation. The survivor syndrome described
above, in which people stop working because of concern about losing their job, parallels the earlier comments about employees'
being physically but not mentally on the job.

However, executives also discussed the concurrent infusion of
social programs, such as diversity and work-family, into the work
environment. Work-family initiatives mentioned were on-site day
care and increased acceptance of family leave, flexible work hours,
and telecommuting:

> Speaking in broader terms, there is more recognition that the
> employees' nonwork life affects their work life. There is more will-
> ingness on the part of the corporation to take care of employees'
> time needs, child care needs, elder care, and so forth.

> We are much more flexible to recognizing employees' other com-
> mitments. We have gone to more job-sharing situations, part-time
> and flexible hours. We have had to be more open minded about
> how work gets done. For example, people can be effective working
> at home.

In addition, more women and people of color are moving into
the workforce and into management positions, allowing for openness and awareness of varying perspectives.

> One aspect of the social contract that has changed is in recognition
> of diversity—there are cultural differences and gender differences.
> Under the old style, we had homogeneous groups, and in many
> ways they are easier to manage. We are finding that heterogeneous
> groups may be harder to manage but produce better results. Having

an Asian or African-American and a woman's perspective on product design is very important.

While this last executive's comments point to an integration of diversity into the new social contract, the majority of other respondents noted that the impacts of diversity and work-family trends have not yet been taken into account. Several expressed hope that these programs would counterbalance and humanize some of the harsher new tenets of the evolving social contract.

Other trends were noted in the balance between economic and social roles and responsibilities of the corporation. Many of the socially oriented programs, such as work-family and flextime, were initiated before resource scarcity and downsizing pressures became acute. In some companies, these programs have continued, becoming part of the culture and an economic tool for recruiting and retaining talented employees:

> The company gets good PR. It makes us a preferred employer, [and] is a recruiting tool. It makes employees' morale better, allows them to better balance work and family life.

In other corporations, lean times have caused these programs to be cut back. One executive who had previously worked for a company undergoing major downsizing, and who now works for a company in a better economic situation, spoke to the contrast, again in terms of the pendulum metaphor:

> At my old company, up until three years ago we were really pushing things like work-family balance, diversity. On a continuum, things were neutral to positive. Then when the bottom fell out economically, things shifted very quickly to the negative side. The issues they now are dealing with concern the survivors. I personally think the pendulum has gone too far toward strictly economics and not enough attention paid to the employee. At my new company, because we are growing at a clip, it is more to the neutral to positive side. The company has just made some decisions lately that reinforce this. Like on benefits, we just decided to keep the current pay-in percentages. Most other companies are shifting the burden more to employees; we consciously are leaving it where it is. This is very employee responsive.

Implications for the Workforce

A major trend is the shift to a more temporary workforce. The implications of a highly temporary workforce play out on several levels. From an individual perspective, it allows more flexibility:

> The whole question of what is loyalty becomes paramount. A good career is defined differently, people are moving around more. At the same time, life-style issues are coming into play. Employees are saying they want to work less, particularly if working all the long hours still won't guarantee them security.

At a managerial level, it is more difficult to manage this workforce effectively. Unplanned turnover increases and workforce and succession planning become more important and more complicated:

> You need staffing models with lots of options. We use more temporary employees. More people are willing to do the contract work, either through a consulting company or independently. A lot of people are saying, I don't mind working as an independent contractor, that way I can control how much work I can do.

> It's harder as a manager to manage this workforce. It's not like dealing with the permanent, stable workforce of the past. It is a more complicated work environment. One negative is that you may have a temporary employee representing the company on the front lines with customers. Does this employee understand the company way of doing things? How do customers view this person, how do you train them so that the fact that they are not a regular employee is invisible to the ultimate customer?

At a societal level, there was concern expressed that people changing jobs more often and a larger temporary workforce might bring down standards of living. This could negatively affect selected populations, specifically women and minorities. In addition, people will have less provisions made for them in retirement and will be underemployed, and corporations will have unstable workforces:

> I have real long-term societal concerns with use of temporary workers. I am old fashioned but find it bothersome that Manpower is now the largest employer in the country. There is not the same

level of loyalty, commitment, willingness to train people, as what we
have traditionally known.

I have some concerns about what this is doing to our society. We
have a lot of people losing jobs, and they don't show up on unemployment because they found a job at a lower rate with no benefits.
These people are going to stop spending money, and it will be a
vicious cycle. I am not sure what the answer is.

There was a general concern expressed about the quality and
skills of labor in the future and a sense that while there might be
sufficient numbers of people available, the pools would not have
the right mix of critical labor skills. There was consensus on the
need for radical reform in the educational system and recognition
that corporations will be required to take on a larger role. Many of
the corporations represented in these interviews are already contributing significant resources to school programs.

The most commonly identified benefit of the new social contract was employees becoming more independent and taking more
responsibility for their own work futures. Related advantages were
more opportunities, more entrepreneurism, people becoming
more self-directed and self-reliant, and employees taking control,
being "healthier." This transition was described by two executives:

On the up side, if you can get employees beyond the storm, can get
them more self-reliant, one could argue that the previous feelings
they had regarding security and all were illusions. Moving to a new
stage can be liberating for employees. Being in State A is okay. State
B is okay. It is the transition in between that is difficult. In State B,
employees begin to view themselves as companies of one. Working
here becomes one of choice, not habit.

When layoffs first happened, employees felt violated; the contract
was shattered. Once they recovered, some experienced tremendous
gains in terms of breaking the cycle of dependence. The transition
packages initially were very lucrative, and it spurred a great deal of
entrepreneurial activity. Eventually, over the long term, this will all
be about self-reliance and resiliency.

These executives described other benefits of the new social
contract that are promoting business efficiency. There is increased

"fluidity" or ability to move people around as different business units need varying personnel levels or skill sets. There is also an improved ability to remove marginal performers; it is both easier and more readily accepted to get rid of people based on performance. Better ability to recruit and retain high performers was noted as a side effect of this heightened emphasis on performance:

> We are far more likely to attract high performers. We have given up the golden handcuffs, which couldn't allow us to get rid of low performers. This has helped our survival; we couldn't survive with the marginal employees, but before we couldn't get rid of them. This is all in the survival interests of the business.

The interviewees also suggested that employees have not been treated appropriately through all the recent downsizing and reengineering. A minority felt very strongly that the pendulum had swung too far toward the economic side. They felt that corporations that seek to maintain a competitive advantage in the future must treat their employees differently.

> We think the only source of sustainable advantage in the marketplace is people. We have misread things in the way we have handled our people through all this. There is a downward cycle; once you start hacking at the cost structure, you are serving the customers worse. Another downside is that we have lost a lot of talented people.

> What has been done in the past ten years can't continue; we can't handle employees as commodities and expect innovation. This needs to change. If you believe organizations are big information-processing machines, then how does my workforce differ from yours? If this is only an exchange transaction, then employees have no incentive for loyalty, employees only need to build their résumés. We talk about organizational learning. At an organizational level, it requires a rich fabric of employees; you can't gain competitive advantage with an organization of strangers. You need networks of people inside and outside the organization that can innovate; it requires a relationship we are currently walking away from.

The implications—positive and negative—of the changing employee-employer social contract are summarized in Table 2.2.

Table 2.2. Impact of the 1990s Social Contract on Work Environment and Workforce.

Positives	Negatives
More fluidity: can move people around	Bad morale
Increased ability to remove marginal performers	Reduced productivity
Better ability to recruit and retain high performers	Employee mistrust of corporation
Temporary workforce allows for more flexibility	Temporary workforce is more difficult to manage; may result in reduced standards of living
Employees are more independent, self-directed, entrepreneurial	Increase in unplanned turnover
Infusion of social programs, such as diversity and work-family	Future workforce may not have the right skills

Undercurrents in the Research

The comments from executives point to a frustration level among some managers who participated in our survey concerning the human consequences of the downsizing process and deep reservations about the tenets of the new social contract. Although these executives were quite open about such feelings, many other executives interviewed expressed similar sentiments in more subtle ways. Throughout interviews conducted in this research, direct responses were accompanied by side comments expressing personal frustration at finding the appropriate balance in the corporation's treatment of employees. These emotional undercurrents revealed that a majority of the executives were not comfortable with the new social contract as it is being played out, even though it has produced some noticeable benefits. The executives were struggling with what the social contract should be and how to achieve it. The expressions of "aha!" and the sudden realizations that took place during the interviews gave evidence that the executives used the interview process to make sense of certain issues in a way that their day-to-day crisis orientation rarely allows them to do. Many were eager to know how other companies were handling these issues.

Analysis

To better understand the data and the undercurrents we have presented in this chapter, we now return to the three questions stated in the introduction: (1) What do executives on the "front lines" see as the ramifications of the current "contract" between employers and their employees? (2) Does this 1990s social contract represent a fundamental shift in American businesses' conceptualization of their economic and social responsibilities? (3) What is seen as the appropriate balance of corporate economic and social roles and responsibilities?

To analyze the significance of respondents' thoughts about these questions in a broader context, we have integrated the empirical interview data with other research on corporate social responsibility and management theory.

Ramifications of the Current Employer-Employee Contract

The social contract between corporations and their employees is undergoing a transformation as corporations continue to downsize. The numbers of jobs lost, the continued restructuring, and persistent downsizing pressure illustrate the profound challenges American industry is facing. The proliferation of reengineering initiatives attests to the need for large-scale institutional design changes to compete now and into the future. A large part of this change involves the employment relationship corporations offer their employees.

The relationship or "contract" between individual employees and their corporations has been an important theme in management research. MacNeill (1985) proposes a framework, used frequently in this literature, which defines "transactional" versus "relational" contracts. Transactional contracts are close ended, narrow in scope, and exchange based. Relational contracts are socioeconomic, open ended, and subjective. The term *psychological contract* was coined in the 1960s (Argyris, 1960) and is used to describe a phenomenon based on an individual's interpretation of the employment contract. (For an additional perspective on the "psychological contract," see Chapter One in this volume.) Early in an employee's tenure, this relationship is transactional in nature. Recent research on psychological contracts looks at the complex relational aspects of the employee contract that build over time. These include actions that promote corporate loyalty, such as heavy socialization into a corporate culture and promises of security and career advancement. Studies point to the emotional burden individuals endure when they feel the psychological contract has not been met (Rousseau and Parks, 1992). Research on layoffs shows that perceived violation of co-workers' contracts can produce similar emotional effects in survivors (Brockner, 1988, 1992).

The term *psychological contract* is framed at the individual-corporate level. A similar term, *social contract,* has been used to describe the unstated contract that exists between the corporations and all their constituencies, including employees, communities, shareholders, and society at large (Donaldson and Dunfee, 1994). Using MacNeill's framework, this type of contract is inherently relational. The specific elements of such contracts are not well defined in this literature; however, it is normative in stipulating that ethical societal norms govern acceptable versus unacceptable behavior. For example, Carroll (1991) defines three types of managerial orientations toward employee stakeholders. "Immoral" management treats employees as factors of production to be exploited, "amoral" management treats employees as the law requires, and "moral" management treats employees as a resource, with respect and mutual trust.

The exchange tenet of the new social contract is strictly transactional, whereas the previous social contract contained both relational and transactional components. The relational components upon which the psychological contract is heavily based are now much more precarious, perhaps even nonexistent. As the survivor studies show, the breaking of the old contract and its relational components, such as security and advancement with the firm, can have devastating impacts on worker morale and productivity. The survey data discussing employees being physically but not mentally on the job confirm this phenomenon.

The second new contract tenet—employees bearing more responsibility—also reflects a lessening of the relational bonds and a trend toward a strictly transactional relationship. The third tenet, employability, moderates the strictly transactional nature of the 1990s contract by requiring corporations to bear some responsibility for employees' securing jobs elsewhere if work is not available in that corporation.

From a normative perspective, the 1990s contract falls in between "immoral" and "amoral" management on Carroll's scale of moral management. Employees are treated as a factor in production; however, there is no evidence to support the intention to exploit. Again, the concept of employability moderates a more extreme "immoral" stance by implying a minimal level of corporate responsibility for employees securing employment elsewhere if necessary.

A Fundamental Shift?

The notion of a corporation's moral responsibilities to its stakeholders and society is a central theme in the broader corporate social responsibility literature. The question of whether and to what extent corporations bear societal responsibility beyond that of a narrow-purpose economic institution has been debated. Management theorists have made a strong and continuing case that corporate roles and responsibilities include both economic and social domains and that the two domains can be successfully merged (for a literature review, see Wood, 1991). *Fortune* has published annually since the 1970s a peer review of major corporations' ratings on key aspects of social responsibility, attesting to the importance of this dimension of business operations. Large corporations, such as Merck and IBM, have staked high value on performance and reputation in the social arena. Numerous nonprofit organizations provide awards and other recognitions to socially responsive businesses.

Bipolar trends of corporate social responsibility are emerging in the 1990s. Samuelson (1993), in a controversial essay in *Newsweek*, declared the "Good Corporation" to be dead—"We thought all companies could marry efficiency and social responsibility. We were wrong" (p. 41). Despite Samuelson's claim, there is broad evidence to support the alternative proposition—that the socially responsible firm is alive and well. New investment firms and mutual funds have been created using social performance as the determining factor in investment recommendations. A 1993 estimate attributes more than $600 million in investment decisions as based on some combination of social and economic factors (Sodeman and Carroll, 1994). A consortium of companies has been formed called "Businesses for Social Responsibility," and over six hundred companies nationwide are members. Successful "new age" businesses, such as Tom's of Maine, explicitly place social responsibility first in their credos of corporate values (Chappell, 1993).

All of the respondents in this survey acknowledged that the corporation has both social and economic roles to play. Striking the proper balance between these roles is the challenge; where the final balance will lie remains questionable. In this study, the economic role was most clearly in focus when respondents discussed the cutbacks necessary to meet shareholder goals and the low morale and productivity that downsizing has caused. The social role became clear when respondents discussed the social programs that have been put in place, such as diversity and work-family initiatives. Figure 2.1 puts these elements in the context of a seesaw metaphor similar to the pendulum metaphor described by survey respondents. As reflected on the seesaw, the difficult economic choices companies are currently facing are driving many of the "dehumanizing" influences in the work environment; the counterbalancing social side is bringing in the "humanizing" elements. (Two additional perspectives on how these forces may balance out appear in Chapter One's discussion of the possibility of the new contract combining transactional and relational approaches via a contract "with a heart" and in Chapter Six, which offers ways that caregiving relationships can mitigate the negative impacts of the new contract.)

Seeking a Balance

Management thinkers over the past twenty years have tried to define an appropriate balance between economic and social roles. Many advocate the view that both are needed for corporate success. The

Figure 2.1. Balancing the Work Environment.

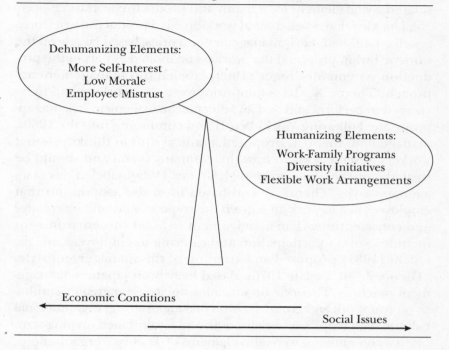

current bipolar split—some firms opting for a pendulum swing toward economics, others toward social values—tells us that perhaps we are no further along in resolving this problem than we were twenty years ago. The set of corporations represented in this survey exhibit a complex combination of both trends in this bipolar split. On the surface, much of the data from this research study support Samuelson's notion that the "good corporation is dead" and that dehumanizing elements are producing a transactional employer-employee relationship. The undercurrents in the research, however, point to executives' discomfort with this current state of affairs. The 1990s contract as it has been portrayed in this chapter may be in a transitional state. The social contract that this group of executives wants to create is one that integrates the benefits of a more independent and flexible workforce with one that has some relational ties—but not up to the level of the 1970s. Relational ties—and the psychological benefits that accompany them—still seem to be considered a vital element for a happy and productive workforce.

The idea that a well-treated workforce is a productive workforce is well established. Early management theories, based largely on the work of Taylor, proposed that workers be treated as part of the production system. McGregor (1960) labeled this management approach "Theory X." Its assumptions were that workers had to be coerced to perform and that an autocratic management style was appropriate. Following World War II and continuing into the 1960s, management theorists proposed a radical shift in thinking—that workers deserve a say in how the company is run and should be treated more compassionately. McGregor (1960) labeled this management style "Theory Y" and based it on the assumption that employees like to work and, given the responsibility, will be creative and conscientious. The management style for this environment includes worker participation and catering to employees' needs. Ouchi (1981) proposed an extension of this management style, "Theory Z," in the late 1970s. Based heavily on Japanese management practices, Theory Z organizations place even greater emphasis on teamwork and group decision making. A strong organizational culture, high employee socialization, and loyalty based on long-term mutual commitment were also elements of Theory Z organizations. Many of the best-selling management books of the 1980s, geared to excellence, endorsed a Theory Z management style.

Many in this group of executives surveyed in this study still agree with the managerial theories of the 1970s and 1980s that a happy workforce is a productive workforce. They are concerned that the 1990s social contract may create employees who are both unhappy and unproductive. Government statistics show that productivity is not rising or not rising as fast as some companies have claimed. The strongly transactional nature of the 1990s social contract is evidence of a shift back to the days of Taylorism and Theory X, when employees were a factor in production; so says at least one survey respondent.

An Evolutionary Perspective

The undercurrents of uneasiness with the current state of affairs lead us to believe that we are not seeing a permanent throwback to Theory X. Rather, American corporations are in a transition period toward a future state that incorporates many of the elements described here but ultimately "looks" like none of the organizational cultures described in prevailing theories. (Chapter Three's discussion of the implications of the new contract on organizational forms offers an additional perspective on this issue.) From the 1970s through the 1980s, American executives recognized and saw the benefits of balancing social and economic roles. Now that economic realities are making it harder to maintain that balance, we have seen a pendulum swing toward a more economically defined model. The pendulum is starting to swing back again, however, toward a recognition that without social programs and integration of people's lives and respectful treatment, corporations may be "throwing the baby out with the bathwater."

It is our contention that this evolutionary cycle is part of the continuing socialization of business organizations. Figure 2.2 depicts this cycle along a time line beginning with the 1950s. The sample of organizations reflected in this survey follows an evolutionary line from the "good" corporation to the reengineered corporation to an emergent "socioeconomically balanced corporation." Under this future scenario, corporations maintain contracts with employees that promote loyalty and productivity, even though the workforce is more "temporary" in character and careers involve numerous organizations.

There is an alternative evolution as well, as the more entrepreneurial "new age" businesses (for example, members of Businesses for Social Responsibility) demonstrate more acceptance of economic realities. Many observers were startled, for example, when Ben & Jerry's, a classic example of a values-driven company whose corporate credo and operations have underscored progressive social values, decided to recruit a professional CEO and break their long-standing rule that the CEO's salary would not exceed seven times that of the lowest-paid employee (Kaufman-Rosen, 1994). This decision is evidence of a shift toward economics.

As illustrated in Figure 2.2, the models of the socially oriented new age corporations and the reengineered good corporations are converging as companies and managers seek to hold on to core values while being responsive to real economic and social pressures.

Figure 2.2. The Evolutionary Cycle in Corporate Balance of Social and Economic Purposes.

	up to 1950s	1960	1970	1980	1990	The Future
Corporate Balancing of Social and Economic Purposes	The corporation as an economic institution →	Corporations start to develop enlightened self-interest →	"Good" Corporations →	Reengineered corporations →	"Socioeconomically balanced" corporations	
				Rise of entrepreneurship →	"New age" businesses ↗	
Underlying Management Theories	Taylorism Theory X	Theory Y Psychological contract Social contract	Corporate social responsibility (CSR)	Theory Z	New trends in CSR	Communitarianism Sustainable development Caring organizations
Timeline	up to 1950s	1960	1970	1980	1990	The Future

Conclusion

New social trends and theories support the emergence of a socioe-conomically balanced corporation. "Communitarianism" is a social movement that has been adopted by a wide-ranging group of social scientists. Its statement of "truths" calls for "creating a new moral, social, and public order based on restored communities" (Etzioni, 1993). The environmental movement's call for "sustainable development" envisions a similar holistic approach to environmental issues that takes into consideration all aspects of economic and social life. For business organizations, this means redefining "the rules of the economic game in order to move from a situation of wasteful consumption and pollution to one of conservation, and from one of privilege and protectionism to one of fair and equitable changes open to all" (Schmidheiny and Business Council for Sustainable Development, 1992). Etzioni (1993) links these social movements: "Communitarians are dedicated to working with our fellow citizens to bring about the changes in values, habits, and public policies that will allow us to do for society what the environmental movement seeks to do for nature: To safeguard and enhance our future" (p. 3).

The adaptation of these broader social movements into the management world is just beginning. Many of the new age businesses discussed earlier subscribe to similar principles; they have committed publicly through membership in Businesses for Social Responsibility. A growing number of organizations (more than eighty by the end of 1994) have committed to principles of sustainable development through becoming signatories of the Coalition of Environmentally Responsible Economics (CERES) Principles or through their own statement of principles.

Practicing managers predict the struggles to become socio-economically balanced will continue:

> Being a good corporate citizen will continue to be important. The aging population will force us to deal with it; so will the new baby boomlet. There will be more gray areas, company and employee responsibilities will blur more, like companies providing more day care. At the same time, though, companies will be continuing to downsize. Those trends tend to be on a collision course and that will be a struggle.

Despite these struggles and some of the grim assessments of current organizational life depicted by survey respondents, they also express a tremendous optimism about learning from past mistakes, the creativity of American business, and getting beyond these difficult times:

> What will happen when we are back in shape? We probably won't return to the fabulous days of the '70s, but things will get better.

> I don't think we, or other companies, are going to make the same mistakes twice. Everyone is putting their houses in order.

> It is an exciting time for those who have the courage and conviction.

Recommendations for Managerial Action

Harry, our representative human resources director in the opening vignette, is engaging in the kind of reflective and institutional-level thinking that is needed concerning the issues we present in this chapter. (Chapter Ten offers some new perspectives on how to engage in such reflective activities.) As our empirical research brought to light, the crisis management mode of today's human resources professionals is not conducive to thinking through the implications of the new social contract. Take time to think about the ramifications of your company's social contracts—with your employees, with the communities where you have a presence, and with society at large. Are you comfortable that the balance your company is striking between economic and social roles and responsibilities is appropriate and in line with your organizational values? Do you feel confident that you know the viewpoints of all your stakeholders on these issues? It might be an opportunity for group reflective sessions and/or focus groups to bring these issues out in the open for discussion.

References

Argyris, C. P. (1960). *Understanding organizational behavior.* Homewood, IL: Dorsey Press.

Brockner, J. (1988). The effects of work layoffs on survivors: Research, theory, and practice. In B. Staw & L. Cummings (Eds.), *Research in organizational behavior* (pp. 213–255). Greenwich, CT: JAI Press.

Brockner, J. (1992, Winter). Managing the effects of layoffs on survivors. *California Management Review,* 9–28.

Byrne, J. S. (1994, May 9). The pain of downsizing. *Business Week,* 61–67.

Carroll, A. B. (1991, July-August). The pyramid of corporate social responsibility: Toward the moral management of organizational stakeholders. *Business Horizons,* 46.

Chappell, T. (1993). *The soul of a business: Managing for profit and the common good.* New York: Bantam Books.

Donaldson, T., & Dunfee, T. W. (1994). Toward a unified concept of business ethics: Integrative social contracts theory. *Academy of Management Review, 19,* 252–284.

Etzioni, A. (1993). *The spirit of community: Rights, responsibilities, and the communitarian agenda.* New York: Crown.

Kaufman-Rosen, L. (1994, October 17). Being cruel to be kind. *Newsweek,* 51–52.

McGregor, D. (1960). *The human side of enterprise.* New York: McGraw-Hill.

MacNeill, I. R. (1985). Relational contract: What we do and do not know. *Wisconsin Law Review,* 483–525.

Ouchi, W. G. (1981). *Theory Z.* Reading, MA: Addison-Wesley.

Rousseau, D. M., & Parks, J. (1992). The contracts of individuals and organizations. In L. Cummings & B. Staw (Eds.), *Research in organizational behavior* (pp. 1–47). Greenwich, CT: JAI Press.

Samuelson, R. J. (1993, July 5). R.I.P.: The good corporation. *Newsweek,* 41.

Schmidheiny, S., & Business Council for Sustainable Development. (1992). *Changing course: A global perspective on development and the environment.* Cambridge, MA: MIT Press.

Sodeman, W. A., & Carroll, A. B. (1994). Social investment firms: Their purposes, principles, and investment criteria. *Proceedings of the Fifth Annual Meeting of the International Association for Business and Society,* 339–344.

Wood, D. J. (1991). Corporate social performance revisited. *Academy of Management Review, 16,* 691–718.

Chapter Three

New Organizational Forms and the New Career

Philip H. Mirvis
Douglas T. Hall

1. Your objective in a job is not self-expression but to put bread on the table. Knowing this will save you painful disillusionment later.
2. Staying happy on the job is your own responsibility.
3. There is only one perfect definition of doing a good job: making your boss look good.
4. Don't expect thanks for a job well done. That is taken care of by the person who brings around your paycheck ["How to Get a Job," 1977, p. 37].

This is the sort of grit that substitutes for career counseling in today's downsized, dog-eat-dog corporate environment. With all of the cutbacks in firms that have been the most paternal providers of security to employees—firms such as IBM, Digital Equipment Corporation, General Motors, Japanese industrials, and Lloyds of London—the notion of a career as a series of upward moves based in a long-term employment relationship has been shattered. However, if we think of a career more in terms of skill development, initiative, and personal freedom, then today's turbulent work environment provides far greater opportunities than one ever would have imagined in the heyday of the big blue-chip firms.

In this chapter, we explore this paradox with reference to emerging new forms of organization. We look for a synthesis in a new strategy of career development—continuous, lifelong learning—embedded in an employment context that emphasizes and rewards flexibility over the life course. In lieu of offering security to the worker, this new approach challenges companies to invest in a portfolio of skills and develop people through work assignments, learning regimens, and flexible arrangements. It also puts added responsibility on working people to "learn a living" and prepare themselves for ups and downs throughout their work lives.

Central to our argument is the realization that traditional definitions of work, nonwork, and careers are changing in America, Japan, and Europe. A decade and a half of corporate downsizing and broad-based deindustrialization has seen employers reduce staff, shut down facilities, and make more use of consultants and the contingent workforce. At the same time, lead companies are recognizing that human resources are their prime source of competitive advantage (Lawler, 1993). Given rapid advances in price per performance, firms are finding that technological advantages are shorter lived and easier to copy than in the past. Furthermore, any company can downsize and reengineer; there is no unique or sustained advantage in these methods of managing. Also, the idea of contracting out work or renting a workforce, although it has applications, cannot substitute for the advantages that come from having skilled and dedicated employees aligned with the organization. As a result, employers are searching for a workable mix of employment options and development tools to respond to the needs and build the capability of today's workforce.

New Environmental Conditions

Some thirty years ago, specialists in organization theory found a mismatch between changes in the environment and the design of formal organizations (Emery and Trist, 1965; Lawrence and Lorsch, 1967; Bennis and Slater, 1968). Their research confirmed that tightly structured, autocratic organizational forms were indeed effective in relatively simple, stable environments. However, when tasks become complex and the environment changes rapidly, a centralized structure cannot access enough original source information to figure out what is going on, and standard operating procedures limit the organization's capability to respond with innovation. In order to adapt quickly and effectively to turbulence, they reasoned, companies need more flexible work arrangements where those closest to the action are involved in assessing the situation and responding to it.

On the contemporary scene, Hall (1993) argues that firms best suited to adapting to complexity and rapid change in today's environment are free, fast, and facile—what he terms a *3F organization.* *Free* means having components (work units and people) that are autonomous and able to respond to problems and opportunities in market segments. *Fast* means having the capability to assess and respond quickly to these situations. *Facile* means being able to change thinking practices and established routines in light of new information or developments.

Prototypes of the free, fast, and facile organization date from the 1960s when, for example, Bennis and Slater (1968) argued that "democracy is inevitable" and advised organizations to devise "temporary" structures to respond to rapid change in their environments. The 1970s witnessed "collateral" forms of organization where temporariness would be built into project groups, "parallel" structures where semipermanent committees of, say, workers and managers would oversee change efforts, and the "matrix" organization, which institutionalized cross-functional linkages to accomplish complex tasks (Zand, 1974; Galbraith, 1977; Davis and Lawrence, 1977). By the 1980s, organizations began an era of restructuring exemplified by new work designs, reengineering and continuous improvement programs, and increased numbers of mergers and cross-company ventures in service of reinventing the corporation (see Lawler, Mohrman, and Ledford, 1992; Mirvis and Marks, 1992, for reviews). Continuing to evolve, corporate giants such as General Electric are described today as "boundaryless organizations" and increasing numbers of "virtual" corporations and project groups are coming into being. Futurist Alvin Toffler (1990) has coined the term *flex-form* to encapsulate the key design principle that will mark the new workplace.

In this evolutionary context, traditional career paths have become dinosaurs. Environmental changes are the cause of their demise. In the dinosaur's case, a comet hit the earth and climactic upheaval proved deadly to a physiology that had adapted dinosaurs to one kind of earth and constrained their adaptability in another. In the case of traditional careers, the force of destruction comes from complex, rapid, and powerful global developments that have upset the prevailing industrial order and chilled employment relations. When it comes to physiology, we are discovering that the one-life, one-company career is too rigid and unwieldy to survive in today's world.

However, the dinosaur metaphor inspires hope. Scientists are learning, for instance, of extraordinary diversity that enhanced the adaptability of dinosaur species of ages ago and allowed for successive generations to reign as planetary conditions changed. It should not surprise, then, that National Public Television serves up "Barney and Friends" to provide lessons on getting along with others and coping with the complexities of life—or that the popular book and movie, *Jurassic Park*, is a cautionary tale about resurrecting old life forms in a new environment. One message in this metaphor is that it is unlikely we can resurrect the traditional career; the other is that the career concept can possibly evolve and adapt to new environmental conditions. Indeed, there are likely as many dinosaurs on earth now as there were at the height of the creatures' prehistoric dominance: they are just smaller and fly through the air! Can careers go through such a dramatic metamorphosis?

The Flex-Firm

The future will favor *3F* organizations with their multiple divisions as well as joint ventures, regional alliances, and private-public partnerships. The large firms will dominate major markets while entrepreneurs, franchisers, and small businesses provide raw materials and technologies, handle support services, distribute goods, and at the same time reach niche markets with their own products and services. The future will see companies routinely reshaping and resizing themselves, regularly buying and selling off businesses, and periodically partnering with other institutions.

Flexible Size and Shape

Charles Handy (1989) configures the organization of tomorrow in the form of a shamrock with three leaves. The first leaf, and the most important for continuity and organizational survival, contains a core staff of managers, technicians, and professionals. These are.

highly skilled individuals who are expected to make a major commitment to the organization and derive a lot of their sense of identity from it. The second leaf is contractors, specialized people and firms, often outside the organization, who serve a variety of needs, including supply, distribution, and routine control functions. Their work is not part of the essential core technology and competence of the firm and can usually be done better, faster, and cheaper by someone else in a smaller, more specialized, and autonomous position. The third leaf is the contingent labor force. These are part-timers and temporary workers who provide a "buffer" to the core workforce of a firm.

Already there is considerable movement in this direction in corporate America. Over 350 of the Fortune 500 companies of fifteen years ago disappeared from the New York Stock Exchange via mergers and acquisitions. Over three thousand substantial joint ventures involving large public companies were formed during this period and the number of strategic alliances, joining information system and entertainment companies in the "infotainment" business, is growing exponentially. More and more companies are "outsourcing," say, their printing and publication work to contractors such as Xerox. Meanwhile, Xerox has turned over its telecommunications function to another contractor, EDS. A final indicator on how quickly things are changing: Manpower, the temporary employment service, is now the nation's largest employer.

Flextime and Flexspace

Work within organizations is also becoming more flexible. Surveys of company practices find that a majority of large companies are offering flextime hours and flexible work schedules, part-time work for managers and professionals and staff, as well as a variety of child-care and work-family–related services and leaves (Mirvis, 1993a). In addition, many more employers are expected to offer job-sharing opportunities for some of their employees and give them the option to work at home (flexplace).

At present, these flexible options come under the heading of "people programs" in many companies and serve the purpose of helping firms to attract and retain working parents and employees seeking more balance in their lives. Hall and Parker (1993), however, see other strategic benefits in this move toward more work-place flexibility. Changes in customers' life-styles and expectations, for instance, have already altered the traditional nine-to-five work-day and five-day workweek. More and more retail stores, grocers, and customer service help lines are open twelve, sixteen, even twenty-four hours a day, seven days a week. There is also the mat-ter of doing business globally and adjusting to the ebb and flow of project-type work. In this context, a case can be made that firms able to do business any time gain an important competitive advan-tage from their flexible work schedules.

Furthermore, the global village will be increasingly wired to-gether and businesses around the world are expected to increas-ingly profit via electronic commerce. Advances in technology (hardware and software) already afford increasing numbers of peo-ple the chance to work from their homes, cars, and suburban of-fices. The expense of downtown office space, the wear and tear of commuting (not to mention the environmental impact), and the costs of business travel and meetings could be reduced substan-tially by further development of telecommuting and -conferencing capabilities and their widespread use. When businesses are fully wired to their suppliers, distributors, and customers and into the homes of potential customers around the nation and world, those who are best positioned to do business any place could be at a decided advantage.

Flexible Jobs and Staffing

Olmsted and Smith (1994) make the point that flextime and -place, when complemented by flexible staffing, make for a flexi-ble company strategy. Firms are already investing in flexible tech-nology and office space and setting up flexible arrangements with suppliers, distributors, and vendors—under the rubric of just-in-time service delivery. Hence many experts contend that just-in-time staffing, through contracted and contingent labor, is the wave of the future.

In a future of continuous restructuring and reengineering, temporary agency employees will be called on to fill in during peri-ods of high demand for clerical support and customer service that heretofore would have been met by regular employees. In-house pools of part-timers, increasing throughout industry, will rotate from area to area as workloads rise and fall. These workers all represent the third leaf of Handy's shamrock organization and will help to protect the job security of full-time, core employees. In addition, we foresee companies relying more on outside business service firms and highly paid independent contractors to handle much of the work currently done by corporate staff and in-house technicians and professionals. The "outsourcing" of hiring, training, and other personnel services, of communications and public relations, of billing and payments, and even of accounting and financial analyses to firms on the second leaf of the shamrock organization has increased dramatically in the past few years. This enables companies to shop around for better service and lets permanent employees focus on "value-added" work. Independent consultants and consulting firms are positioning themselves to help companies organize and staff new projects and ventures and then withdraw as the effort matures or is completed. They say it is easier and less expensive long term for companies to staff up and down with independent contractors rather than permanent, full-time employees.

Finally, there is good reason to believe that the work of tomorrow's full-time employees will also change dramatically. Bridges (1994), for one, contends we are entering a "post-job" era. He points out that the very idea of a job, with prescribed duties and hours, arose as a means to "package" work in the factories and bureaucracies of an industrialized nation. As we move ahead into postindustrialization, the argument goes, work will be packaged in the form of time-bounded projects and temporary assignments. Lacking a better term, some experts refer to this as a *virtual* job in the sense that people, individually and in teams, will have to define their tasks and work assignments and determine when and how they work, and they are apt to "interface" electronically more often than face to face.

Needed: A Flexible Workforce

This move toward flexibility has several implications for the management and staffing of companies' workforces. For instance, firms are beginning to abandon the idea that strategy consists of a comprehensive picture of the environment, translated into a master plan of action, and implemented top-down by redirecting organizational units and people. Based on the new sources of competitive advantage we have discussed, strategy is best understood as a corporate outlook and direction that emerges from continuous information processing about environmental conditions accompanied by coordinated responses by people, units, and the organization as a whole.

A Portfolio of Skills

From this vantage, rather than thinking of a business as a set of work units with preestablished structures and responsibilities, it is useful to see a company as having a portfolio of skills that can be applied to the demands of varied situations. This means keeping a cadre of generalists, as well as technical specialists and skilled workers, in the core of a company and having flexible and variably skilled second- and third-leaf resources at the ready to deploy as needed. The most successful companies will be able to rearrange their skill portfolio by moving people quickly into new assignments, forming new work structures for them, and having them hit the ground running.

Clearly, new competencies will be required of working people in this scenario. To staff the core of company and to build a more flexible workforce overall requires that firms select and develop people who have an appetite for continuous learning and the capacity to cope with the ambiguity and challenge of shifting job assignments. Companies have traditionally hired only a select group of "high-potential" employees with this mind-set and then groomed them through carefully selected job assignments and training programs. Many more multiskilled workers of this type will be needed at every level for tomorrow's work.

This puts a premium on working people becoming multiskilled and comfortable moving into and out of new settings and situations. Traditionally, training has come at fixed points in a career and often at the initiative of the employer. Looking ahead, it will have to be more or less continuous and largely self-motivated by those hoping to remain full-time employees. Even those contingent workers filling third-leaf jobs will need increased flexibility in their personal schedules and skill sets to adapt to frequent changes in work hours and duties.

Self-Designed Jobs

Many companies tomorrow will abandon rigid job descriptions and classification schemes along with their reliance on standardized work rules, fixed work hours and locales, and, of course, the oversight of employees by layers of supervision. Instead, the new imperative will be to give people the freedom to create self-designing relationships among co-workers and with relevant customers, suppliers, distributors, and so on. This will put much more flexibility into people's work roles and regimens.

The thinking here is that as organizations become more decentralized and functions gain local autonomy, their ultimate resource will be people who have the skills and discretion to manage the demands of novel work situations. Thus more and more employees will come to be viewed as semiautonomous, self-managing professionals whose security is not in corporate career paths but in their core competencies.

What competencies will become more important? Certainly, companies will need many more people with the abilities to plan and organize their work, set priorities and time lines, and supervise their own work. In addition, self-pacing and self-discipline will become crucial competencies for people staffing short-term projects or working out of their homes on the electronic highway. Interpersonal skills and the ability to work as part of a team will also be essential in the organization designs of tomorrow.

Continuous Learning

With frequent job rotation, short-term assignments, lateral career moves, and the necessity of moving from the first leaf of a flexible company to the second and third leaves, the new career involves a good deal more than simply earning a living. Instead, it will require *learning* a living. Tomorrow's versions of "color your own parachute" will emphasize the importance of varied experience and advise jobholders to continually network and take advantage of formal development and education programs that are offered.

Those seeking higher-skilled employment will obviously have to continue to learn more about computer technologies and their applications in business processes. Upgraded skills will also be needed for those hoping to fill techno-service jobs, which are projected to increase dramatically in the future. The larger point to make is that continuous learning will not simply be needed for people to get ahead in their careers; it will be essential to having one.

Personal Implications for Career Development

Seymour Sarason (1977) makes the point that many people who came into the workforce in the 1950s had a "one life/one career" outlook. Those who have entered the workforce in the past thirty years have, to some extent, recognized the necessity of more frequent job changes. Most, however, are still imbued with the idea that a career is marked by constant progress and that occupational success is defined by mastering a job and then savoring the recognition and perks that follow from seniority.

We contend that more and more careers in the future will involve periodic cycles of skill apprenticeship, mastery, and re-skilling. In addition, we expect that lateral rather than upward movement will constitute career development and that late careers will increasingly be defined in terms of phased retirement. The problem is that this model of career progress is new and not yet accepted as the norm by many workers and managers. Indeed, it seems the antithesis of the onward-and-upward ideal that fires the American success ethic. Furthermore, it does not fit the more conservative but realistic notion that through hard work and diligence one can "make it" in a chosen field of endeavor.

Naturally, as the careers of more and more people unfold in peaks and valleys, and cross-functional moves gain currency as essential to multiskilling and continued employability, career progress of this sort will come to be acceptable to and respected by the American workforce. During this period of transition, however, it will be essential for working people to adjust their expectations about career progress and to savor the intrinsic rewards and psychological success that come from challenging new assignments.

It seems inescapable, too, that workers will have to change jobs, companies, and even careers over their life course in the decades ahead. With frequent job rotation, developmental assignments, lateral career moves, and the option of going from the first leaf of the adaptable company to second and third leaves, the "new career" in corporations promises to tax even the most adaptable worker. Workers who cannot adapt to this kind of change will likely find themselves downwardly mobile at an earlier than expected age or simply ushered out.

This means people will have to learn how to adapt to new situations. One way is to keep people moving through a number of career cycles rather than trying to prolong the maintenance stage of their career. Companies can do this by encouraging exploration of new areas of work even while a person is thriving in the present one; and they can legitimize the process of planning for disengaging and moving on even while one is still performing well in one's current work. Indeed, we can foresee a time when employees might move in and out of their organizations by, say, working in core areas for a time, taking a job in a supplier company or consulting firm, working as an individual contractor on selected projects, and then returning to the fold as a senior core contributor.

There is simply too much uncertainty about future organizational needs to chart out prospective career paths and steer people through precise developmental sequences. Also, there is ample evidence that many working people today recognize that promises of future promotions are illusory. They would rather "pack their own parachute" than move through their corporation's definition of career development (Hirsch, 1987). All of this means that the individual is truly on his or her own in developing a career. Thus people are well advised to conduct self-assessments, network, and participate in self-development programs to upgrade their skills and marketability. Hakim (1994) advises that people think of themselves as self-employed. In this context, what, if anything, can the organization do to promote career growth?

Career Development Practices

What exactly would it look like if a firm were more flexible in managing careers as it goes about continually restructuring itself? As a start, we have to consider seriously the idea that an organization should not be in the business of career planning—at least as it has been conventionally defined. Based on the adaptive requirements we have discussed, it is instead incumbent upon firms to ensure employees are exposed to a variety of challenging work assignments, develop both short-term performance-related skills and the meta-skills needed for long-term adaptability, and have the freedom and support to self-design their careers in line with the contours of a changing organization.

1. *Selection and placement are crucial to development.* The competencies required to manage and staff the adaptable company will differ from those needed in steady-as-she-goes companies. Many firms, for instance, hire people primarily for today's jobs and put a premium on their having today's skills. Professional assessments are reserved for "high-potential" employees who are then groomed through carefully selected job assignments. In the future, by contrast, companies will be well advised to scientifically select a larger proportion of their workforce and then offer the same sort of enriching on-the-job development.

Indeed, our feeling is that the best form of development is providing jobs that challenge and stretch workers over their life course. A large body of research has shown that the best source of development is the job itself (Hall and Associates, 1986). Rather than spend so much time worrying about what kinds of training and retraining programs are needed to keep people's skills current, we think it advisable to focus instead on providing information and support to help people get into jobs that will provide intrinsic opportunities for self-training and self-learning.

2. *Job assignments provide "real-time" learning.* The silver lining in the cloud of difficulties in promoting lifelong learning for workers is a critical finding that has emerged from years of research on career learning: the best development occurs on the job (Hall and Associates, 1986; McCall, Lombardo, and Morrison, 1988). Therefore, a critical task is to promote such learning through participation in projects emphasizing adaptive skills. For example, action learning programs at 3M, Motorola, and GE have utilized a variety of formats to incorporate personal development into work projects. Eli Lilly has for years utilized real-work projects, often related to a total quality or continuous improvement process, which are chosen by the individual for the purpose of learning new skills. How-

ever, they are done in addition to the person's regular work assignments, and the person enlists the aid of other people (coaches) for help as needed.

In most of these applications, workers cum trainees operate in project teams, thus building skills in managing complex relationships. So-called 360-degree feedback (because it comes from multiple sources and directions), teamwork and leadership skill training, and change management concepts are usually included as part of the learning program. In addition to such specialized assignments, real-time learning is also enhanced in companies that feature team-based work and encourage employees to help each other learn the new skills.

This approach to continuous learning differs substantially from programs aimed simply at retraining people for new jobs (see Table 3.1). In the case of retraining, the instructor is typically an expert, an academic or professional trainer, and the pedagogy is more or less programmed, featuring simulations, case studies, and/or discussions of theory. The costs of these kinds of programs is comparatively high. By contrast, real-time learning makes the worker the agent, and the learning comes from the task itself. Here, lessons come just in time as new tasks are performed, and the cost is lower than for classroom instruction or off-site seminars and is partially offset by the value of productive work.

We contend, too, that learners are more empowered in the case of continuous learning and more apt to enhance their adaptability and sense of identity when learning from job assignments. Retraining may or may not prepare them for future jobs; continuous learning unfolds in rhythm with change in the workplace. As such, we think it a better way to think about preparing people for the kinds of new jobs that will be created in the years ahead (see Hall and Mirvis, 1995).

3. *Career moves should be valued.* Finally, we would argue that turnover in companies needs to be viewed as a positive, not a negative. Of course, there is always a risk that companies, having continuously enriched the skills and experiences of their employees, will lose them before these investments have been recouped. In this sense, firms that do not invest in their people but perhaps pay top dollar for talent would seem to be "free riders." Our feeling is that, on the contrary, firms with developmental cultures are more

Table 3.1. Continuous Learning, Not Retraining.

	Retraining	Continuous Learning
Agent	Expert	Self
Time, Cost of Delivery	High	Low
Pace	Programmed	Just in Time
Task	Theoretical or Simulated	Real Work
Learner Empowerment	Low	High
Development of Learner Identity	Variable	High
Development of Learner Adaptability	Low	High
Link to Future Jobs	Variable	High

apt to retain talented people and certainly be attractive to eager learners of all ages who have reached a plateau in firms that do not emphasize development.

Another consideration concerns the appropriate skill mix within work units in a company. To this point, many firms strive to have peak performers in place in all of their work units. We would contend that the adaptable corporation will need a culture where it is just as valued to be a learner as to be a peak performer. Indeed, key criteria in selection decisions should be a person's ability to learn and move rapidly and easily from job to job.

This raises a complication in organizations that offer skill- and performance-based pay. If, for example, there is too much stress placed on skill mastery within a specific job, this could create a disincentive for moving to a new job where the person would be starting over as a learner. This problem might be addressed through the payment of a "learning bonus" and a premium for the new skills that are mastered. In addition, companies that primarily compensate current performance will have to find ways to reward developmental work. The point is to put less stress on skill mastery and current performance (as ends in themselves) and more emphasis on learning and developing in new areas.

Responding to Tomorrow's Workforce

These ideas on how companies can contribute to career development have a generic flavor. There are also steps to be taken to respond to the specific needs of segments of tomorrow's workforce.

School-to-Work Transitions

Looking ahead, as developed nations continue their transformation from "brawn" to "brains" industries, studies project that the bulk of jobs created will require more education of jobholders than current ones and higher levels of language, math, and reasoning skills (Johnston and Packer, 1987). Meanwhile, the educational preparation of high school and even college graduates in the United States is declining, and nearly half the entry workers in today's labor market cannot read well enough or do the math necessary to meet job demands. What can American businesses do?

Many are taking on the role of educators, offering remedial education and basic skill training to their high school graduate hirees. The more proactive ones have become more involved in the education system. In Los Angeles, for example, 125 Arco Oil & Gas Company employees volunteer time at the Tenth Street Elementary School. Also, Honeywell sponsors a summer "teachers' academy," where high school math and science teachers team up with industry people to develop work-relevant projects for students ("Needed: Human Capital," 1988).

Furthermore, there are growing numbers of "adopt-a-school" programs, where employers provide high school students with training and part-time work plus a job after graduation, as well as such community-based efforts as the Boston Compact, a consortia of Boston-based companies who create summer jobs for three thousand high school students and hire a thousand interns annually. In addition, companies are taking an interest in apprenticeship programs, such as those that have worked so successfully in Germany and Sweden. Surveys find that one in three employers say it is very likely their companies will institute such programs in the next five years (Mirvis, 1993a). Still, the success of the European apprenticeship programs has been highly dependent on cooperation—lacking in the United States—among regional industry groups and multiple trade unions and has not proved an anti-dote to the shortage of scientifically trained talent on the continent. The implication, then, is that nothing short of a sweeping overhaul of the education system in this country may be required to truly close the skills gap.

Interestingly, as firms develop partnerships with, say, local school systems, this provides people with the opportunity to take on new and challenging assignments that promise to expand their horizons and give fuller expression to their personal interests and values. In Rochester, New York, for example, Kodak and the school board launched a wholesale restructuring of the local school system (Marshall and Tucker, 1992). Hundreds of Kodak people worked on task forces and volunteered time in schools to improve school performance and create apprenticeship-type programs for students in local industries. This may not seem to be the core work of Kodak, but it is essential to upgrading its future workforce, it enhances the attractiveness of the local community to Kodak employees, and we believe it enhances the personal development of Kodak contributors.

Valuing Diversity

In an area where U.S. industry faces unique challenges, companies will have to take account of changes in the racial and ethnic makeup of the workforce. For instance, African-Americans, Hispanics, and Asians will be the fastest-growing segments of the U.S. employee mix in the next decades. There will also be a steady increase in the number of working women who will be as well educated as men. How will companies respond to this diversity?

Surveys of employers find nearly four of five companies either now or will offer training on managing a diverse workforce. Until recent years, the employment needs of women and minorities were seen in terms of equal opportunity or affirmative action. In most instances, the personnel function was charged with "policing" employment practices and ensuring that managers followed the letter and spirit of the law. Today, companies are taking more pro-active measures to acknowledge and respect differences in the temperament, needs, and style of women, blacks, Hispanics, and other minorities rather than forcing them to conform to the prevailing white, male, corporate mold. This corporate commitment is not a matter of social work or political correctness. On the contrary, the underlying thinking is that a person is simply more productive when bringing the "whole self" to work (Hall and Parker, 1993).

As a result, leading firms are striving to create a multicultural work environment. In Corning, New York, for example, members of a quality team at Corning Glass worked with nonprofits in housing, education, and social service to enhance the attractiveness of the area for African-Americans, a growing segment of their workforce. This was part of a larger effort in Corning to value diversity. A recent survey finds that a fifth of the minority workers in the United States believes that they have been discriminated against by their employer. In addition, over half of the workforce prefers working with people of the same race, gender, age, and education as their own (Galinksy and Friedman, 1993). At the same time, employers who understand the demographic trends see programs aimed at managing diversity as competitive necessities. As a result, mentoring programs aimed at minority workers and training for all employers on the management of diversity are becoming commonplace in these companies. Such efforts, exemplified by the outreach undertaken by Corning, help to promote social integration within companies, have a competitive payoff for the organization, and provide employees with new and rich experiences integral to success in the multicultural workplace of the future (Cox, 1993).

Opportunities for Older Workers

The age segment fifty and over will grow faster than any other in the United States during the next several decades. What will their employment prospects be? Certainly, periodic downsizing will mark the adaptable corporation. Rather than just emphasizing cost cutting in these efforts, adaptive companies will also put considerable time and money into retraining and redeploying their workers over the life course. At present, companies faced with the choice between retiring their older workers at any early age or retraining and redeploying them generally favor the seemingly more cost-effective option of getting rid of them. The rationalization is that because older workers have fewer remaining years of employment, the benefits of further investment may not be recouped before their retirement (Barth, McNaught, and Rizzi, 1993).

This economic logic will be turned on its head in companies who promote more or less continuously. We expect that as employees age through several career cycles, companies will apply cost-benefit criteria to their continued employment and development. Ironically, older workers, having benefited from continuous development, may prove to be more expensive to replace than early career employees. In addition, companies may have more options about where to redeploy aging workers. Given that corporations will have closer relationships with supplier plants, distributors, and other firms on their second leaf, it is possible that movement of older workers to these organizations could become part of a phased retirement career plan. Indeed, it is not hard to imagine companies using these firms much like the "farm system" in professional baseball: drawing in young people after they have gained some seasoning and sending back older workers who might well serve as mentors and coaches in addition to performing day-to-day chores.

Helping Working Parents

The dramatic rise in employment of women means an increase in the number of working parents in the United States. Nearly three-fourths of employed women are of childbearing age and 60 percent have school-age kids. In turn, nearly three-fifths of employed men have wives who work. This makes work-family issues a matter of concern to most couples and single-family heads. One recent survey finds that three in five American workers rate the effect of a job on their personal and family life as "very important" in making employment decisions—far more so than wages, benefits, and even job security (Galinsky and Friedman, 1993). With 87 percent of the American workforce living with at least one family member, finding time for spouses, children, parents, or partners is a priority for more and more people. The survey also reports that nearly half of the workforce rates the family-supportive policies of employers as a key consideration in their job choice.

What are the implications for careers? The option of entering, say, a "mommy track" or "daddy track" has of course been advanced as one means of accommodating the career preferences of working parents (Schwartz, 1989). We also estimate that the very temporariness of work assignments in adaptable companies coupled with advances in telecommunication technology will afford many more people the opportunity to work part-time, or from their home, or on a seasonal basis. This kind of flexibility will help people to manage their work time and location. It will also help them manage their commitment and psychic energy. Research on social identity by Lobel (1991) suggests that work-family conflicts can be minimized to the extent that people achieve some congruence with their work and nonwork roles. Workplace flexibility makes this easier.

High- and Low-Involvement Career Tracks

Beyond the identifiable needs of demographic segments of the workforce, it must be recognized that there are great individual differences in what employees look for from a job—in general and at particular points in their career (Hall and Rabinowitz, 1988). For some, the goal might be a continuously high level of challenge, growth, and development—the so-called intrinsic rewards of work. Accordingly, they would be oriented to a "high-involvement" career path. However, another segment of workers is keyed to extrinsic rewards: steady pay, good benefits, congenial working conditions, and the like. The solution, where feasible, is to find ways to match these people to jobs suited to their talents and needs. Certainly, companies will continue to have jobs in the future that are less demanding psychologically. These might offer flexible work schedules, job rotation for variety, the option of work at home, and, in later career stages, the opportunity for jobholders to move down to lower-level, less demanding positions. Thus a low-involvement career path, although likely not as remunerative as in the past, could nonetheless provide a feasible, low-stress alternative to staying on the fast track (see Figure 3.1).

What is important to recognize, however, is that an exclusively high- or low-involvement career is not the answer. Already, companies are making informal accommodations for parents of young children that enable them to take on less demanding assignments for a period of years (in lower-involvement jobs) and then resume more intensive work (in high-involvement jobs). In addition, more

Figure 3.1. Two-Path Career Model.

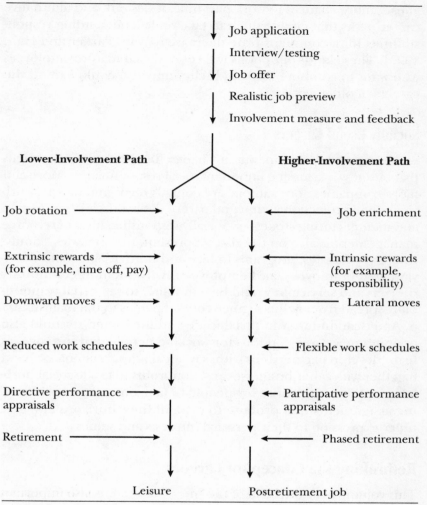

Job application
Interview/testing
Job offer
Realistic job preview
Involvement measure and feedback

Lower-Involvement Path   **Higher-Involvement Path**

Job rotation   Job enrichment

Extrinsic rewards   Intrinsic rewards
(for example, time off, pay)   (for example,
                                                     responsibility)

Downward moves   Lateral moves

Reduced work schedules   Flexible work schedules

Directive performance   Participative performance
appraisals   appraisals

Retirement   Phased retirement

Leisure   Postretirement job

companies are expected to offer sabbaticals to workers in the years ahead, more chances to work part-time, if desired, and alternative career paths that enable them to take on less demanding responsibilities for a commensurate decrease in pay (Parker and Hall, 1993). These kinds of options will certainly aid mature employees who want to combine work and schooling and could extend the careers of older workers.

Socially Useful Careers

As Altman and Post point out in Chapter Two, there are some signs that business is assuming important social responsibilities. More and more companies, for example, are going "green" and making environmental protection an integral part of their sourcing, packaging, and manufacturing strategies. Socially responsible human resource management is also on the rise. At present, this includes "family-friendly" practices, programs to hire and train disabled and disadvantaged employees, and employee involvement in community projects and service. It would be ennobling to see social responsibility spread from a thin segment of companies to the mainstream of American industry in this decade and thereafter. It would also open up new career options for working people. For instance, as firms develop partnerships with, say, local school systems or band together with other businesses and nonprofits to tackle social problems, opportunities arise for people to take on new and challenging assignments that promise to expand their horizons and give fuller expression to their personal interests and values.

Rethinking the Concept of Careers

This volume hails the birth of the "new" career. It is also important to look at its downsides. By now, members of the young, "new-breed" workforce of the late 1960s and 1970s are well along in their careers. Surveys in those times found many of them infused with the belief that interesting and challenging work was central to their identity (Yankelovich, 1981). This trend seemed to hold through the 1980s as the "new achievers" (Pascarella, 1984) moved up in organizations or else moved out to entrepreneurial ventures. Today, the new generation makes up the lion's share of the workforce and

Maccoby (1988) finds a new character type, the self-developer, emerging among them. Self-developers, he reports, balance mastery and play, strive for knowledge but also seek balance in their lives. They are the problem solvers in organizations, the most customer centered, and the most suited to the techno-service work that will increasingly be the work of the future.

As such, they have taken hold of what we have termed the *new* career. The question that we must confront, then, is why self-developers are often unhappy with their circumstances and find themselves making repeated and unsatisfying compromises (Sarason, 1977). It may be, of course, that work is simply not that much fun and that self-developers simply have not grown up and accepted this unpleasant reality. Alternatively, it could be that not enough organizations have yet accepted the notion advanced by Harman and Hormann (1990) that in a technologically advanced society "employment exists primarily for self-development" (p. 26). Certainly, many executives, pressed to compete globally, would quarrel with that notion.

A third hypothesis, and one that needs imaginative study, is that interesting and challenging work is simply not the end-all and be-all of self-development. Current aspirations to get more time with family and pursue personal goals hint at other dimensions to self-development. Moreover, if we in this country can set aside the assumption that self-actualization is our highest goal, we can consider whether community, transpersonal connectedness, and even spirituality are the transcendent aims of human development.

The new stage of career research we are pointing to concerns not only the development of one's work but also one's life work. The two, in our view, connect deeply in the work-life intersection— a subject given only the barest scrutiny by career researchers. In this light, of course, distinctions between, say, career and life stages, and indeed between career and self-development, may prove arbitrary and ultimately meaningless.

In this frame, a person's work career consists of a whole set of activities (part-time jobs, self-employed undertakings, temporary assignments, three-year team projects, work-at-home periods, sabbaticals, and so forth) that may not and probably will not come neatly packaged and defined as a "job" in one organization but that can constitute full employment, provide adequate compensation, and afford deep satisfaction to the individual. Furthermore, a focus on life's work also takes account of how one's activities as spouse, parent, neighbor, friend, and volunteer shape work choices, add to skills, promote or tax adaptability, and otherwise influence one's self-picture.

Conclusion

In this broadened conception of life's work, the company's role in career development needs careful consideration. On the one hand, the claim can be made that as companies become a prime venue for personal development, take care of people's health and family needs, and attend to their communal needs and spiritual centering, they take on the character of "total institutions" (Mirvis, 1993b). This raises the specter of corporate mind control, blurs the boundary between people's private and corporate selves, and puts "Big Brother" in charge of people's lives. On the other hand, companies have the resources and motivations to fill in the gaps missed by families and community institutions and, in partnership with parents and community groups, have much that is good to offer to their employees and society.

In a different light, the future corporation we have been describing may seem cold and calculating in its human resource outlook—welcoming, perhaps, of its "fittest" workers but rather indifferent in its handling of the seemingly less adaptable and able. Yet studies find consistently that companies who take a lead in responding to new environmental conditions facing their business also tend to be human resource leaders in all respects (Mirvis, 1993a; Denison, 1990). What characterizes flexibility in these leading firms? The survey in Exhibit 3.1, developed by the Families and Work Institute with our assistance, highlights factors worth considering: (1) Does your company have stated values about the importance of people? (2) Does your company's culture respect human needs? (3) Does your company invest in employee development? (4) Does your company actively promote career development? (5) Does your company provide flexible employment options? and (6) Does your company have policies and programs that respond to the concerns of a diverse workforce? Answers to these diagnostic questions provide some guidance to working people on whether or not they will be supported while handling the ups and downs—or "chutes and ladders"—of the new career in their organization.

Exhibit 3.1. Chutes and Ladders: Corporate Readiness for Alternative Career Paths.

Please indicate the extent to which you agree or disagree with the following statements in terms of the organization in which you work. While your answers might vary depending on which job level, department, site, or subsidiary you focus on, please provide your best answer for the majority of people working for your organization.

	Strongly disagree	Disagree	Agree	Strongly agree
Culture and Values				
1. The mission of the organization reflects a concern for people in the organization.	1	2	3	4
2. The leadership at the top "walks the talk" when it comes to the values of the organization.	1	2	3	4
3. My organization really understands the needs and priorities of people.	1	2	3	4
4. Top management is committed to empowerment and gives managers the freedom they need to run their divisions/units.	1	2	3	4
5. There are role models at senior levels of the organization who have worked nontraditional hours or who have had nontraditional career paths.	1	2	3	4

Subtotal Score _____

People

6. Human resources is involved in the strategic planning of the organization.	1	2	3	4
7. My organization views people as *the* key to long-term success.	1	2	3	4
8. My organization values diversity in all its forms: age, gender,				

Exhibit 3.1. *(continued)*

	Strongly disagree	Disagree	Agree	Strongly agree
race, life-style, culture, ability, etc.	1	2	3	4
9. My organization is sensitive to the personal/family responsibilities of employees.	1	2	3	4
10. My organization believes employees should bring "the whole person" to work (e.g., people can be open about the nonwork aspects of their lives).	1	2	3	4

Subtotal Score _____

Training and Learning

11. My organization is focused on continuous improvement.	1	2	3	4
12. There are core training and education programs that help develop people and communication skills.	1	2	3	4
13. My organization believes that jobs and assignments provide more learning opportunities than formal training programs.	1	2	3	4
14. Cross-training occurs for a large proportion of workers.	1	2	3	4
15. There are opportunities for people to learn in everyday work activities.	1	2	3	4

Subtotal Score _____

Career Development

16. The process of evaluation involves feedback from a variety of co-workers, subordinates, and supervisors.	1	2	3	4

	Strongly disagree	Disagree	Agree	Strongly agree
17. A facet of development involves personal development (e.g., helping people become flexible, learn quickly, and be resilient when experiencing setbacks and failures).	1	2	3	4
18. Managers and supervisors are evaluated on their efforts to coach and develop talent.	1	2	3	4
19. There is sufficient recognition for those who have served as coaches, role models, or mentors throughout their careers.	1	2	3	4
20. People are rewarded for their skills, competencies, and adaptability.	1	2	3	4

Subtotal Score _____

Flexibility

	Strongly disagree	Disagree	Agree	Strongly agree
21. There are no career penalties if people take personal or family leaves.	1	2	3	4
22. People do not have to give up pay or status in order to get the flexibility they need.	1	2	3	4
23. Lateral moves are valued in my organization.	1	2	3	4
24. Career advancement in my organization does not have to occur at the expense of a personal life.	1	2	3	4
25. Managers and supervisors are evaluated on their efforts to be flexible in response to employees' needs.	1	2	3	4

Subtotal Score _____

Exhibit 3.1. *(continued)*

	Strongly disagree	Disagree	Agree	Strongly agree
Policies and Programs				
26. My organization offers flextime, which employees are encouraged to use.	1	2	3	4
27. My organization offers sabbaticals, which people have used without penalty to their careers.	1	2	3	4
28. My organization offers child-care and elder-care supports, such as referral services, flexible spending accounts for dependent care, and seminars and educational programs on a range of topics.	1	2	3	4
29. Job assignments are based, in part, on the development needs of individuals.	1	2	3	4
30. My organization encourages employees to explore both internal and external career opportunities.	1	2	3	4

Subtotal Score _____

Score

Culture and Values Subtotal _____

People Subtotal _____

Training and Learning Subtotal _____

Career Development Subtotal _____

Flexibility Subtotal _____

Policies and Programs Subtotal _____

Total Score _____

Bonus Points: Do you agree with the following?

In my company, people have the freedom
to plan out and manage their own
careers.   → If yes, add 5 points   _____

In terms of my own career decisions, I am willing to do what's
right for me and my family. → If yes, add 5 points   _____

FINAL TOTAL SCORE   _____

Source: These questions were developed in collaboration with Dana Friedman
and the Families and Work Institute.

References

Barth, M. C., McNaught, W., & Rizzi, P. (1993). Corporations and the
  aging workforce. In P. H. Mirvis (Ed.), *Building the competitive workforce.* New York: Wiley, 156–200.

Bennis, W. G., & Slater, P. (1968). *The temporary society.* New York: Harper-
  Collins.

Bridges, W. (1994). *Jobshift.* Reading, MA: Addison-Wesley.

Cox, T. (1993). *The multicultural organization.* San Francisco: Berrett-
  Koehler.

Davis, S. M., & Lawrence, P. R. (1977). *Matrix.* Reading, MA: Addison-Wesley.

Denison, D. (1990). *Corporate culture and organizational effectiveness.* New
  York: Wiley.

Emery, F. E., & Trist, E. L. (1965). The causal texture of organizational
  environments. *Human Relations, 18,* 21–32.

Galbraith, J. R. (1977). *Organizational design.* Reading, MA: Addison-
  Wesley.

Galinsky, E., & Friedman, D. (1993). *National study of the changing workforce.* New York: Families and Work Institute.

Hakim, C. (1994). *We are all self-employed.* San Francisco: Berrett-Koehler.

Hall, D. T. (1993). The "new career contract": Wrong on both counts.
  Technical Report, Executive Development Roundtable, School of
  Management, Boston University.

Hall, D. T., & Associates. (1986). *Career development in organizations.* San
  Francisco: Jossey-Bass.

Hall, D. T., & Mirvis, P. H. (1995). Careers as lifelong learning. In
  A. Howard (Ed.), *The changing nature of work.* San Francisco: Jossey-
  Bass, 269–289.

Hall, D. T., & Parker, V. A. (1993, Summer). The role of workplace flexibility in managing diversity. *Organizational Dynamics,* 4–18.

Hall, D. T., & Rabinowitz, S. (1988). Maintaining employee involvement in a plateaued career. In M. London & E. Mone (Eds.), *Career growth and human resource strategies: The role of the human resource professional in employee development* (pp. 67–80). New York: Quorum Books.

Handy, C. (1989). *The age of unreason.* Boston: Harvard Business School Press.

Harman, W., & Hormann, J. (1990). *Creative work.* Indianapolis: Knowledge Systems.

Hirsch, P. (1987). *Pack your own parachute.* Reading, MA: Addison-Wesley.

How to get a job. (1977, July). *Esquire, 37.*

Johnston, W. B., & Packer, A. E. (1987). *Workforce 2000.* Indianapolis: Hudson Institute.

Lawler, E. E., III. (1993). *The ultimate advantage: Creating the high-involvement organization.* San Francisco: Jossey-Bass.

Lawler, E. E., III, Mohrman, S. A., & Ledford, G. E., Jr. (1992). *Employee involvement and Total Quality Management: Practices and results in Fortune 1000 companies.* San Francisco: Jossey-Bass.

Lawrence, P. R., & Lorsch, J. W. (1967). *Organization and environment.* Cambridge, MA: Harvard Graduate School of Business Administration.

Lobel, S. A. (1991). Allocation of investment in work and family roles: Alternative theories and implications for research. *Academy of Management Review, 16*(3), 507–521.

McCall, M. W., Jr., Lombardo, M. M., & Morrison, A. M. (1988). *The lessons of experience: How successful executives develop on the job.* Lexington, MA: Lexington Books.

Maccoby, M. (1988). *Why work.* New York: Simon & Schuster.

Marshall, R., & Tucker, M. (1992). *Thinking for a living.* New York: Basic Books.

Mirvis, P. H. (Ed.). (1993a). *Building a competitive workforce: Investing in human capital for corporate success.* New York: Wiley.

Mirvis, P. H. (1993b). Personal development programs in corporations: Do they gain loyalty or exploit suckers? In F. Heuberger & L. Nash (Eds.), *The fatal embrace?* New Brunswick, NJ: Transaction.

Mirvis, P. H., & Marks, M. L. (1992). *Managing the merger.* Englewood Cliffs, NJ: Prentice Hall.

Needed: Human capital. (1988, September 19). *Business Week,* 100–141.

Olmsted, B., & Smith, S. (1994). *Creating a flexible workplace.* New York: Amacom.

Parker, V., & Hall, D. T. (1993). Workplace flexibility: Faddish or fundamental? In P. H. Mirvis (Ed.), *Building the competitive workforce.* New York: Wiley, 122–200.

Pascarella, P. (1984). *The new achievers.* New York: Free Press.

Sarason, S. (1977). *Work, aging, and social change.* New York: Free Press.

Schwartz, F. (1989). Management women and the new facts of life. *Harvard Business Review, 67*(1), 65–76.

Toffler, A. (1990). *Powershift.* New York: Bantam Books.

Yankelovich, D. (1981). *The new rules.* New York: Random House.

Zand, D. (1974). Collateral organization: A new change strategy. *Journal of Applied Behavioral Science, 10,* 63–89.

Relational Influences on Career Development

So, in this strange new world, how do we help people hold on amid the chaos and make sense of their work lives?

In Part Two, we introduce to the career literature the concepts of *relational development*. Chapter Four lays the theoretical ground for a relational approach to development, based on concepts such as interdependence, mutual respect and benefit, and reciprocity. It also challenges us to recognize relational career assistance when it is given and to value or reward it, as it often passes unnoticed. Chapter Five carries these relational concepts further, into the world of organizations, jobs, and work relationships. It gives us a theoretical road map for diagnosing and facilitating relational factors in career development.

The other three chapters in Part Two describe more specific ways of providing relational support for development and specific people who might give and receive it. Chapter Six offers the concept of the secure base as a holding environment for development and talks about how such a space might be provided in a chaotic organization. Chapter Seven expands our view of career-enhancing relationships by looking at extra-organizational relationships (GROWs, as author Victoria Parker calls them). As this chapter shows so clearly, the resources for learning are all around us (the silver lining in the clouds of turbulence); we just need help in becoming aware of them and in tapping their growth potential.

We conclude this part with something else that is new to the field of careers: the identification of single adults without dependent children (SAWDCs) as an important group with much relational support to give. In fact, as Chapter Eight points out, they are often asked to give too much at the office, and we must recognize their needs to *receive* more from their colleagues.

Thus each of these chapters represents new, unexplored, and high-potential terrain for the career practitioner. Understanding these concepts will add greatly to the practical resources of the innovative counselor, coach, consultant, or human resource professional. At this point, the possibilities are limited only by our own creativity in seeing their implications.

Chapter Four

A Relational Approach to the Protean Worker

Joyce K. Fletcher

Andrea: So, this guy from another division calls me up the other day and describes a problem they're having and asks if I can help him out. I don't really have the time but I say okay. So we meet and I end up spending a couple of hours with the guy. Turns out it's pretty much the same thing we ran into—heck, my team's been working on this thing for six months and we finally figured it out. So, I mean, even though I really didn't have the time, I'm glad I met with him. We shouldn't keep reinventing the wheel around here. But the thing is, last night after I got home I started to not feel so great about it. I started to feel like I'd been taken down the garden path. I mean I did him a big favor. But I don't have any trust that I'm going to get anything back for that. So I'm frustrated that I spent the time helping him . . . and yet when I think about it, should I not have helped him? And made him spend six months learning the stuff on his own? Helping him was the right thing for the company . . . that's got to be right . . . and yet it doesn't feel so great.

Barbara: Look, you're right, you've got to watch out for yourself. You should have told him no and then waited until you can put something in writing describing what your team did, and send it to his boss.

Andrea: No, I don't want to do that because it would feel like I was telling him he shouldn't have come and asked me the question. And I did feel he was behaving appropriately by not trying to reinvent the wheel. So I support that process. It's just that I had to spend the time and now he's going to look good and I don't think he should look as good as he's going to look! The thing is, why can't we reward someone who says, "So and so's team did all this work and here is some of the output." And if the boss could say, "That was good of you to not reinvent the wheel" . . . and you could actually get recognized for the *way* you got the job done rather than just getting it done. But that's not the way things work. Just getting it done is what is important—*you're* the one who got it done, so it becomes your deliverable and you *alone* get the credit.

Introduction

Andrea has a problem. According to the rhetoric, her behavior is right in line with calls for the new worker who will succeed in the reinvented organization—one who is flexible and team oriented (Peters, 1990), a continuous learner who can share knowledge and learn from others (Byham and Cox, 1994; Watkins and Marsick, 1993; Wheatley, 1992), and a systems thinker who can anticipate consequences and is empowered to accept ownership of problems and work to solve them (Hammer and Champy, 1993; Senge, 1990). By sharing her know-how with a co-worker in another division, she is operating in a holistic, collaborative fashion, thinking of the overall project and putting the long-term benefits of sharing the information ahead of her own time and independent "deliverables." In fact, this routine, informal transfer of knowledge could be seen as the essence of organizational learning (Jacques, 1992; Nonaka, 1994). But because of her past experience watching who gets promoted and how people get recognized as competent, she intuitively knows that this behavior is out of sync with the organizational culture and reward system. In this culture, achievement is credited to individuals; as Andrea says, if you come up with the deliverable, it is assumed that "you're the one that got it done . . . so you alone get the credit for it." So enabling another, especially another not even in her division, is not something for which she is likely to get credit. Although the overall project stands to benefit, both she and her co-worker Barbara recognize that she is likely to "get disappeared" from the other team's final product. Moreover, since the positive effects of her behavior are invisible in the current reward structure, her effort and skill in enabling others is unlikely to be used as an "ability signal" (Rosenbaum, 1989) in future career decisions about her as a top performer.

Of course, the organization also has a problem. If it unwittingly "disappears" the very behavior it would like to encourage in its workers, there is little chance of achieving the goals of reengineering. The problem seems to be that although it is clear that the reinvented organization will need holistic, systems thinkers such as Andrea, it is unclear how to develop these new workers and how to reward and encourage this kind of behavior. Indeed, the discussion Andrea and Barbara are having suggests that organizational models of success and development have not kept pace with the rhetoric and remain rooted in structures and practices that reproduce and reinforce old images of competency. The argument presented in this chapter is that creating an environment in which individuals can grow and develop into the protean workers organizations need will require a rethinking of organizational norms, assumptions, and beliefs about adult development, about the role of organizational structures and practices in supporting this development, and about reward and recognition systems that determine the organizational definition of competence. More specifically, it argues that if, as Hall and Mirvis suggest in Chapter One, the protean worker requires a blend of mastery and relational skills, then this rethinking of organizational norms—norms that traditionally have privileged mastery, individualism, and a "vertical" model of success—will benefit from an explication of the more relational, communal, and "horizontal" aspects of success and organizational achievement.

The goal of this chapter is to add this relational piece to our thinking about the protean worker by offering an alternative model of growth and development in organizations, one that is rooted in women's psychology (Miller, 1986). This model is based on a set of assumptions and beliefs about organizational achievement that differs from traditional organizational thinking and has the potential to add different skills and attributes to our image of the "ideal" worker. To address the need and potential benefits of this addition, we will present a brief overview of traditional models of adult growth and development in organizations, giving particular attention to the skills these models implicitly emphasize. Then we will explore an alternative model—a relational model of growth-in-connection (Jordan et al., 1991)—with particular attention to the beneficial additions this model offers to traditional notions of what it takes to grow, develop, and succeed in organizations. Lastly, we will discuss the implications for individuals waging a new employment contract with organizations, and we will suggest concrete, practical steps individuals and career professionals within organizations might take to apply these concepts to the workplace.

Traditional Models of Growth, Development, and Achievement

In general, traditional models of psychological growth and development view maturity as a process of differentiating, integrating, and redefining the relationship between self, others, and the external world (Alexander, Druker, and Langer, 1990). Growth is conceptualized as moving from a state of dependency and embeddedness with others to relative states of independence and psychological autonomy. From this state of autonomy, new ways of integrating with others becomes possible. The hallmark of growth in this process of individuation and integration is an increasingly differentiated sense of self—a self who is capable of relating to others and to the external world in more complex, sophisticated ways. There are many different models describing how this growth occurs. Whether the image is one of stages or seasons (Levinson et al., 1978; Erikson, 1963), of different levels of cognitive complexity (Kegan, 1982; Loevinger, 1976; Perry, 1970), or of stages of moral development (Kohlberg, 1976), the emphasis in most of these models is on the differentiating process itself and the goal of establishing a strong sense of self-identity. Thus, although the growth process is conceptualized as occurring in relationship to others and as movement through different phases of individuation and integration, the goal of psychological autonomy has led to what is more recently being characterized as an overemphasis on independence, cognitive processes, formal operations, and deductive, syllogistic reasoning (Alexander, Druker, and Langer, 1990). In other words, it has led to an emphasis on the mastery dimensions of growth and largely ignored the relational dimensions. Building primarily on work in women's psychology (Gilligan, 1982; Miller, 1986), which emphasizes interdependence, contextual reasoning, and affective development, these traditional models of growth are in the process of being revised and extended to what Souvaine, Lahey, and Kegan call "development beyond autonomy" (1990, p. 233). The important point for this chapter is that despite these new formulations (see, for example, Alexander, Drucker, and Langer, 1990; Gallos, 1989; Kegan, 1994), organizational models of career success continue to reflect more traditional notions of growth. The result is that career and self-developmental programs in organizations tend to emphasize mastery, individuation, and personal autonomy as the hallmarks of maturity and competence.

Career Implications

As other contributors to this book note (see Chapter Two; Chapter Three; Chapter Five) career development theory, whether based on life-span models (for example, Super, 1957), individual differences models (for example, Holland, 1973; Schein, 1978), or models of cognitive complexity (for example, Dalton and Thompson, 1986), tends to view development as a vertical, hierarchical process and the career as a linear, age-related progression that is assumed to occur within stable organizational or occupational settings. Summaries of these models (Cytrynbaum and Crites, 1989; Hall, 1976; Osipow, 1983) suggest that, despite some differences among them, they envision career as movement through set stages. In early career, one is socialized and proves oneself, then moves on to a period of full membership and contribution where one grows in personal power and influence, followed by late career experiences, where one passes on expertise through generative activities such as mentoring. The progression finally ends with a period of decline, in which work takes on a less important role in one's life. Models of success from this perspective tend to focus on task learning and mastery as the primary site of personal and professional growth. For example, Bandura's models of self-efficacy (1986) envision growth as movement along a continuum of tasks that are just challenging enough to require new strategies for success without being so challenging that success is unlikely. In the same vein, Hall's model of psychological success (1976) stresses the ways in which the independent achievement of challenging tasks and goals can lead to a spiraling process of growth not only in task competence but also in self-confidence and in a willingness to take on additional challenges.

These three concepts—age-related career stages, linear career movement within a stable organization or occupation, and an emphasis on challenging tasks as the primary sites of learning—traditionally have defined the landscape of career development initiatives in organizations. For example, many prestigious management trainee programs are noted for their focus on challenging, stress-filled assignments that demand high effort and long hours to succeed. Presumably, the assumption is not only that the early career years of high potential workers are years in which they will be willing, able, and eager to put high energy into their work but also that this is the best way to develop and assess potential leaders and put them on the "fast track."

Skills and Definition of Competence

The key point for this discussion is that these models of the ideal career within the stable hierarchical organization lead to a focus on developmental programs and experiences that foster a certain set of skills and behavior in workers—skills and behavior that are assumed necessary for individual and organizational success. For example, the notion of career stage suggests that ideal workers are those who can move from dependency relationships where they learn the ropes from others to an optimal state in which they are independent, high achieving, full contributors and finally, as their own drive to achieve declines, to a state where they contribute to the development of others. This concept of self-development as moving along a continuum of needing help to not needing help to giving help implies that the skills needed in navigating this journey will be skills in overcoming dependency and skills in proving and/or distinguishing oneself from others. It is assumed that this experience and these skills, which are implicitly competitive and individualistic, will somehow develop the generative, more relational skills needed to successfully negotiate the last career stage: contributing to the individualistic development and socialization of the next generation of workers.

The assumption that professional growth is primarily a process of individuation that occurs through successfully negotiating increasingly challenging tasks has been translated, in many organizational settings, to developmental programs that focus on proving oneself through the demonstration of individual task proficiencies. Moreover, these task proficiencies often become the "ability signals" (Rosenbaum, 1989) that define organizational competence. Since demonstrating these proficiencies typically is rewarded by movement of the "winners" up the hierarchy, this situation tends to foster competitive behavior and skills in self-promotion (McIlwee and Robinson, 1992). More specifically, it tends to idealize individual heroics over collaboration, independent achievement over collective output, and winning short-term contests over contributing to the collective advancement of more long-range goals (Martin, 1995).

The result is a self-reinforcing cycle in which organizational models of individual development, although based on theories of growth that implicitly include aspects of both mastery and relational development, tend to reward task proficiency and ignore the process, development, and/or rewarding of relational proficiencies. This, of course, is the organizational reality with which Andrea and Barbara are grappling. On the one hand, Andrea's co-worker in another division has the makings of a protean worker. He recognizes his own inadequacies in dealing with a problem and is appropriately seeking an in-house source of expertise to increase his knowledge and skills. He is operating as a continuous learner should and is enacting the kind of interactive, on-line knowledge transfer typical of "communities of practice" and touted as exemplary behavior in a learning organization (Brown and Duguid, 1991; Huberman and Hogg, 1994). The problem Andrea has, on the other hand, is the intuitive recognition that although continuous learning is valued and is likely to be rewarded, the relational practice of continuous teaching enjoys no such organizational dividend. On the contrary, taking the time from her independent tasks to enable another makes her feel that she has been "led down the garden path," diverted from the real work of individual achievement and distinguishing oneself from others.

This is not to say that the relational practice of enabling others is completely absent from the organizational screen in this or any other large company. What it does suggest is that the old stage model of careers—the entry phase where you learn, the high-achieving period where you distinguish yourself as competent, and the generative phase where you pass on knowledge to others—positions the practice and skill of enabling others not as a routine, continuous practice but as a function of hierarchy and seniority. Coaching, supporting, and enabling others is a responsibility reserved for managers, who in more progressive companies are rewarded for developing subordinates, and mentors, who are recognized for teaching newcomers the ropes (Kram, 1983). Continuous, on-line peer development, or situations in which subordinates support, care for, and enable supervisors, are rarely afforded the same level of recognition (see for example, Kahn, 1993). Thus the skills, motivation, and organizational conditions that would foster this kind of behavior not only are off the organizational screen but also tend to be undertheorized and underexamined in the organizational literature.

Recent research (Fletcher, 1994; Jacques, 1992) suggests that enabling others is not the only relational skill that is unrewarded in organizational settings and unexamined in organizational theory. Rather, there are a whole host of behaviors associated with relational interactions—behaviors that could potentially add value to organizational goals—that typically are invisible in workplace settings.

As Hall and Mirvis suggest in Chapter One, the reason relational skills have been unexamined in the workplace is perhaps because these skills are more strongly associated with the private, family sphere of one's life (traditionally the domain of women) rather than the public, work sphere (traditionally the domain of men). In fact, the skills needed to be successful in private life are assumed to be different from—and perhaps in direct conflict with—those needed for organizational success. Yet as noted earlier, the call for a new kind of worker—one who is holistic, collaborative, team oriented, and able to operate in a flatter organizational structure—emphasizes skills that are relational in nature. In fact, early in the history of reengineering it was noted by many that these skills traditionally have been associated with stereotypical feminine traits (Helgeson, 1990; Peters, 1990; Rosener, 1990). More recently, Michael Hammer (1994, p. 24) observes, "To be a good re-engineer, not only do you need process thinking and imagination and creativity and stick-to-it-iveness, but you need team skills, communication skills and the ability to have a holistic perspective. For whatever reasons, whether cultural or psychological, I don't know, women seem to have an advantage in those areas."

During the past decade, the field of women's psychology, particularly the work of Carol Gilligan (1982) and Jean Baker Miller (1986), has begun to explicate the psychological determinants of these relational skills. As noted earlier, their work is just beginning to influence mainstream theories through the suggestion that the growth process that results in relational skills and attributes, although traditionally associated with the feminine, is applicable to all human development. Most important for this discussion of the protean career, their work suggests that our current models of human development are overly masculine in nature and are imbalanced in their underexamination of the ways in which humans— both men and women—can "grow-in-connection." To begin to address this imbalance in the organizational literature and to more fully understand and explore the organizational conditions that might foster, support, and encourage the development of relational skills in today's workers, it will be necessary to understand the theory of growth-in-connection from which these skills spring.

Relational Models of Growth, Development, and Achievement

Relational models of growth and development (Jordan et al., 1991; Miller, 1986) emphasize the role of relational interactions in the growth process. Although all models of growth include the importance of relationships and human intimacy in the maturation process, relational theories subtly recast the nature of what constitutes growth-enhancing relational interactions. For example, relational theory is based on a slightly different model of the role of "other" in self-development. Miller (1991) asserts that traditional views of growth-enhancing relational interactions are too one-directional, conceptualizing one party as selflessly giving while the other gradually outgrows the dependency relationship through repeated instances of separation and individuation. She claims this does not reflect the early experiences of females *or* males and that early infant development actually occurs in a context of connection and mutual influence. She cites several studies that indicate that even in the earliest days of life an infant influences the emotional field between self and caretaker and begins to develop an "interacting sense of self." As noted in more detail elsewhere (Fletcher, 1994), this recasting of even early relational interactions as more fully two-directional suggests that the process of adult growth might be more accurately described less as a process of outgrowing dependency and more as a process of movement through increasingly complex states of interdependence. Self-development in this model is less a process of differentiating oneself from others as it is understanding oneself as increasingly connected to others in more complex and sophisticated ways. The "other" and relational interactions with this "other" are conceptualized as sites of growth, development, and achievement in which each party is potentially teacher *and* learner and both parties benefit and grow. Importantly, growth is conceptualized as occurring not in *any* engagement but through a specific kind of relational interaction. If we generalize from this theoretical base, it would appear that the distinguishing features of growth-fostering relational interactions include the following:

1.   *Interdependence.* Growth-fostering interactions are characterized by a belief that interdependence, rather than autonomy, is the ideal state in which to achieve, grow, and develop. This belief system emphasizes interdependence over autonomy and recognizes vulnerability, need, and inadequacy (in oneself and in others) as part of the human condition. More specifically, it views autonomy and independence as fluid rather than sequential states and, as Jean Baker Miller (personal communication) puts it, accepts as a universal truth that "much of our strength lies in [our relationships with] other people." Implicit in this belief in interdependence is an acceptance of the responsibility to contribute to the development of others and a recognition of the opportunity to grow through these enabling interactions. Thus seeing others as a source of strength and achievement is only half of the growth potential in relational interactions. Just as important is recogniz-

ing the potential self-growth, development, and achievement inherent in contributing to the development of others. This leads to the second characteristic of relational practice, mutuality.

2. *Mutuality.* Relational growth depends on both parties approaching the interaction expecting to grow and benefit from it. This belief in a two-directional model of growth is the essence of mutuality. When one is contributing to the growth of another through, for example, teaching or enabling interactions, it is assumed that the "student" grows because of this intentional action while the "teacher" grows either because of enhanced self-esteem at using her relational skills to enable another's achievement or through the learning that takes place in listening to, identifying with, or adopting the student's perspective. Achieving mutuality in relational interactions, then, depends on both parties having two sets of skills—skills in enabling others (ability to assume the expert role in guiding, teaching, explaining) and skills in being enabled (ability to step away from the expert role in order to be influenced by and learn from others). This expectation of "fluid expertise" leads to the third characteristic of growth-fostering relational interactions: reciprocity.

3. *Reciprocity.* Reciprocity refers to the expectation that both parties will have the skills to achieve this two-directional model of growth and will be motivated to use them. That is, it assumes that both parties feel a responsibility and a desire to be both teacher and learner. Thus, if at some point someone is put in the "expert" role and makes the effort to enable another's growth and achievement, the natural expectation in this belief system is that the other would be similarly motivated to engage in future interactions in which the roles were reversed. Thus, rather than a sequential approach to relational interactions in which status, position, and role determine who is teacher and who is learner, reciprocity implies a willingness to transcend these boundaries. In this belief system, the "dependency" that characterizes being a learner and the "independence" that characterizes being a teacher are both natural but temporary states. This fluidity, of course, is the essence of interdependence and implies that both parties are responsible to give and entitled to receive benefits from relational interactions.

Career Implications

This view of relational interactions suggests a very different role of the "other" in career and adult development in organizational settings. The key assumption underlying what Miller and Gilligan would call "overly masculine" models of the development process in organizational settings is that the growth that occurs in interactions with others is primarily a one-directional, sequential process where you start on one side (learner) early in your career and end up on the other (teacher). Growth-in-connection models of career development, on the other hand, focus on the two-directional nature of interactions, on the development of "fluid expertise" and the ability to move easily—not only over time but even within the space of one interaction—from teacher to learner and back again.

Skills and Definition of Competence

As noted earlier, the process of growth-in-connection relies on skills, behaviors, and competencies that are more commonly associated with the private or personal side of life. This creates some problems in applying these models to organizational life because for most of us, these attributes are intuitively viewed as somehow "inappropriate" to the workplace. In fact, it is increasingly being noted how the management literature has tended to focus on separating these two facets of a worker's life (Fletcher and Bailyn, 1996; Friedlander, 1994; Kegan, 1994) and on the ways in which the two roles are in conflict (see, for example, Greenhaus and Beutell, 1985; Hall, 1972; Hennig and Jardim, 1978; Harragan, 1977). The result is that we assume people will act differently at work than they do at home, particularly in how they deal with others. The goal of applying relational theory to organizational behavior is not to suggest that workplace interactions should mirror personal, intimate relationships. On the contrary, the goal is to build a bridge between the two spheres that extends our understanding of personal interactions outside of a context of love and intimacy.

Recent fieldwork applying a relational model of growth to workplace interactions has done just that (Fletcher, 1994; Jacques, 1992). The findings from this fieldwork suggest that relational growth is not dependent on strong affection between the parties.

That is, relational interactions characterized by interdependence, mutuality, and reciprocity have some structural elements that can be engaged and can lead to growth for both parties regardless of their level of mutual intimacy or affection. Indeed, the data gathered from observing female design engineers (Fletcher, 1994) suggest that workers operating from a relational belief system look to relational interactions in the workplace not so much to enhance their affective personal relationships with others but rather to enhance their own and others' achievement and work effectiveness. This way of working, called "relational practice," is motivated by a belief that relational interactions are presumed to be sites of growth, development, and professional achievement for both parties. It is characterized by work practices and strategies that differ in significant ways from conventional "strategies for success" and uses a set of skills not commonly associated with organizational effectiveness.

This study of engineers found four types of relational practice. The first is related to task and has to do with keeping the project connected to the people and resources it needs to survive. This includes things such as using informal channels to pass on key information to other groups, working behind the scenes to create relational bridges between people who need to be connected for the sake of the project, or picking up the slack and doing whatever it takes to·get the job done.

The second type of relational practice is related to empowering or enabling others' achievement. This includes things such as "other-centered teaching," which is a way of teaching that takes the other's intellectual and emotional reality into account when passing on information by, for example, sitting down rather than standing over someone when giving instruction or using everyday examples to illustrate complex concepts. The motivation to engage in this type of enabling activity has to do with a willingness to work for what Cato Wadel (1979) calls "embedded outcomes." These are outcomes embedded in other people such as increased competence, know-how, or self-confidence.

The third type of relational practice has to do with using relational skills to create conditions that enable one's own growth and professional accomplishment. This includes activities such as using one's relational skills to keep working relationships on an even keel, being aware of the emotional context of situations, and strate-gizing appropriate responses and "relational asking"—asking for help in a way that takes the helper's perspective and interests into account, increasing the likelihood that you will actually get the help you need.

The final practice associated with this way of working is related to enhancing team spirit and a sense of collaboration in the work setting. This includes things such as affirming and acknowledging others; building on rather than attacking others' ideas; listening to others' feelings and responding to their preferences or unique circumstances by, for example, taking on a minor aspect of a job someone else dislikes or offering to work at a time that will allow someone else to make it to day care on time. The willingness to undertake these activities appears to stem from an expectation of reciprocity—those who engage in this activity expect to be treated the same way—and a belief that individual and collective achieve-ment occurs best in a context of connection.

Summary

The point in overviewing this study of relational practice is to sug-gest that this way of working is especially appropriate for what Jack Welch calls the new "boundaryless" organization (Slater, 1994). In fact, it appears to encompass many of the traits describing the new ideal worker for today's faster, flatter, more flexible organizations. For example, many of these relational practices routinize activities traditionally reserved for upper levels of hierarchy. Generalizing these functions and ensuring that all workers have these skills will be essential to the success of flatter organizations composed of empowered, self-managed teams who can make decisions and move quickly to implement them. These generalized management activities include things such as enabling and developing others, thinking systemically, anticipating consequences, and connecting across functions. They are activities that encompass continuous learning *and* continuous teaching and depend on skills not com-monly associated with organizational success—skills such as paying attention to emotional data, sensitivity to others' emotional reali-ties, self-reflection, and an ability to move easily and repeatedly, even in the course of one interaction, from the role of novice to the role of expert. Most interesting to this discussion of developing the protean worker, these relational practices appear to depend on skills that are a blend of those commonly associated with the public work sphere and those commonly associated with the private, family sphere. This suggests that if organizations want to develop protean workers such as Andrea, their reward systems as well as their developmental programs should be more integrative, reflecting and encouraging skills that are a blend of those commonly associated with the public sphere (technical competence, autonomous action, competitiveness, and linear thinking) and those commonly associated with the private sphere (empathy, enabling, collaboration, trust).

The Challenge

The primary contribution relational theory makes to traditional adult development is that it offers a two-directional model of growth that is based not on dependency (implicitly hierarchical) but on interdependency (implicitly nonhierarchical). More specifically, it suggests that growth, development, and professional achievement can occur in a relational context of connection rather than an individuated context of separation and competition and that it is in the organization's best interest to encourage these kinds of growth-fostering relational interactions and the skills they require. Thus the primary challenge this model presents to organizational models of individual development is a challenge to the task-focused, hierarchical nature of current career and self-developmental activities in organizations.

Unfortunately, challenging this focus is easier said than done. Indeed, the findings from the study of design engineers indicate that people who engaged in relational practice were not simply unrewarded for the value their approach added to organizational goals. In fact, in many cases they were misunderstood or exploited or suffered negative career consequences for engaging in these activities. Engineers such as Andrea who enabled others were often characterized by co-workers not as competent workers who were contributing to organizational learning but rather as "helpful" or "nice" people. While being viewed as a nice person is hardly grounds for complaint, both Andrea and Barbara recognize that it does have some negative career consequences. The skill in explaining complicated ideas so that others will be able to understand them is trivialized when labeled as merely "helpful." In the same vein, the holistic view that time spent in enabling another is time well spent gets noted not as a competency or an ideal way of working but rather as evidence that the enabler is nice and perhaps likes to do this sort of thing. The result is that these skills are dismissed as personal attributes rather than being counted as personal competencies. It is not only the relational practice of enabling others that gets disappeared in this way. Some engineers who, for example, wrote notes of appreciation to other groups who were providing important resources to the project tended to be seen as "thoughtful" or "caring" people who were concerned about others' feelings. Their efforts in maintaining relationships that were critical to the life and well-being of the project went largely unrecognized as a value-added activity, one that potentially prevented future problems and project delays. Others, who spoke of avoiding confrontational interactions because they wanted to create an environment where people would feel free to express their ideas, were often characterized not as collaborative team players but as people with a dependency need who were afraid of confrontation because they had a "need to be liked."

The point of these examples is simply to suggest that rewarding relational skills and creating systems that will foster and enhance their development is no easy task. Behavior of this type runs so counter to organizational definitions of competence that simply calling for a new kind of worker is unlikely to lead to change. Instead, it will require some changes in structural practices to create new ways of developing, rewarding, and recognizing the blended skills needed to succeed in the context of the reinvented organization and the protean worker. The following are some suggested strategies to begin to move in this direction and to build a bridge between the mastery and relational skills needed for success.

Strategies for Individuals

The goal is to assume primary responsibility for your career by focusing (on and off the job) on growth-in-connection activities to develop relational *and* technical skills. Because of the present imbalance in the organizational focus on mastery, this will require a conscious, personal decision to emphasize relational skills by creating learning opportunities to develop these skills in yourself and supporting their development in co-workers. Strategies for achieving these goals could include the following:

• *Redefine the role of "other" in your own development.* As the description of relational practice indicates, operating in a context of growth-in-connection will entail adopting a somewhat different stance toward others. This means approaching work relationships from a standpoint of mutuality and implicit reciprocity rather than one of autonomy and competition. One way of making progress in this regard is to consciously seek out opportunities to contribute to the growth, well-being, or achievement of another. This could be accomplished in a formal way, by offering to share something you have learned with another, or more informally, by interacting with others in ways that communicate your willingness to learn from them, thereby increasing their feelings of self-confidence and self-esteem (see Chapter Five for a more detailed description of relational mentoring). More broadly, seek out opportunities to blend rather than dichotomize the public and private aspects of your life by modifying and using at work the skills you have learned in your private life. This could include using your feelings to strategize a response to a situation. It could include empathic listening, in which you try to understand another's emotional context or anticipate what others might feel in response to some action you are considering. Additional strategies to hone relational skills might include consciously making an effort to build on rather than compete with others' ideas or suggestions and consciously trying to engage with others in ways that will affirm and validate their contributions. An even more challenging developmental task would be to make a concerted effort to not "disappear" the help—including the outcomes embedded in you—that others have contributed to your achievements.

• *Develop a language of competence in describing relational practice.* Developing and practicing these skills in an organizational setting is tough work. As noted above, your new skills might be misunderstood. Thus it is important to use language that captures the skill dimensions of your behavior. For example, on hearing these findings, one of the engineers in the study described earlier decided to make one of the roles she played for her team more visible by talking about it differently. Rather than simply working behind the scenes to make sure people key to the team's output were doing their jobs and not feeling exploited, she started to talk of her role as one of "interfacing." At team meetings she gave status reports on her efforts in this regard and eventually got it put on the agenda as one of the key checkpoints in gauging project progress. In this way, she rescued the activity from obscurity and made it visible as work practice. Other ways of using language might include talking of "continuous teaching" as part of organizational learning and noting when you observe others practicing this skill. The point is that language is a powerful way of bringing these skills and behaviors into the organizational domain, where they can be recognized and rewarded as evidence of competence.

Strategies for Career Professionals

The task for career professionals is to create organizational conditions and practices that would encourage the development of skills needed for growth-in-connection. This could include the following initiatives:

 • *Clarify and communicate the value of relational skills.* To be effective, organizational commitment to relational self-learning cannot be communicated by directive but instead must be modeled from the top down. In fact, a first trigger for change would be showing the organizational benefits of such change in top-level executives. Certainly, there is ample evidence that executives who are self-aware, reflective, and skilled in interpersonal relations are more effective in their work and in leading others (Bennis and Nanus, 1985).

One way then of beginning to change the culture would be to invest in personal development programs such as those suggested by Robert Kaplan and colleagues (1991) for key executives. These one-on-one executive development programs encourage self-reflection by exploring the parallels between behavior patterns in one's work life and those exhibited in one's private life. The purpose is to help individuals begin to understand the origins of their individual character and makeup and to move beyond the externalization of problems. Such self-awareness encourages change that goes beyond the surface, behavioral modifications usually addressed in executive development programs.

However, communicating the value of self-learning must also include a recognition that an inability to engage in this kind of growth is a deficiency that has serious consequences for the organization. It must be clear that relational skills are not simply nice things to have but also are critical to organizational effectiveness. One way to communicate the importance of relational skills in the workplace would be to hold training sessions and workshops to develop these skills. These workshops in "continuous teaching" or "collaborative communication" would send a powerful message that relational skills can be taught and that there is organizational value in learning them. Unlike some of the human relations training sessions that focus on "how to treat people you manage," relational skill building sessions could focus on the *process* of mutual growth-in-connection. These sessions could be structured to give individuals specific techniques, such as the kinds of questions to ask or the proper internal attitude to assume in attempting to understand another's experience in the way that person experiences it. Practice in using collaborative language skills or in actively minimizing status differences can build this type of relational skill that can then be used in understanding and ultimately integrating other perspectives into a new, enlarged understanding of self and other. As others have noted (Drath, 1990), this enlarged understanding is a critical step in moving from a mind-set in which interpersonal relationships are objectified and autonomy is the highest goal to a mind-set in which interpersonal relationships are seen as a site for growth and interdependence is the highest goal.

- *Recognize and reward the value that relational activity currently adds to organizational effectiveness.* In addition to the study mentioned earlier, which detailed relational practice, there have been a number of recent studies that make visible the hidden relational work that gets done in organizations (Huff, 1990; Jacques, 1992; Harvey, 1993; Kolb, 1991). Each of these studies emphasizes that the current paradigm of organizations-as-instrumental-entities is an incomplete representation of organizational life. Each identifies different ways in which organizations depend on and reap the benefits of relational activity. However, the fact that these activities are systematically devalued and their effect on the efficiency and effectiveness of organizational action remains invisible and unrewarded mitigates against organizations taking positive actions to promote more of this activity in certain of its members. Yet with a workforce that has been trained to overvalue the instrumental aspects of self, that is exactly what organizations would have to do to promote self-learning in the workplace.

In the early 1990s, a project at Digital Equipment Corporation undertook just such an initiative. Working with members of the Stone Center for Developmental Services and Studies at Wellesley College, one group of software engineers undertook a program to bring relational strengths into the mainstream of DEC's organizational values and structures. The project drew on employee experience, particularly the experience of women, to identify relational activities that were unrecognized and unrewarded in the current structure. The resulting eighteen recommendations for change—ranging from rewards for teamwork to the establishment of support groups—have made a noticeable difference in the culture of the participating work group. Those involved in the project speak of a sense of empowerment and an ability to bring "more of themselves" to work (Harvey, 1993). Organizations that undertake initiatives such as this in which the present value of relational activity is recognized will go a long way toward legitimizing and thereby encouraging the type of "self-learning through connection" that we have described.

- *Address the issue of work-life integration.* Although the detailing of relational practice suggests that growth-in-connection occurs in organizational contexts, it is also true that this type of learning often occurs in personal relationships and is then transferred to organizational settings. For example, those who have studied the sociology of parenting (Ruddick, 1989) suggest that the skills learned in the process of caring for and caring about others are unique. Acquiring these skills gives one the ability to enable and empower others while enhancing one's own self-esteem (Miller, 1986). The change in self-identity, the stretching and growing that occurs for both parties in caring relationships, is an essential developmental task. If inhibited by, for example, organizational conditions that (even unintentionally) discourage family or community caring activity, individuals will be limited in their ability to grow in these ways. On the other hand, organizations whose practices, structures, and policies encourage work-life integration are more likely to have employees who can bring fully developed, integrated selves to the workplace. For example, companies such as American Express, Du Pont, and AT&T have recently instituted voluntary sabbatical programs offering employees from nine months' to two years' leave without pay to work on community service projects. Although these programs were initiated as a short-term answer to downsizing, they have the potential to offer a unique opportunity for personal development. A modified program, for example three or six months' leave at half pay, could be a unique component of a self-learning effort. The stated goal of the leave would be to encourage the kind of relational self-learning that comes from contributing to the welfare of others whether that be in the family or broader community.

Taking this a step further, one could imagine, for example, that in a work environment where relational skills were on a par with task mastery skills, developmental programs might include some form of family or community involvement as a necessary condition of advancement or continued employment. Performance appraisals could include suggestions for meeting this relational developmental need by the use of "outside consultants" (children, elderly parents, members of shelters, schools, hospitals, and so on). This admittedly radical idea would be self-reinforcing. The experience of caring for others could potentially develop the type of relational skills we have been discussing. Transferring these skills to the workplace, where they would be rewarded and noted as evidence of competence and effectiveness, would further encourage their development; these skills would no longer be considered inappropriate but instead would be viewed as a source of career enhancement.

Other initiatives could include organizational support for public policy incentives, such as those recently adopted by some of the Scandinavian countries (Rapoport, 1995) to encourage paternity in addition to maternity leaves. This would help to make the skills and competencies that are developed in caring for others less traditionally "feminine" as it would encourage fathers to be more involved in their children's development. This in turn would lessen the likelihood that demonstrating these skills in the workplace would be considered inappropriate, because a broader range of people would practice them.

Some U.S. companies are making strides in this same direction not through public policy initiatives but rather through linking work-family integration to reengineering. For example, for the past several years the Xerox Corporation has been cosponsoring an action research project with the Ford Foundation in which work-family is a "catalyst for change" in the reorganization of work practices and processes (Bailyn et al., 1995; Fletcher, 1995). They found that using a work-family lens to identify general work practices that make it difficult for all employees—not just women—to integrate their work and personal lives resulted in work process innovations that had a significant positive effect on the bottom line. Moreover, not only did these innovations benefit both work and personal goals, these initiatives depended on well-integrated individuals to engage the process and achieve the results. It appears that organizing work in ways that assume all employees are involved in family and community life not only legitimates this type of integration in members of the workforce but it is also a path toward improved productivity and business effectiveness.

Conclusion

The goal of this chapter has been to address the imbalance in current organizational practices, reward systems, and developmental programs by focusing not on task mastery but on more relational dimensions of growth and professional achievement in organizational settings. This discussion suggests that organizations have much to gain by encouraging, rewarding, and developing relational skills in its workforce. It also suggests, however, that addressing the current imbalance in organizational models of success in this way is not an easy task. In many ways, rewarding relational skills violates many deeply held assumptions about what it means to be a competent, productive, effective worker. It follows that simply calling for this new kind of worker is unlikely to do the job. Instead, what will be required is an organizational effort to break down the barriers and assumed separation among skills associated with the public, work domain (such as technical competence, autonomous action, competitiveness, and linear reasoning) and those associated with the private, personal, or family domain (such as empathy, support, interdependence, and contextual reasoning). As the strategies suggested above indicate, breaking down this barrier will require some innovative, out-of-the-box thinking in terms of designing reward systems that recognize fully integrated individuals who use both sets of skills in doing their work. It will also require individual initiative in developing a language of competence to describe and articulate these skills and practices.

More radical perhaps is the suggestion that developing these skills in new workers will require some relaxation of the work-family boundary as it is typically experienced in organizations. Designing work so that *all* workers can integrate work and personal life is one way to address this issue. This means, of course, addressing some of the cultural determinants of work behavior and design that reinforce the image of an "ideal" worker as someone with no outside responsibilities and a firm boundary between work and personal life. Redefining the ideal worker as someone who is a blend of public *and* private, work *and* family, rational *and* emotional, masculine *and* feminine is quite a departure from organizational norms. Yet if the concerns of the new organization are to be met, it appears that this is exactly what needs to take place.

In summary, this chapter suggests that addressing the discrepancy between a call for a new, "blended" protean worker of the future and many of the current organizational reward and development systems is a key challenge facing organizations today. Rising to this challenge will require some new ways of thinking that call into question many deeply held assumptions about individual and organizational paths to success. Although the road map for developing and rewarding the new protean worker is not clear, what is clear is that initiatives that encourage and support changing, evolving individuals, accompanied by environments that use these changes as catalysts for innovation, will free people to enthusiastically engage in the kind of relational self-growth activities organizations will ultimately find beneficial.

References

Alexander, C. N., Druker, S. M., & Langer, E. J. (1990). Major issues in the exploration of adult growth. In C. Alexander & E. Langer

(Eds.), *Higher stages of human development*. New York: Oxford University Press.

Bailyn, L., Kolb, D. K., Eaton, S., Fletcher, J. K., Harvey, M., Johnson, R., Perlow, L., & Rapoport, R. (1995). *Executive summary. Work-"family" partnership: A catalyst for change*. Cambridge, MA: School of Management, Massachusetts Institute of Technology.

Bandura, A. (1986). *Social foundations of thought and action: A social cognitive theory*. Englewood Cliffs, NJ: Prentice Hall.

Bennis, W., & Nanus, B. (1985). *Leaders: Strategies for taking charge*. New York: HarperCollins.

Brown, J. S., & Duguid, P. (1991). Organizational learning and communities-of-practice: Toward a unified view of working, learning and innovation. *Organization Science, 2*(1), 40–57.

Byham, W. C., & Cox, J. (1994). *HeroZ*. New York: Harmony Books.

Cytrynbaum, S., & Crites, J. (1989). The utility of adult development theory in understanding career adjustment process. In M. B. Arthur, D. T. Hall, & B. S. Lawrence (Eds.), *Handbook of career theory*. New York: Cambridge University Press, 66–88.

Dalton, G., & Thompson, P. (1986). *Novations: Strategies for career development*. Glenview, IL: Scott, Foresman.

Drath, W. (1990). Managerial strengths and weaknesses as functions of the development of personal meaning. *Journal of Applied Behavioral Science, 26*(4), 483–499.

Erikson, E. (1963). *Childhood and society* (2nd ed.). New York: W.W. Norton.

Fletcher, J. K. (1994). *Toward a theory of relational practice in organizations: A feminist reconstruction of "real" work*. Doctoral dissertation, Boston University, Boston.

Fletcher, J. K. (1995, August). *The work-family business imperative: Where's the beef?* Symposium talk presented at the Academy of Management Annual Meeting, Vancouver, B.C.

Fletcher, J. K., & Bailyn, L. (1996). Challenging the last boundary: Reconnecting work and family. In M. Arthur & D. M. Rousseau (Eds.), *Boundaryless careers*. Oxford, England: Oxford University Press.

Friedlander, F. (1994). Toward whole systems and whole people. *Organization, 1*(1), 59–64.

Gallos, J. (1989). Exploring women's development: Implications for career theory, practice and research. In M. B. Arthur, D. T. Hall, & B. S. Lawrence (Eds.), *Handbook of career theory*. New York: Cambridge University Press, 110–132.

Gilligan, C. (1982). *In a different voice*. Cambridge, MA: Harvard University Press.

Greenhaus, J., & Beutell, N. (1985). Sources of conflict between work and family roles. *Academy of Management Review, 10,* 76–88.

Hall, D. T. (1972). A model of coping with role conflict: The role behavior of college educated women. *Administrative Science Quarterly, 17,* 471–486.

Hall, D. T. (1976). *Careers in organizations.* Glenview, IL: Scott, Foresman.

Hammer, M. (1994, January). Interview with Michael Hammer. *Computer-World, 28*(4).

Hammer, M., & Champy, J. (1993). *Reengineering the corporation: A manifesto for business revolution.* New York: HarperBusiness.

Harragan, B. (1977). *Games mother never taught you.* New York: Warner Books.

Harvey, M. (1993). *The Stone Center Project at DEC.* Unpublished report, The Stone Center, Wellesley College, Wellesley, MA.

Helgeson, S. (1990). *The female advantage.* New York: Doubleday.

Hennig, M., & Jardim, A. (1978). *The managerial woman.* New York: Pocket Books.

Holland, J. L. (1973). *Making vocational choices: A theory of careers.* Englewood Cliffs, NJ: Prentice Hall.

Huberman, B. A., & Hogg, T. (1994). *Communities of practice: Performance and evolution.* Working paper, Palo Alto Research Center, Palo Alto, CA.

Huff, A. (1990, May). *Wives—of the organization.* Paper presented at the Women & Work Conference, Arlington, TX.

Jacques, R. (1992). *Re-presenting the knowledge worker: A poststructuralist analysis of the new employed professional.* Doctoral dissertation, University of Massachusetts, Amherst.

Jordan, J. V., Kaplan, A. G., Miller, J. B., Stiver, I. P., & Surrey, J. L. (Eds.). (1991). *Women's growth in connection.* New York: Guilford Press.

Kahn, W. (1993). Caring for the caregivers: Patterns of organizational caregiving. *Administrative Science Quarterly, 38,* 539–563.

Kaplan, R., with Drath, W. H., & Kofodimos, J. (1991). *Beyond ambition: How driven managers can lead better and live better.* San Francisco: Jossey-Bass.

Kegan, R. (1982). *The evolving self.* Cambridge, MA: Harvard University Press.

Kegan, R. (1994). *In over our heads.* Cambridge, MA: Harvard University Press.

Kohlberg, L. (1976). Moral stages and moralization: The cognitive developmental approach. In T. Lickona (Ed.), *Moral development and behavior.* Troy, MO: Holt, Rinehart & Winston.

Kolb, D. (1991). Women's work: Peacemaking behind the organizational scene. In D. Kolb & J. Bartunek (Eds.), *Conflict in the crevices: New perspectives in organizational conflict.* Newbury Park, CA: Sage.

Kram, K. (1983). Phases of the mentor relationship. *Academy of Management Journal, 26*(4), 608–625.

Levinson, D., with Darrow, C. N., Klein, E. B., Levinson, M. H., & McKee, B. (1978). *Seasons of a man's life.* New York: Knopf.

Loevinger, J. (1976). *Ego development: Conceptions and theories.* San Francisco: Jossey-Bass.

Martin, P. (1995, August). *Mobilizing masculinities.* Paper presented at the Academy of Management Meeting, Vancouver, B.C.

McIlwee, J., & Robinson, J. G. (1992). *Women in engineering: Gender, power and workplace culture.* Albany, NY: State University of New York Press.

Miller, J. B. (1986). *Toward a new psychology of women* (2nd ed.). Boston: Beacon Press.

Miller, J. B. (1991). The development of women's sense of self. In J. V. Jordan, A. G. Kaplan, J. B. Miller, I. P. Stiver, & J. L. Surrey (Eds.), *Women's growth in connection.* New York: Guilford Press, 11–26.

Nonaka, I. (1994). A dynamic theory of organizational knowledge creation. *Organization Science, 5*(1), 14–37.

Osipow, S. H. (1983). *Theories of career development.* Englewood Cliffs, NJ: Prentice Hall.

Perry, W. (1970) *Forms of intellectual and ethical development in the college years.* Troy, MO: Holt, Rinehart & Winston.

Peters, T. (1990, September). The best new managers will listen, motivate, support: Isn't that just like a woman. *Working Woman,* 216–217.

Rapoport, R. (1995, March). *Global forces and corporate responses.* Symposium presented at the WorkLife Issues Conference, Northeastern University, Boston.

Rosenbaum, J. E. (1989). Organization career systems and employee misperceptions. In M. B. Arthur, D. T. Hall, & B. S. Lawrence (Eds.), *Handbook of career theory.* New York: Cambridge University Press, 329–353.

Rosener, J. (1990). Ways women lead. *Harvard Business Review, 68*(6), 119–125.

Ruddick, S. (1989). *Maternal thinking.* Boston: Beacon Press.

Schein, E. (1978). *Career dynamics: Matching individual and organizational needs.* Reading, MA: Addison-Wesley.

Senge, P. (1990). *The fifth discipline.* New York: Doubleday.

Slater, R. (1994). *Get better or get beaten!* New York: Irwin.

Souvaine, E., Lahey, L., & Kegan, R. (1990). Life after formal operations: Implications for a psychology of the self. In C. Alexander &

E. Langer (Eds.), *Higher stages of human development*. New York: Oxford University Press.

Super, D. (1957). *The psychology of careers*. New York: HarperCollins.

Wadel, C. (1979). The hidden work of everyday life. In S. Wallman (Ed.), *The social anthropology of work*. New York: Academic Press, 365–384.

Watkins, K., & Marsick, V. (1993). *Sculpting the learning organization: Lessons in the art and science of systemic change*. San Francisco: Jossey-Bass.

Wheatley, M. (1992). *Leadership and the new science*. San Francisco: Berrett-Koehler.

Chapter Five

A Relational Approach to Career Development

Kathy E. Kram

Richard is a fifty-one-year-old white middle manager who has enjoyed a long career with a public utility. He now confronts more uncertainty in his career than ever before: dramatic changes in the marketplace have resulted in restructuring that may eliminate his position; and, as a result of recent diversity initiatives in the company, promotions in the last two years have consistently gone to qualified women and people of color. He wonders how he can continue to grow and find satisfaction at work, and in bleaker moments he experiences considerable fear and anxiety about what lies ahead.

Helen is a thirty-year-old financial consultant of Asian decent who has launched a fast-track career on Wall Street. Although her performance appraisals have been quite good in the first five years, her bosses have consistently noted that she needs to be more assertive in her dealings with clients and colleagues if she is to advance further. This feedback contradicts her natural style, which is confident yet reserved, consistent with her cultural heritage. She

Note: I am grateful for several colleagues' comments on the first draft including those from Joyce Fletcher, Tim Hall, Jane Hodgetts, Bill Kahn, Victoria Parker, Cynthia Piltch, and Mary Young.

wonders how she can effectively respond to this feedback and feels quite alone with the problem because neither her mentor nor her peers fully appreciate the difficulty that she faces. Helen is ambitious and dedicated to hard work; these traits, however, do not help to alleviate the sense of isolation she feels in trying to reconcile strong organizational norms about appropriate style with her own views of herself.

Richard and Helen exemplify increasingly common scenarios in today's work settings. In stark contrast to career experiences in earlier decades, these two individuals face challenges posed by an ever more turbulent and diverse environment. The purpose of this chapter is to examine how a relational approach to career development provides a useful framework for helping individuals such as Richard and Helen address and move beyond the challenges that they currently face.

A relational approach to career development explores the ways in which individuals learn and grow in their work-related experiences through connections with others, taking a holistic view of individuals and the nature of their interactions with assignments, people, organizations, and the social context in which they work. In this chapter, we will focus on one aspect of this array of relational activities, the dyadic relationships that individuals have at work, which can support learning (acquiring new skills and competencies) and development (advancing one's career and/or developing self-esteem or a new sense of one's identity).

In some ways, this relational approach is not new: since the earliest studies of boss-subordinate relationships (for example, Berlew and Hall, 1966) and throughout the last two decades of research on mentoring (for example, Kram, 1983; Levinson, Darrow, Levinson, and McKee, 1978; Dalton and Thompson, 1986), the important role of relationships in career development has been consistently demonstrated.

The earliest work on the role of relationships in career development emphasized the importance of mentoring and coaching for individuals in the establishment stage of their careers (Hall, 1976; Super, 1957; Dalton and Thompson, 1986). More experienced colleagues—both bosses and mentors—provide challenging assignments, regular constructive feedback, exposure and sponsorship, which help novices establish a work identity, learn the ropes, and successfully advance to positions of greater status and responsibility. Fairly early on in this stream of research it became clear that bosses and mentors also benefit from these relationships.

For example, Dalton, Thompson, and Price (1977) demonstrated how providing mentoring and sponsorship are part of the essential developmental tasks that they associated with stages three and four of professional careers. Stage three, the mentor stage, is a phase when individuals begin to teach, coach, and develop others. Stage four, the sponsor stage, is a time when managers have sufficient experience and influence to shape the future direction of their organization. Similarly, it has been demonstrated in more recent studies of mentoring that experienced professionals and managers gain new competencies, loyal followership, and recognition from peers and superiors for developing talent for the organization, and they also gain personal satisfaction from enabling younger colleagues to flourish (Kram, 1988; Thomas, 1990, 1993).

Recent and dramatic changes in the workplace (as delineated in earlier chapters in this book) render this established view of mentoring and other developmental relationships insufficient. In today's context, individuals of all ages, organizational tenure, and career stage find themselves to be novices—having to learn a radically new job, acquire new technical skills, or work with people of vastly different backgrounds and world views. As with the young novice just starting out, relationships are a critical resource for learning in these instances; without them, a sense of isolation and/or despair are all too likely.

In addition, in contrast to periods characterized by stability and linear careers, potential mentors in the current context—individuals with more than ten or fifteen years of experience—no longer hold the expertise and security to serve as trusted advisers in the traditional sense. Their role in developing less experienced colleagues is necessarily being transformed into one of colearner (Kram and Hall, 1996). The learning and coaching that evolves between junior and senior colleagues in today's environment must be necessarily more mutual and reciprocal. Given the pace of change, such relationships are likely to be of shorter duration.

Initiating and maintaining relationships that facilitate learning are more difficult in today's context. The uncertain and fast-paced context poses unique obstacles to forming new developmental relationships because potential mentors are as consumed as their less experienced colleagues with surviving in this new environment (Kram and Hall, 1996). Also, more often than not, individuals (regardless of their age, gender, or race) will face the challenge of forming productive alliances with others who differ from them in some fundamental way. Thus the natural rapport and mutual identification so commonly experienced in mentoring relationships between individuals who share common values and backgrounds no longer provide the impetus or the glue for mutual learning and development (Kram and Bragar, 1992; Thomas, 1993; Ibarra, 1993; Thomas and Alderfer, 1989).

Finally, these trends are further amplified by increasingly resource-constrained environments that inevitably reduce the time available for relational activity. This reality only serves to extend the complexities and challenges involved in making relationships central and effective in career development. Current research and writing on this subject clearly suggest that the current career context requires individuals to acquire a new set of relationship competencies (Fletcher, 1994b; McCauley and Young, 1993). Without these, the potential of relationships to support learning and development will not be realized.

In order to help individuals benefit from relational activity at work, career practitioners must first understand their clients' current concerns. After briefly reviewing how these differ from those in traditional contexts, I will outline what I consider to be the necessary conditions for a relational approach to career development: (1) relationships that are characterized by interdependence, mutuality, and reciprocity, (2) a willingness to see relationships as important sites of personal learning and development, (3) interpersonal competencies including self-reflection, self-disclosure, active listening, empathy, and feedback, and (4) opportunities to develop multiple developmental alliances at work. (See Chapter Seven in this volume for consideration of developmental relationships that occur outside of the work setting.) I will end with several guidelines for career practitioners who want to model and facilitate relational activity that enhances their clients' development (as well as their own).

Career Development in the New Context

Until recently, career theorists and practitioners had developed fairly consistent views about how individuals' careers unfold over time (Dalton, 1989). Although a number of different perspectives had emerged (for example, life-span models, organizationally based models, individual differences models), all of these tended to take a developmental view of individuals' career-related experiences. Thus, if one knew a person's age, tenure (in the organization or in a particular career), personality, values, and/or learning style, one could predict fairly accurately what that person's salient career concerns and developmental tasks might be (Super, 1986).

The new career context, however—characterized by persistent turbulence and ever-increasing diversity—renders these developmental models less effective in understanding, predicting, and responding to a particular individual's career concerns. A closer look at Richard and Helen (introduced earlier) helps to illuminate the new challenges and concerns that individuals face at various points in their careers.

First, Richard's circumstances at age fifty-one help us to see firsthand that one's identity and self-concept are no longer necessarily stabilized during the early career period. While age-related and organizational-based models of career development would have predicted considerable clarity of identity (combined with perhaps some reassessment and redirection at midlife), Richard finds himself propelled back to what we might consider concerns of the novice. Changes in the environment have stripped away the familiar parameters of Richard's occupational identity, leaving him with considerable uncertainty about his niche, his value to the organization, and even his self-worth.

Although we might expect identity confusion in someone at Helen's age and career stage, she faces a unique challenge created by being Asian and female in a historically white male-dominated workplace. Although traditional adult and career development perspectives suggest that relationships with mentors and more experienced peers would effectively guide a young professional toward greater clarity of identity and style, Helen has yet to find such connections. Those who are sponsoring and coaching her and providing her with challenging assignments are helping her learn critical technical skills, but they are not able to help her discover a style that is congruent with her personal values and also acceptable to the organization.

More specifically, the gender expectations (be nurturing, supportive, and accommodating) and cultural messages (be polite and responsive) regarding appropriate behavior for an Asian female professional are powerful influences on Helen's behavior and largely unclear (if not invisible) to her mentors and other colleagues of dominant group backgrounds. These same messages are also in conflict with the dominant organizational culture that expects assertiveness and willingness to confront conflict head-on from its high performers. Thus the path to a clear sense of identity and an effective style is uncharted for employees such as Helen.

Even young white males face a more complicated path toward a sense of identity in their chosen occupation. The "dream" first articulated by Levinson and colleagues (1978), for example, is far more difficult to envision and to realize in a world that is filled with pervasive uncertainty. Young white men cannot aspire to emulate their fathers, grandfathers, and mentors because these role models received satisfaction and various measures of success from things that no longer exist. Instead, these novices face a set of obstacles never encountered by their seniors.

Although traditional career development models predict that relative newcomers (such as Helen) would be striving to develop a sense of competence in their chosen occupations, we would not historically predict equally substantial concerns about competence for a midcareer individual such as Richard. It is precisely the organizational turbulence—including downsizing, restructuring, emergent markets, and new technology—that quickly makes Richard's knowledge, skills, and perspectives obsolete. What once made him a well-respected expert worthy of serving as a mentor to those younger than himself—his accumulated wisdom and organizational history—now leave him vulnerable to unemployment and a range of negative reactions associated with such a loss.

These brief illustrations demonstrate how developing a sense of identity and developing competence are tasks that are likely to resurface regularly for individuals in today's career context. In one sense, this is not new. Levinson and his colleagues illuminated the concept of "life structure"—and associated structure building and structure changing periods—as typical of adult lives over time (Levinson, Darrow, Levinson, and McKee, 1978). They demonstrated how such fundamental questions about identity and competence predictably resurface during structure-changing periods as individuals altered external circumstances, reoriented their internal relationship to particular facets of the life structure, or experienced major events over which they had little or no control (such as loss of a parent or job).

What is different in today's more turbulent context is the pace at which external circumstances change and affect the existent life structure (Mirvis and Hall, 1994). Though not yet empirically documented, it appears that stable and transitional periods are necessarily of shorter duration. As a consequence, such fundamental questions about identity and competence are likely to resurface more often than traditional models would have us anticipate. Thus minority and majority group members, young and middle age are equally likely to have to wrestle with these fundamental questions many times during their lives. The only certainties are that the texture of these concerns will vary from individual to individual and the pathways to mastery will be equally unique.

Traditional models of career development and adult development have offered interdependent relationships as a critical vehicle for addressing these fundamental developmental tasks. These models predict that experienced, midcareer individuals can offer guidance and support to novices and in doing so enhance their own self-esteem, self-worth, and value to their organizations. Yet it seems obvious that the stability and security once thought to be a prerequisite for enacting the mentoring role is no longer readily achieved—even by midlife. Newcomers and experienced individuals alike, in the absence of stable jobs and organizations, are that much more dependent on relationships as a vehicle for developing a sense of identity and for developing new skills and competencies. (See Chapter Six in this volume for further discussion of how relationships provide a secure base.)

We can expect individuals' reactions to this new reality to vary. Those with career concepts characterized by autonomy and excitement will not find the new context particularly disturbing, and in some instances they may thrive on it. In contrast, those with career concepts characterized by security or balance may have a difficult time coming to terms with the new reality (Driver, 1982; Derr, 1986; Schein, 1978). Indeed, individuals who primarily value security or life balance may find persistent change to be quite disruptive to an overall sense of well-being. Regardless of one's career orientation, however, relational activity that provides opportunity to regularly reflect on these inevitably recurring and fundamental questions of identity and competence have the potential to support individuals' efforts to cope with the challenges they face.

As the ability to lead becomes increasingly essential to organizational competitiveness, individuals at all levels and career stages are likely to encounter opportunities to develop this capacity (Kanter, 1989; Handy, 1989; Kiechel, 1994). Traditional theories of career development consistently suggest that only with years of experience and the requisite analytical, interpersonal, and emotional skills are individuals able to exercise power in the service of organizational vision and strategy (Schein, 1978). It seems to me that the capacities needed to engage in relational activity that supports career development are nearly the same as those required to lead. If so, this relational approach to career development will enhance organizational development as well.

Addressing Career Concerns Through Relational Activity

What does it mean to address career concerns through relational activity? Several scholars and practitioners have already partially answered this question through their work on leadership development (McCall, Lombardo, and Morrison, 1988); learning organizations and the dialogue process (Senge, 1990; Isaacs, 1993; Schein, 1993), and women's development (Jordan et al., 1991; Miller, 1991). Common to all of these works is the important role of a variety of relationships in learning and development and the conditions that enable personal learning through connection with others.

A relational approach suggests that regardless of age or career stage, when individuals face concerns about their identity and value at work (triggered by external events such as organizational downsizing or internal shifts such as a desire for more work-family balance), they will benefit from conversations with others who have dealt with similar issues. Similarly, when rapid changes in work role, technology, and/or the marketplace require learning new skills, competencies, or perspectives, individuals can create and enhance the learning process through relationships with others that have experience in relevant areas.

While research on mentoring has delineated the developmental functions of such relationships and the value of peer relationships as well (Kram, 1988; Thomas and Kram, 1989; Thomas, 1990), it is the more recent work on women's development that illuminates the necessary conditions for such relationships to foster personal growth (rather than only career advancement). Most relevant here are the capacities for self-reflection, empathy, and listening as well as the willingness to be vulnerable that are essential for meaningful personal learning to occur (Fletcher, 1994a, 1994b; Miller, 1991; Jordan et al., 1991).

Relational models of growth and development (derived from studies of women's development) are based on a different set of assumptions and beliefs than traditional models of career development. In contrast to traditional theories that conceptualize growth as a process of individuation and achievement in which individuals move from a stage of dependency to one of independence, a relational model conceptualizes growth as movement through increasingly complex states of interdependence. (Miller, 1986; Jordan et al., 1991; Fletcher, 1994b). Thus development is viewed less as a process of differentiating oneself from others as it is understanding oneself as increasingly connected to others. (See Chapter Four in this volume for further elaboration.)

This perspective on growth and development implies that relational activity that supports learning is two-way (rather than one-way), and both parties enter the interaction expecting to be both expert and learner, to give and receive, to enable and be enabled. A relational approach to career development (Figure 5.1) assumes that individuals at every career stage can learn and contribute to others' learning, and the over-arching goal is interdependence (as opposed to independence) that supports task accomplishment as well as personal learning. Interestingly, this view is highly consistent with the role of mentor as colearner that has necessarily evolved in increasingly turbulent and uncertain environments (Kram and Hall, 1996).

Figure 5.1. A Relational Approach to Career Development.

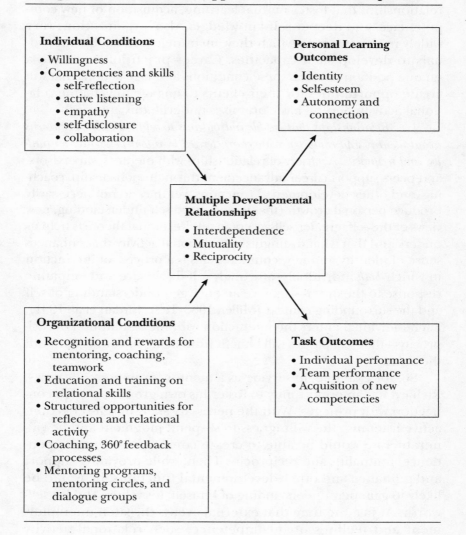

Individual Conditions

- Willingness
- Competencies and skills
  - self-reflection
  - active listening
  - empathy
  - self-disclosure
  - collaboration

Personal Learning Outcomes

- Identity
- Self-esteem
- Autonomy and connection

Multiple Developmental Relationships

- Interdependence
- Mutuality
- Reciprocity

Organizational Conditions

- Recognition and rewards for mentoring, coaching, teamwork
- Education and training on relational skills
- Structured opportunities for reflection and relational activity
- Coaching, 360° feedback processes
- Mentoring programs, mentoring circles, and dialogue groups

Task Outcomes

- Individual performance
- Team performance
- Acquisition of new competencies

Not all individuals have the capacities to build developmental relationships that foster mutual learning, acquisition of new competencies, and deeper self-knowledge. Also, organizations vary widely in the extent to which they encourage and enable individuals to develop such capacities. Career practitioners are in a unique position to assess these conditions and take actions that will create opportunities for their clients to engage in valuable relational activity. Several basic premises underlie this approach.

1.   *Relationships that enable individuals to address central concerns about identity and competence are characterized by interdependence, mutuality, and reciprocity.* A variety of relationships with mentors, supervisors, and peers support career advancement through sponsorship, coaching, and other developmental functions; yet they do not necessarily produce personal growth (that is, enhanced self-understanding, new views of the self, greater self-acceptance). Relational theorists help us understand that what distinguishes relational activity that enhances sense of identity and new competencies is a process of interaction in which *both* individuals—through self-disclosure and empathic response to the other—achieve an enlarged understanding of self and the surrounding context (Miller, 1986, 1991; Jordan et al. 1991). Each individual enters the interaction with the assumption of reciprocity—that *both* parties will benefit from being in connection with the other.

So, for example, in serving as a mentor for junior colleagues, Richard has an opportunity to foster his own growth through connection with protégés. With the necessary skills of self-reflection, active listening, the willingness to suspend judgment and be vulnerable, he would be able to create conditions of interdependence, mutuality, and reciprocity. Then, while providing support and guidance and other developmental functions, he would be likely to gain new understanding of himself, his values, and his self-worth. At just the time that external events threaten unemployment and feelings of incompetence, such relational activity enhances self-esteem and personal empowerment.

Similarly, Helen is likely to gain insight into the challenge of defining a personal style that is congruent with her personal values as well as compatible with the organization's culture; she will accomplish this through interaction with others that is characterized by interdependence, mutuality, and reciprocity. Here she has the opportunity to hear others' personal stories and to tell her own, to reflect on both, and to incorporate new views of what is possible. Helen might hear in a colleague's story, for example, a novel approach to managing relations with high-profile clients, one that is characterized by a unique combination of politeness, collaboration, and assertiveness. The individual's personal account might also shed light on how to integrate vastly different aspects of one's style into a style that is effective in challenging client interactions. Indeed, support groups, peer relationships, and dialogue groups have in common a process that enables self-reflection and self-transformation through the relational activity that is fostered. (See Chapter Eleven in this volume.)

2. *Individuals vary in their willingness to see relationships as sites of personal growth and in their ability to participate in such relational activity.* There is considerable evidence that as a result of gender socialization, women (more than men) have a tendency to see the potential of growth-in-connection with others (Miller, 1986; Jordan et al., 1991; Kram and McCollom, in press). Other cultural forces can also shape the extent to which individuals look toward relationships for personal learning. For example, the expression of a wide range of feelings and the willingness to discuss problems and concerns openly may be more acceptable in some cultures than others (Adler, 1991).

Even with the willingness to see relationships as a source of personal growth, individuals may not have the skills required to foster interaction characterized by interdependence, mutuality, and reciprocity. For example, if Richard lacks the capacities for self-reflection, self-disclosure, vulnerability, active listening, and/or empathy, he will not benefit from the potential in his connection with protégés or peers. If this is the case, he will experience considerable self-doubt and alienation as the organization is restructured and his job is eliminated. Rather than discovering a new identity through connection with others, he will primarily experience loss of status and esteem.

There is some evidence to suggest that individuals can develop both the willingness and the ability to engage in relational activity through exposure to the opportunity for such interaction and the guidance and coaching to practice unfamiliar interpersonal skills (Schein, 1993; Isaac, 1993; Walker and Hansen, 1992). Whether in the context of therapy, executive coaching, management training, mentor training, dialogue groups, or some other learning vehicle, individuals discover the value of mutuality and reciprocity and learn through experience how to create such growth through connection.

3.   *Individuals benefit from fostering multiple developmental relationships, experiencing unique potential for growth in each.* Recent initiatives designed to foster mentoring and coaching relationships have a tendency to foster the misconception that individuals should seek out one primary developmental relationship (Kram and Bragar, 1992; Murray and Owen, 1991; Mink, Owen, and Mink, 1993). This is particularly true in programs where individuals are formally matched with others who have the potential to provide appropriate guidance and support given their complementary career stage. Thus, for example, newcomers are matched with more experienced peers or with middle managers who can help them learn the ropes and begin to develop a clearer sense of their role in the organization.

Although this approach is certainly helpful in addressing predictable challenges of the early career period, such programs, if not carefully positioned, may cause participants to overlook the value of fostering multiple relationships with seniors, peers, and subordinates who can promote personal learning in a variety of ways. Recent research shows that successful black managers have benefited from relationships with both black and white senior colleagues, a good example of the importance of developing multiple relationships (Thomas, 1990, 1993). Similarly, women have found it invaluable to be in connection with other women as well as with male colleagues as they strive to develop a relationship to their work that is congruent with personal values and also acceptable in the corporate culture (Kram, 1988; Morrison, White, and Van Velsor, 1987; Morrison, 1992).

Nontraditional employees who have multiple developmental alliances experience unique sources of learning in each relationship (Ibarra, 1995). It seems that in relationships with those who share common background characteristics (such as gender or race), individuals find confirmation and a reduced sense of isolation, and they come to value and be empowered by what makes them different from the dominant culture (Ely, 1994; Bell, 1990). At the same time, relationships with individuals from the dominant group not only open doors and enable career advancement but also provide opportunities for individuals to practice critical skills of communication, negotiation, collaboration, and managing conflict with key colleagues. Both types of relationships enhance sense of identity and development of new competencies.

Helen, for example, has just begun to experience the value of being in dialogue with other women and Asian women in particular about the challenges that she faces in developing a work style that is acceptable to her organization and also congruent with her personal values. At a dinner for women professionals in her division, she heard other women speak of their difficulty with the "macho" culture of their firm and strategies that they employed to demonstrate their value as team players while also maintaining their personal integrity. She left this meeting with new hope about surmounting the challenge she faces in developing a satisfying career within the firm and with new connections to plug into when she again feels isolated or confused in response to feedback from her superiors.

In recent years, opportunities for similar types of experiences, on an ongoing basis, have expanded for women and minority group members (Kram and Hall, 1996). Networks of various kinds, housed both inside and outside particular organizations, are becoming commonplace. The durability of these forums seems to be a consequence of the significant personal learning that occurs over time for those who participate. As a group of Boston-area executive women in health care recently noted, their ongoing connection with each other for over a decade resulted in regular promotions for all of them as well as consistent support and personal empowerment that continues to enhance self-esteem and personal satisfaction (Gabor, 1995).

The value of multiple developmental relationships is not limited to those from nontraditional backgrounds. In the context of assessing the value of a formal mentoring program, for example, several white male mentors commented that relationships with female protégés had resulted in unexpected and welcomed learning about how to effectively coach those of different backgrounds. Some also commented on their personal discovery of new ways of relating to work, expanding their styles to include more active listening and collaborative problem solving as a result of being in relationships with female protégés. These cross-gender relationships complemented the homogeneous alliances that had fostered their career advancement for years and made unique contributions to their development in midcareer.

Finally, for individuals who are no longer part of the full-time core of an organization but rather in a contract or part-time relationship with one or several organizations, multiple relationships that support one's sense of identity and development of competencies are essential. Without these sources of feedback, guidance, support, and fresh input on a variety of task and personal issues, individuals who are working independently are vulnerable to a sense of isolation and myopic views of their own work.

4. *A relational approach to career development also supports the accomplishment of work-related objectives.* It is quite evident how mentoring and coaching relationships support work-related objectives by facilitating newcomers' learning and socialization into their work roles and more generally developing talent for an organization. What is less obvious, perhaps, is how a relational approach to career development can contribute to a wide range of work objectives—including, in particular, projects that must be accomplished through effective teamwork (Handy, 1989; Kanter, 1989).

Viewed through a relational lens, work teams have great potential to support individual development and organizational performance. When members view other team members as resources for both task and personal learning, their connections with each other have the potential to produce outstanding work products as well as opportunities to develop new competencies and to confirm one's value to the organization. This kind of synergy is most likely to occur when a team's objectives include task accomplishment as well as personal and organizational learning.

In practice, team leaders and members must bring the same relational skills noted earlier to their work together. This has been most recently referred to as relational practice (see Chapter Four in this volume). In doing so, group norms that encourage brainstorming, active listening, open disagreement, consideration of novel and embryonic ideas, minimization of status differences (in other words, experienced members have much to learn from newcomers), and role flexibility are likely to take hold. Then conditions are created for excellent team performance (Eddy, 1985; Katzenbach and Smith, 1993) and for growth through connection (Miller, 1991; Jordan et al., 1991).

As with one-on-one relationships, team members bring to their work together a willingness to learn in relationships with each other. Team interactions are governed by the fundamental assumption that dialogue characterized by self-disclosure and active listening will result in self-learning and creative work outcomes (Isaacs, 1993; Schein, 1993). We have begun to see evidence of this synergy in the automobile industry (for example, in Chrysler's platform teams), the computer industry (Hewlett-Packard), and the pharmaceutical industry (Du Pont). Creativity is enhanced, cycle times are reduced, and personal learning that supports a positive sense of identity and development of new competencies thrives.

5. *Organizations encourage a relational approach to career development (and task accomplishment) when their cultures recognize, reward, and support self-reflection, peer learning, mentoring, and teamwork.* Although the new context for careers is plagued with considerable uncertainty and turbulence, some organizations are creating conditions that support a relational approach to career development. In particular, we see efforts to recognize and reward efforts to mentor and coach less experienced colleagues as well as peers in the performance appraisal process. In addition, it is increasingly common to see relational education and training providing individuals with opportunities to sharpen self-reflection and interpersonal skills that enable growth-in-connection with others (Kram and Hall, 1996).

These initiatives combined with the availability of internal and external coaching, 360-degree feedback processes, mentoring programs, mentoring circles, and dialogue groups all serve to create a "developmental culture" (Kram and Hall, 1996). Such practices encourage individuals to build developmental relationships by facilitating relevant interpersonal skill development, rewarding behaviors that support others' learning, and making relational activity central to the work itself (such as in teamwork).

Individuals who work in contexts that are lacking most (or all) of these conditions may find it difficult to build relationships that support learning through connections with others. Forces such as increased competitive pressures and rapid changes in technology, which demand shorter cycle times, are likely to undermine efforts to be self-reflective and to take time to actively listen to those from whom one might develop a new sense of identity or new competencies. It seems that only with counteracting forces—ones that encourage self-reflection and learning through relationships—will individuals have a chance to benefit from relational activity that supports career development.

Guidelines for Career Development Professionals

Career development professionals are in an excellent position to provide the encouragement and tools that individuals need in order to benefit from relational activity. Indeed, helping clients to engage in relationships that enhance self-understanding, sense of identity, and development of new competencies is both challenging and exciting. Whether inside a large organization or working independently, the professional will be involved in several core activities: diagnosing current career concerns, modeling relational activity, coaching, and facilitating action.

Diagnosing Current Career Concerns

In working with clients in today's context, I suggest that we assume that concerns about identity, self-worth, and personal values and meaning necessarily are more readily addressed through connections with others than through stability in a work role. Part of the task early on in work with a client, then, is to assess to what extent the individual is oriented toward building relationships that support his or her development (see Exhibit 5.1).

In assessing current concerns, the career professional undoubtedly has a range of questions regarding the client's current job, current concerns, visions of the future, and so forth. In addition, questions about relationships are essential. So, for example, in beginning to work with someone such as Richard, who may face loss of his current job, we would want to ask to what extent he mentors junior colleagues, to what extent he has shared his current concerns with peers, his superior, and others inside or outside his organization. Richard's responses would help us know whether relational activity—in which he discloses his own concerns, actively solicits others' perspectives on the challenges he faces, derives self-esteem from serving as a sounding board to others—is part of his repertoire.

If possible, it is also of value to solicit information about the client's career and life history. Reflection on past job experiences,

Exhibit 5.1. Diagnostic Questions for the Career Practitioner—The Relational Approach.

1. What are the individual's current career concerns?
   - Current job fit
   - The future
   - Work-personal life balance
   - Competence, values, identity

2. How does the individual's history influence current career concerns and relationships?
   - Jobs and organizations
   - Family background
   - Relationships with parents and other authority figures
   - Critical events

3. Does the individual seek out relationships for personal learning?
   - As a mentor
   - With a mentor
   - With peers
   - With subordinates
   - With seniors
   - Outside of work

4. Does the individual demonstrate the skills necessary for effective relational activity?
   - Self-disclosure
   - Self-reflection
   - Empathy
   - Active listening
   - Collaboration

5. Does the current work context provide opportunities for relational activity?
   - Teamwork
   - Mentoring, coaching, and 360-degree feedback
   - Education and training
   - Rewards and recognition for relationship building
   - Current business challenges (such as downsizing, restructuring)

one's family background, and past relationships with family members and authority figures throughout childhood and early adulthood lends insight into established patterns of relating that either facilitate or undermine the potential of current relationships at work. For example, trusting and close relationships with parents generally engender greater willingness to ask for help (that is, seek developmental alliances) in relationships at work. In contrast, the individual who has been estranged from authority figures earlier in life will be more inclined to maintain distant relationships that do not support learning. Making these patterns visible helps to create the possibility of change in one's stance in the future.

Modeling a Relational Approach

Throughout all phases of career counseling, the career professional has the opportunity to model effective relational activity that supports personal learning. In doing so, we demonstrate through active listening and empathy the value of engagement and the potential of growth through connection with another. For some individuals, such as Richard, this may be a relatively new and somewhat threatening experience. For others, it may come more naturally. As in a therapeutic relationship, it is essential to create a safe environment of confidentiality and acceptance if the interaction is to promote self-learning and relational activity back at work.

The texture of this relationship-building process will vary. From my own experience, for example, I have learned that the gender, age, and racial background of my client greatly influences how I go about establishing a growthful connection. I am more willing to disclose my own experience (and be vulnerable) with young women that I counsel because I have a sense that this will be helpful to them and that they will value such disclosure. In contrast, I find myself somewhat at a loss when some of my male clients find it difficult to be self-disclosing and responsive to my diagnostic questions. In these instances, I need to listen patiently and work to develop some level of empathy with how they approach career challenges. In doing so, I find opportunities for us to jointly explore the concerns that prompted them to meet with me.

Clearly, it is easier for me to facilitate and model growth for those with whom I more closely identify. A relational approach to career development, then, requires us to do the work and develop the competencies that we expect of our clients. Self-awareness and self-reflection are essential so that we can continuously learn how our own background, assumptions, and relational skills shape interactions with particular clients. We must also acknowledge the limitations of what we have to offer and encourage clients to seek other sources of growth-in-connection that complement what we bring to the alliance.

Coaching

The coaching process implied by a relational approach to career development can take several forms (Kinlaw, 1993; Mink, Owen, and Mink, 1993; Hall and Otazo, 1995; Pryor, 1994). First, based on a thorough diagnosis of a client's current concerns, a career professional might help clarify strategies for redefining a job, seeking a new position, or developing new skills. This more traditional aspect of career assistance is certainly of value to those who may lose their job through downsizing and who are in a poor fit. In defining such strategies, it is critical to aid clients in identifying individuals who could be helpful to them.

Second, and less obvious perhaps, is coaching on how to go about building new relationships not only for the purpose of finding new job opportunities but also to clarify one's needs, sense of identity, and self-worth in a context of continuous change and ambiguity. For example, in discovering Helen's struggle with defining a style that is acceptable to her and to the financial services culture and that helps her to respond to feedback from her superiors, a counselor might encourage her to talk with other women who may have encountered similar challenges. Helen's reactions to this kind of coaching will depend in part on her general stance toward relationships and whether growth-in-connection with others is a familiar experience.

A third aspect of coaching involves the willingness to give feedback to a client who may not have the relational skills or the necessary openness and confidence to initiate such dialogue with others. Helping an individual to see the need to develop skills such as active listening and self-reflection is not easy. However, it is essential, particularly for individuals who have not historically experienced growth-in-connection with others. Here again, as in therapeutic relationships, the career professional can draw upon the here-and-now interaction to demonstrate how to be self-reflective, self-disclosing, and empathic and how to actively listen to another.

Facilitating Action

Ultimately, the career professional is in a position to prompt clients to take action. In addition to encouraging a client to initiate dialogue with others who might enhance sense of identity and/or development of new competencies, the counselor may find opportunities to recommend relevant educational programs, support groups, or networks. Furthermore, acting on occasion as a broker of sorts, the career professional's own network of colleagues and clients can be a source of referrals that may result in a mutually beneficial connection.

The career professional in an internal human resource or organizational development role also has the opportunity to recommend or initiate programs and activities within the organization to enhance relational skill development or create opportunities for relational activity (special interest networks for women, people of color, and others; training and education on mentoring, coaching, relational practice; dialogue groups that bring together people of diverse backgrounds for the purpose of personal learning). There may also be opportunities to educate and influence decision makers who are in a position to establish rewards and accountability for mentoring, coaching, and other kinds of relational activity.

As career professionals, we must choose which core activities are most appropriate for a given client and how best to initiate them. What makes this work so interesting and difficult is that we must be willing to continue our own self-learning if we are to be able to serve our clients effectively. The willingness to be open (and vulnerable) in order to grow through our connections with others is essential to enabling others to do the same. I suppose what most of us have in common is a genuine interest in doing this highly personal and challenging work.

Conclusion

When I was about to leave graduate school and begin my career as a college professor and career researcher/consultant, one of my mentors, Dan Levinson, made a prediction about what I was about to experience. He said that during the next phase of my development, relationships with my peers and with my students would become increasingly important. Having just completed my dissertation on mentoring, and having benefited from several rich developmental relationships with mentors, I was intrigued with his comment.

My research and my life experiences since then have given me insight into Dan's words and have enabled me to expand upon his initial contributions on mentoring. Indeed, my students, clients, and research participants, reflecting on their own experiences, have helped me to describe a variety of relationships that support development at each career stage (Kram, 1988). Whereas my earliest study of mentoring emphasized the potential learning for young managers in their relationships with their mentors, I am clear that interdependence, mutuality, and reciprocity in these relationships are both possible and essential. My current view is that rather than occurring in one primary mentorship, learning is deepened and amplified when individuals seek to build multiple relationships with peers, seniors, and less experienced colleagues (and with individuals outside of work).

As I review Dan Levinson's work today, I find an enduring consistency about the central role of relationships during structure-building and structure-changing periods in both early and middle adulthood (Newton, 1994). Indeed, Dan's biographies (first of men and then of women) demonstrate that it is through relationships with family, at work, and in the community that individuals establish and then revise their fundamental life structure (and identity). In his original study of midlife men, Dan noted how central the mentor relationship is to young men as they strive to define a "dream" and create a satisfying life structure. In his most recent work on women at midlife, relationships are noted to be central to resolving work and family dilemmas that women (in both traditional and nontraditional roles) face.

Concurrently, researchers in the areas of executive development (McCall, Lombardo, and Morrison, 1988), women's development (Miller, 1991; Jordan et al., 1991), and adult development (Levinson, Darrow, Levinson, and McKee, 1978; Newton, 1994) have demonstrated the central role of relationships in personal learning and development. Also, recent work on relational theory (see Chapter Four in this volume) has clarified the competencies required for growth-in-connection with others to happen.

The purpose of this chapter has been to extend our understanding of how relationships can enhance sense of identity and development of new competencies in a career context characterized by turbulence and diversity. Ultimately, the career professional plays a pivotal role in making a relational approach to career development useful. If the reader can meaningfully embrace the core activities of diagnosis, modeling, coaching, and facilitating action in working with those facing challenging career concerns, I am confident that both parties will experience the growth-in-connection that is now so essential.

References

Adler, N. J. (1991). *International dimensions of organizational behavior* (2nd ed.). Boston: PWS-Kent.

Bell, E. L. (1990). The bicultural life experiences of career-oriented black women. *Journal of Organizational Behavior, 11*(6), 459–477.

Berlew, D. E., & Hall, D. T. (1966). The socialization of managers: Effects of expectations on performance. *Administrative Sciences Quarterly, 11,* 207–223.

Dalton, G. (1989). Developmental views of careers in organizations. In M. B. Arthur, D. T. Hall, & B. S. Lawrence (Eds.), *Handbook of career theory.* New York: Cambridge University Press, 89–109.

Dalton, G., & Thompson, P. (1986). *Novations: Strategies for career management.* Glenview, IL: Scott, Foresman.

Dalton, G., Thompson, P., & Price, R. (1977, Summer). The four stages of professionals' careers—A new look at performance of professionals. *Organizational Dynamics,* 19–42.

Derr, C. B. (1986). *Managing the new careerists.* San Francisco: Jossey-Bass.

Driver, M. J. (1982). Career concepts—A new approach to career research. In R. Katz (Ed.), *Career issues in human resource management.* Englewood Cliffs, NJ: Prentice Hall.

Eddy, W. B. (1985). *The manager and the working group.* New York: Praeger.

Ely, R. J. (1994). Organizational demographics and the dynamics of relationships among professional women. *Administrative Sciences Quarterly, 39,* 203–238.

Fletcher, J. (1994a). Castrating the female advantage: Feminist standpoint, research and management science. *Journal of Management Inquiry,* *3*(1), 74–82.

Fletcher, J. (1994b). *Toward a theory of relational practice in organizations: Feminist reconstruction of real work.* Unpublished doctoral dissertation, School of Management, Boston University.

Gabor, A. (1995, January 8). Crashing the "old boy" party. *New York Times,* Section 3, pp. 1, 6.

Hall, D. T. (1976). *Careers in organizations.* Glenview, IL: Scott, Foresman.

Hall, D. T., & Otazo, K. L. (1995). Executive coaching study: A progress report. Boston: Human Resource Policy Institute, Boston University.

Handy, C. (1989). *The age of unreason.* Boston: Harvard Business School Press.

Ibarra, H. (1993). Personal networks of women and minorities in management: A conceptual framework. *Academy of Management Review,* *18*(1), 56–87.

Isaacs, W. N. (1993, Autumn). Taking flight: Dialogue, collective thinking and organizational learning. *Organizational Dynamics,* 24–39.

Jordan, J. V., Kaplan, A. G., Miller, J. B., Striver, I. P., & Surrey, J. L. (Eds.). (1991). *Women's growth in connections.* New York: Guilford Press.

Kanter, R. M. (1989, November-December). The new managerial work. *Harvard Business Review,* 85–92.

Katzenbach, J. R., & Smith, D. K. (1993, March-April). The discipline of teams. *Harvard Business Review,* 111–120.

Kiechel, W., III. (1994, April 4). A manager's career in the new economy. *Fortune,* 68–72.

Kinlaw, D. C. (1993) *Coaching for commitment.* San Diego, CA: Pfeiffer & Company.

Kram, K. E. (1983). Phases of the mentor relationship. *Academy of Management Journal,* *26*(4), 608–625.

Kram, K. E. (1988). *Mentoring at work: Developmental relationships in organizational life.* Lanham, MD: University Press of America.

Kram, K. E., & Bragar, M. E. (1992). Development through mentoring: A strategic approach. In D. Montross & C. Shinkman (Eds.), *Career development: Theory and practice* (pp. 221–254). Chicago: Charles C. Thomas.

Kram, K. E., & Hall, D. T. (1996). Mentoring in a context of diversity and turbulence. In E. Kossek & S. Lobel (Eds.), *Human resources strategies for managing diversity.* London, England: Blackwell.

Kram, K. E., & McCollom, M. E. (in press). When women lead: The visibility-vulnerability spiral. In E. Klein & F. Gabelnick (Eds.), *New paradigms for leadership in the twenty-first century.* New Haven, CT: Yale University Press.

Levinson, D. J., Darrow, D., Levinson, M., & McKee, B. (1978). *Seasons of a man's life*. New York: Knopf.

McCall, M. W., Jr., Lombardo, M. M., & Morrison, A. M. (1988). *The lessons of experience*. Lexington, MA: Lexington Press.

McCauley, C., & Young, D. P. (1993). Creating developmental relationships: Roles and strategies. *Human Resources Management Review, 3*(3), 219–230.

Miller, J. B. (1986). *The new psychology of women*. Boston: Beacon Press.

Miller, J. B. (1991). The development of women's sense of self. In J. V. Jordan, A. G. Kaplan, J. B. Miller, I. P. Stiver, & J. L. Surrey (Eds.), *Women's growth in connection* (pp. 11–27). New York: Guilford Press.

Mink, O. G., Owen, K. Q., & Mink, B. P. (1993). *Developing high performance people: The art of coaching*. Reading, MA: Addison-Wesley.

Mirvis, P. H., & Hall, D. T. (1994). Psychological success and the boundaryless career. *Journal of Organizational Behavior, 15*, 365–380.

Morrison, A. M. (1992). *The new leaders: Guidelines on leadership diversity in America*. San Francisco: Jossey-Bass.

Morrison, A. M., White, R., & Van Velsor, E. (1987). *Breaking the glass ceiling*. Reading, MA: Addison-Wesley.

Newton, P. M. (1994). Daniel Levinson and his theory of adult development: A reminiscence and some clarifications. *Journal of Adult Development, 1*(3), 135–147.

Pryor, S. E. (1994). *Executive coaching: Sign of success or stigma?* Boston: Executive Development Roundtable, Boston University.

Schein, E. (1978). *Career dynamics: Matching individual and organizational needs*. Reading, MA: Addison-Wesley.

Schein, E. (1993, Autumn). On dialogue, culture, and organizational learning. *Organizational Dynamics*, 40–51.

Senge, P. M. (1990). *The fifth discipline: The art and practice of the learning organization*. New York: Doubleday.

Super, D. E. (1957). *The psychology of careers*. New York: HarperCollins.

Super, D. E. (1986). Life career roles: Self-realization in work and leisure. In D. T. Hall & Associates (Eds.), *Career development in organizations*. San Francisco: Jossey-Bass, 95–119.

Thomas, D. T. (1990). The impact of race on managers' experience of developmental relationships: An intraorganizational study. *Journal of Organizational Behavior, 28*(2), 279–290.

Thomas, D. T. (1993). Racial dynamics in cross-race developmental relationships. *Administrative Sciences Quarterly, 38*(3), 169–194.

Thomas, D. T., & Alderfer, C. A. (1989). The influence of race on career dynamics: Theory and research on minority career experiences. In

M. Arthur, D. T. Hall, & B. S. Lawrence (Eds.), *Handbook of career theory*. New York: Cambridge University Press, 133–158.

Thomas, D. T., & Kram, K. E. (1989). Promoting career-enhancing relationships in organizations: The role of the human resource professional. In M. London & E. More (Eds.), *Career growth and human resource strategies.* New York: Quorom Books, 49–66.

Chapter Six

Secure Base Relationships at Work

William A. Kahn

As the chapters in this volume make clear, the relationship between companies and their employees is at a confusing point in modern organizational life. The traditional relationship is one of lifetime employment, in which the employee offers a guarantee of loyalty in exchange for that of job security. Although this contract attaches particular labor forces to particular companies, it is not always fully in the service of the primary tasks of those companies: to locate, train, and promote workers best able to bring their skills to bear on creating the ideas, services, products, and technologies that enable organizations to prosper; and, conversely, to relocate (inside or outside the organization) workers unable to bring relevant skills to bear on organizational tasks. Increasingly, the high costs of doing business prohibit companies from maintaining expensive lifetime employment contracts. Employees must consistently prove themselves marketable within the context of the organization. This constitutes a different sort of company-employee relationship, with consequences intended and unintended. In this chapter, I explore some of the consequences related to organization members' engagement and disengagement at work.

The New Contract

"There will never be job security. You will be employed by us as long as you add value to the organization, and you are continuously responsible for finding ways to add value" (CEO, quoted in O'Reilly, 1994).

In some organizations, members must consistently demonstrate their abilities to contribute to organizational goals. Workers are encouraged to be entrepreneurial: to create ideas, products, services, procedures, and technologies that will manufacture or meet demand within and external to the organization. Each worker must link to a project or projects and account for his or her time. Careers are increasingly defined in terms of ongoing sequences of projects that members are able to justify and work effectively. Workers themselves become responsible for locating, auditioning for, and assuming roles on viable projects.

"Employees become far more responsible for their work and careers: no more parent-child relationships but adult to adult" (manager).

"You own your own employability. You are responsible" (worker).

This shift is a movement away from the traditional dependence and paternalism characterizing the implicit parent-child relationship between organization and worker. Traditionally, the organization manages the employee's career: specifying projects, products, markets, bosses, developmental steps, and training sequences. The paternalistic organization breeds loyalty, safety, and security. Sometimes it breeds counterdependence, as individuals resist the intrusion on their freedom to manage their own work lives and, at some point, leave or in other ways distance themselves from their organizations. But most often it breeds dependence, a greater or lesser acceptance of company policy and decisions. Such dependence manifests itself in conformity—to habits of thinking, acting, dressing, conversing.

The increasing decentralization of organizations renders it more difficult for organization members to simply depend on formal hierarchical relationships—the subordinate following the boss's orders. As Hirschhorn (1990, p. 529) writes, "The leader no longer charts the organization's work, with subordinates lined up to do the bidding. Instead, the leader and the subordinates must collaborate." When organizations are defined as networks, as places of intersection among people who need to collaborate across roles on aspects of various projects, there is an attendant loss of security: not only are organization members no longer sure of their tenure but they also no longer know precisely what to do, with whom to do it, and how it ought to be done. The "new contract" thus offers greater autonomy at the cost of organizationally provided sense of security.

The lack of security is particularly important given the heightened anxiety that some organization members experience working under the terms of the new contract.

"Even if there are no layoffs and his evaluations are good, he cannot relax. His engineering projects typically last a year or two, and when they end he must find another project to work on. If he can't find another job at the company within a few months, he must leave. Now he hustles all the time, concerned that he won't have the necessary skills to win a berth on a new project when the current one ends. It is a persistent worry but not a paralyzing fear so far" (manager).

The portrait here is of organization members who work hard to manage their careers: make the right contacts, develop the appropriate skills, and create the most relevant roles for themselves on viable projects. It is also a portrait of abandonment, in which—relative to the traditional organizational career—workers must fend for themselves.

"The message we're getting now is that the company doesn't owe you anything. Consultants have told us that the company is not there for your emotional support, that they don't owe you raises or job security, just honesty. And that a day's pay for a day's work is honest. Everyone is shocked. The drones are panicking and looking for somebody to tell them what to do. The better ones are looking for opportunity" (worker).

In such organizational environments—networks of members linked through various projects, rich with opportunity, fraught with uncertainty and anxiety, demanding and frightening and exhilarating, in which individuals are ultimately responsible for managing their own careers (Hakim, 1994)—members must be, above all, self-reliant.

The Paradox of Self-Reliance

John Bowlby, a pioneering developmental psychologist, began his article "Self-Reliance and Some Conditions That Promote It" (1973) with the following statement: "Evidence is accumulating that human beings of all ages are happiest and able to deploy their talents to best advantage when they are confident that, standing behind them, there are one or more trusted persons who will come to their aid should difficulties arise. The person trusted, also known as an attachment figure, can be considered as providing his or her companion with a secure base from which to operate" (p. 201).

Bowlby's work explores the paradox inherent in self-reliance: individuals are only capable of being fully self-reliant when they experience themselves as supported by and attached to trusted others. This paradox is relevant to the demands of the new contract. When organizations require members to venture into uncharted territory, create ways to add value and to innovate, members experience themselves as increasingly abandoned by their organizations, left to fend for themselves in the hustle for resources, projects, and customers. That sense of abandonment engenders the sort of anxiety and insecurity that undermines members' abilities to, in Bowlby's words, "deploy their talents to best advantage." It is difficult to take the sort of risks that ventures into uncharted territory require when persistently preoccupied with issues related to security.

There is real irony here. Organizations that require members to create new collaborations, markets, and products in order to justify their continuing employments are those most in need of ways to enable members to feel secure. Yet these organizations cannot help but heighten members' sense of insecurity. Members are required to venture forth into the unknown, to work, as it were, without the sense of a safety net below. The paradox of self-reliance suggests that such work is all but impossible without some sort of base on which, when warranted, to depend—for reinforcements, for help and support, for protection. Such a base is created in the context of meaningful attachments to others. In this chapter, I describe the nature of such attachments and their relevance to the creation of felt security.

Attachment Theory

Attachment theory (Bowlby, 1973, 1980) focuses on how relationships between children and attachment figures (typically parents) facilitate or undermine children feeling secure. The theory, initially developed out of the object-relations tradition in psychoanalysis and drawing from ethology, control theory, and cognitive psychology, continues to receive wide empirical support and elaboration. Empirical evidence indicates that children who receive effective caregiving are able to engage in exploratory behaviors, consisting of movements away from attachment figures, in order to investigate surroundings, gain knowledge and skills, and cope with or control the environment (Ainsworth, 1990). Other children are less able to engage in unworried exploration and are instead anxious, frustrated, or inhibited (Heard, 1982). Ainsworth (1967) coined the term *secure base* to describe the felt security of children who engage in unworried explorations, trusting their parents/attachment figures to come to their aid should difficulties arise.

Attachment figures create secure base relations when they act as effective caregivers—when they consistently perform behaviors that lead their children to feel secure and able to explore. Such behaviors include communicating empathy, respect, warmth, and regard; and helping others to cope with potentially threatening situations by giving encouragement, comfort, practical assistance, appropriate information, and access to essential material resources or information for obtaining them. The effective caregiving attachment figure neither *intrudes* nor *abandons*—in other words, is neither unresponsive (when others seek proximity or help) nor overactive and impinging (when others need to explore and operate on their own). Maintaining such a stance requires sensitivity to the needs, signals, and experiences of others. It requires meeting their reasonable dependency needs while letting them conduct their own journeys of growth and development. It means metaphorically holding others while neither letting them go (abandoning) nor pressing too tightly (intruding). Bowlby (1988, p. 11) writes, "It is a role similar to that of the officer commanding a military base from which an expeditionary force sets out and to which it can retreat, should it meet with a setback. Much of the time the role of the base is a waiting one but it is none the less vital for that. For it is only when the officer commanding the expeditionary force is confident his base is secure that he dare press forward and take risks."

While the secure base concept was developed in relation to children and their attachment figures, it applies to adult relations as well (Ainsworth, 1990; Weiss, 1982). As Bowlby (1988, p. 27) notes, the search for a secure base, "while most obvious in early childhood, can be observed throughout the life cycle, especially in emergencies. To remain within easy access of a familiar individual known to be ready and willing to come to our aid in an emergency is clearly a good insurance policy—whatever our age." The secure base concept offers a particularly useful way to conceptualize relationships in organizations in which members experience themselves, at various moments in their work lives, as children sometimes experience themselves: lost, confused, frightened, anxious, and threatened. Organization members experience moments of regression in the course of their work lives as they feel helpless, confused, or lost and become dependent and frustrated. This is particularly relevant for members of organizations undergoing times of risk, growth, and other sorts of vulnerability.

Organizational Caregiving

Bowlby's work suggests that the creation of security for organizational members hinges partly on their relationships. It is in the context of relationships with others that people may experience themselves as anchored in organizational contexts and situations that are, like high seas, turbulent and frightening. Work relationships have the potential to help people feel connected rather than disconnected, held fast rather than floundering, soothed rather than disquieted. The experience of feeling cared about in the context of role-related work interactions allows people to experience security in organizational contexts that are (particularly under the terms of the new contract) insecure.

In previous research, I developed the concept of *organizational caregiving* to account for role-related interactions that produce a sense of security within organization members (Kahn, 1993). I discovered that organization members become temporary caregivers within work-related interactions when they act in ways that leave others feeling valued and valuable, cared for, and ultimately securely connected within turbulent, insecure situations and contexts. I empirically identified eight behavioral dimensions of caregiving supported by literatures focusing on the philosophical basis of caregiving (Mayeroff, 1971; Noddings, 1984), social support at work (House, 1981), and considerate leaders and supervisors (Bass, 1990). The eight dimensions are defined as follows:

Accessibility: Remains in other's vicinity, allowing time and space for contact and connection

Inquiry: Asks for information necessary to provide for other's emotional, physical, and cognitive needs; probes for other's experiences, thoughts, and feelings

Attention: Actively attends to other's experiences, ideas, self-expressions; shows comprehension with verbal and nonverbal gestures

Validation: Communicates positive regard, respect, and appreciation to other

Empathy: Imaginatively puts self in other's place and identifies with other's experiences; verbally and nonverbally communicates experience of other

Support: Offers information (about salient issues and situations), feedback (about other's strengths and weaknesses), insights (about relationship), and protection (from distracting external forces)

Compassion: Shows emotional presence by displaying warmth, affection, and kindness

Consistency: Provides ongoing, steady stream of resources, compassion, and physical, emotional, and cognitive presence for other

The eight behavioral dimensions are often woven together in daily interactions. In the context of a social service agency, for example (Kahn, 1993), when a new social worker presents a difficult case, a senior social worker listens patiently, asks probing questions, withholds judgment, validates the other's efforts by saying how impressed she is with the sensitivity and judgment displayed, empathizes with the other's struggles by sharing her sense of the frustration and sadness she senses from the other, and supports the other by offering feedback about how she is framing the case in a constraining way. Similarly, the low degrees of these eight qualities are also generally woven together in situations involving the withholding of care. An example is a group supervision meeting in which the supervisor ignores the agenda of discussing social workers' problematic cases and instead emphasizes administrative issues, stares down at her notes for much of the meeting, speaks so softly that the social workers must strain to hear, makes little space for the questions or comments, asks no questions about their experiences or thoughts, displays little empathy or compassion for their overwhelming caseloads, and is unable to provide crucial scheduling information.

The eight dimensions indicate that organizational caregiving is a matter of organization members' witnessing others' journeys—enabling others to experience themselves as joined, as seen and felt, as known, and as not alone. These are the core experiences of feeling cared for (Noddings, 1984). People feel tended to when they feel that others are present for them. Presence entails a constant series of calibrations: movements toward (inquiries into experiences, attentive listening, provision of resources) balanced by movements away from others, such that they feel neither abandoned nor intruded upon as they go about their own processes of regaining a sense of security. Organizational caregiving is thus a state of being present for others (Kahn, 1992) rather than the more paternalistic "fixing" of their problems.

It should be mentioned that there is a distinction between caregiving and caretaking that is not simply semantic but also speaks to the issue of dependency. Caregiving is a gift; the recipients may either receive or deny it. In caretaking, control is overtly or covertly *taken* from care-seekers by dealing with them in ways that deny their abilities to care for themselves and that reduce them to objects (see Noddings, 1984). Organizational caregiving behaviors are those that are in the support of organization members who are temporarily needy—of, for example, support, resources, and validation—but who are assumed to remain ultimately capable of autonomously performing their roles.

Organizational caregiving offers a way to think about secure base relationships at work. The dimensions of organizational caregiving involve behaviors that are performed as part of rather than separate from work interactions. Being present for another worker—inquiring about and attending to her, validating and empathizing with her, supporting and showing compassion for her—may be done consistently in the context of work interactions. It does not require an external, personal relationship or a therapeutic, counseling relationship. What it requires is an attention to and a valuing of the other's self and experiences. When people are present for one another in work interactions, they create meaningful attachments. Such attachments, ideally, do not resemble parent-child attachments, in which one member is perceived as omnipotent and the other as helpless. Rather, secure attachments at work enable adults to move fluidly between caregiving and care-receiving roles, each taking on the appropriate role according to the demands of the current situation.

Such caregiving is ultimately in the service of organizational effectiveness. Organization members, when they are personally engaged in their work, give of themselves to varying extents, emotionally and intellectually as well as physically (Kahn, 1990, 1992). This is particularly true when members perform tasks that involve caring for, serving, or entertaining patients, customers, and clients. Such workers are most clearly in danger of being victims of job burnout, a "syndrome of physical and emotional exhaustion, involving the development of a negative self-concept, negative job attitudes, and a loss of concern and feelings for clients" (Pines and Maslach, 1978, p. 223). Job burnout engenders withdrawal, both physical (absence, turnover) and emotional (alienation, dissatisfaction, depersonalization). Such withdrawals cost both individuals and organizations. Individuals are rendered less effective at their tasks and less personally fulfilled, whereas organizations pay the costs of ineffective task performance (for example, bad products and services) and the training of new workers. My research indicates that such costs are avoided when organization members experience themselves as "filled" more than "drained" in the course of their work. This occurs through acts of organizational caregiving, performed within the context of everyday task-related interactions between co-workers and across functional, hierarchical, and departmental boundaries.

Caregiving in the Workplace

The extent to which organizational members actually experience themselves as cared for in the way I have described it varies widely both across and within organizations. Organizations, and industries more generally, have norms of thought and behavior that shape the extent to which caregiving behaviors are sanctioned. In traditionally male-dominated organizations and industries, such as investment banking and building construction, for example, there is less support for caregiving among members than in traditionally female-dominated systems, such as social work, nursing, and teaching. This is a stereotype, of course, albeit with some underlying validity, and suggests only one of the factors determining whether organization members actually experience themselves as cared for during task-related interactions with others. Other factors include the dispositions and interpersonal skills of individual members; formal and informal mentoring systems; reward systems that encourage collaboration over competition; organizational leadership that publicly models and rewards caregiving behaviors; and, more generally, cultural aspects of departments and organizations that are encoded in the values and norms of how members relate with one another during task performances. These and other factors combine to shape the extent to which organizational caregiving occurs, is absent, is rendered invisible (see Chapter Four, this volume), or is substituted for with pseudo-caregiving (for example, paternalism). What organization members actually experience is, in other words, the luck of their draw.

It is a difficult time for members to have a lucky draw in terms of organizational caregiving. Under the terms of the new contract, workers are busy, stretched thin, trying to keep abreast of new opportunities to exploit—markets to tap, products to develop, sales to make, skills to acquire—that will enable them to be valuable in their internal and external marketplaces. There is less traditional mentoring (see Chapter Five, this volume). There is less time for people to be present with and for themselves, much less with and for one another, and when workers feel a more tenuous connection to their employing organizations and seek meaning elsewhere, they are less emotionally available for others. The new contract may thus lend itself to people disengaging rather than engaging with one another at work, withdrawing from the creation of meaningful attachments. They are left, relative to the traditional organizational worker, isolated and insecure. Ironically, it is precisely when organizational caregiving is most difficult to generate and locate that it makes the most sense. When the traditional formal organization— its hierarchy, its reward systems and career ladders—is increasingly less prominent as the place on which people depend for their sense of security, meaningful attachments at work become more significant. The question is, how can such secure base relationships be created and maintained when organization members experience increasing pressures and inclinations to disconnect from others and focus solely on themselves?

Groups as Secure Bases

Groups with which members identify and in which they are dependent on one another to complete their tasks offer the most likely possibility for secure base relationships at work. Increasingly, organizations are using temporary and permanent groups—teams, task forces, self-managing groups, along with departments—as essential work units. Such work groups offer the most effective locus of caregiving among members as well as a primary source of continuous learning. The group itself can become a secure base to which members can retreat for support and empathy and nurturing, as delivered by various individuals at different times who each assume the role of temporary attachment figure. (Ideally, different members at different times assume the various roles of caregiver and care-receiver, depending on the needs and capabilities of each in any given situation.) The group, temporary or enduring, may assume the pivotal role in shaping employees' experiences, particularly as people feel abandoned by the traditional organizational hierarchy. Work groups can enable organization members to create the sorts of relationships they need in order to feel securely attached, held fast in the midst of turbulence. Take, for example, the following illustration (drawn from my research into a social service agency; Kahn, 1993, 1995).

During a meeting among the social workers of an agency serving homeless youths, Tomas tells the others of his frustration that volunteers serving as mentors for the youths do not return his calls. Clare nods. "I know what you mean. It is frustrating. It sometimes helps to leave messages saying exactly when they can call you, so they don't think they have to waste their time trying." Jen, a senior social worker leading the meeting, turns to Clare. "When you reach them, how do you find the conversations?" Clare says, "Sometimes people don't offer much. I'm afraid to put words in their mouths. I want them to talk on their own."

Stacy agrees. "I know, it can get like pulling teeth. Sometimes it's important just to stay on the phone with them, to build the relationship. After a time, it gets easier." Myra says, "I think that's right. It lets them know that they have some place to go to when they need to. Tomas, what do you do when you do have them on phone?" Tomas talks about what he tries to accomplish in his conversations. Stefan asks how Tomas feels when he is in the midst of those conversations. Tomas says he feels anxious and sometimes catches himself trying to rush off the phone. Sara offers to sit in on his next few phone calls and to share her observations afterwards. Tomas accepts her offer, thanking her and the others for their counsel.

Sara asks if she can get some help with an issue. Jen says, "Of course." Sara speaks hesitantly. "A mother [of a youth served by the agency] called me. She was beside herself because the volunteer was letting her child sit on his lap and drive the car. The more we talked, the more upset she became and the more confused I was." There is a pause. Then Stacy asks Sara why she was confused. Sara tells of feeling paralyzed because of an incident a year earlier, with another youth, when she did not intervene and wished that she had. Responding to questions, she elaborates. The group helps her examine the differences in the two situations. They then return to the issue. Stacy says, "The mother is the one who has to feel okay about her child's match. I would try to affirm and legitimate her perspective and hear what's going on for her. Myra agrees. "You would have to build rapport with her if she is going to work with you to support the match." Tomas notes, "There is so much potential for mothers to sabotage the matches. You have to support her and establish a connection with her, so if she's overly worried you can reason with her later." Sara tells them, "This is exactly my experience with this case. I have been trying to connect with the mother, so she'll have someone like her kid has someone." She looks at the others. "Thanks a lot. I feel more confident about my instincts."

Jane, who has been silent, fills in the pause in the conversation. "Can I ask about a case I have? It involves a sexually abused child who is not talking about it with his volunteer." Jen says, "What's going on?" Jane explains: "The boy just won't open up, and the volunteer is concerned." Clare offers a way of thinking about the child's experience: "It may be that when the kid is with the volunteer he doesn't want to be a victim or a witness, he just wants to be a kid." Jen nods, adding, "And what's probably important here is to get the volunteer himself to talk about his own feelings about the situation. Perhaps the way to help the boy is to make sure that the volunteer isn't pressing him to talk because of his own needs, and that he can be available to the boy when the time comes." Myra concurs, saying, "Which means that you have to be available to the volunteer in the same way, not just pressuring him to talk but letting him know that he's in a difficult situation and he may be having his own reactions to it. And you're there if he needs to talk about it."

Jane says that it has been difficult to do that, partly, she thinks, because the issue is difficult for her personally to talk about. Jen tells her that's understandable, and if she needs some help getting a handle on it, they can talk more about it. Clare makes the same offer. Jane thanks them, thanks the others for their comments, and promises to talk with the volunteer.

Jen looks at her watch. "We need to wrap this up. Anything else?" Clare says, "I'd like to thank you for doing an outstanding job of running the meeting." The others clap. The social workers end their meeting and adjourn to their offices.

As the illustration suggests, the creation of a group into a secure base for its members involves face-to-face group meetings in which members address substantive work issues and experiences, including their own roles, their growth and development at work, and, where necessary, their interactions with one another. Group members attempt to help one another with issues that are raised. They offer advice, support, training. The group becomes a secure base for its members, for whom the combined resources are available to members as needed. There may be elements during these meetings of what Meryl Louis (Chapter Nine, this volume) terms *safe havens,* when members are deeply attentive to one another, and elements as well of what Jane and William Hodgetts (Chapter Thirteen, this volume) term *developmental sanctuaries,* in which people use reflection and mutual support to gather personal insight and the capacity for growth and development. In each of these forms—secure bases, safe havens, developmental sanctuaries—people become more fully present (Kahn, 1992).

As discussed above, the concept of the secure base was developed in the context of parent-child relationships. The imagery is instructive about groups when they exist as secure bases for their members. Groups can, through the consistent actions of their members, communicate empathy, respect, warmth, and regard to the members. Groups can help members cope with potentially threatening situations by giving encouragement, comfort, practical assistance, appropriate information, and access to essential material resources or information for obtaining them. They can be both appropriately responsive, when members seek help, and distanced, when members need to explore and operate on their own. This is to say, groups can act—when individual members temporarily regress, need support, or feel threatened and insecure—like competent parents act with momentarily startled, insecure children. Competent groups may thus be understood in practice as those in which mature acts of asking for and receiving caregiving, as related to collective tasks, are ongoing processes among members.

Provisions and Disruptions of a Secure Base

There are certain conditions under which groups can flourish as secure bases for their members. One set of conditions involves understanding who the members are as individuals. People have different skills and vary in terms of their abilities to provide support for one another at appropriate times and in appropriate ways. They also have different unconscious, internal models—based on their early childhood experiences with their own attachment figures and on subsequent attachment relationships—that continue to shape their perceptions, attitudes, and behaviors related to possible attachments (Kahn and Kram, 1994). These individual factors are more or less amenable to building skills of giving and receiving feedback, active and empathic listening, self-awareness, the management of emotions, and the like. It is clear from the work of those involved in teaching group dynamics, interpersonal competence workshops, and other sorts of individually focused training laboratories that the skills of building and maintaining supportive relationships can be taught and acquired. However, it is also clear that such skills cannot flourish in social systems that do not support their consistent usage.

Organizations—acting through those authorized to manage and facilitate others' work—can create or undermine secure base relationships among work group members. When organizations use reward systems that depend partly on work team performance, the stakes are raised for group members to create effective working relationships. Similarly, when tasks are structured such that group members are required to be interdependent, the possibilities increase for intensive collaboration, communication, and the development of effective support systems—all decent precursors to secure base relationships. Also increased are the possibilities of competition, internal warfare, and self-aggrandizement, each of which is not unknown to work groups and each of which undermines the creation of secure base relations among group members. Whether work groups become secure bases for their members has a lot to do with their leadership and that of the organizations in which they exist.

When groups operate as secure bases, members experience their groups as being safe places to which they can momentarily retreat. People feel safe when they know that there are no potential repercussions to expressing what they really think and feel. Group leaders play important roles in creating such safety by helping to initiate and monitor caregiving interactions among members: pointing out interactions as they occur that are likely to enable or undermine members feeling valued, appreciated, and generally cared for in the context of group meetings. The extent to which leaders themselves model caregiving and care-receiving behaviors also sends powerful messages to group members. Leaders can help ensure safety by enforcing what Shapiro and Carr (1991) identify as the three key elements of the holding environment: the focus on a clearly defined task (enabling members to hold tightly onto the purpose of aiding one another in the completion of a shared mission), the clear delineation of roles (enabling members to support one another without experiencing role confusion and competition), and a clear definition of boundaries (enabling members to differentiate between appropriate and inappropriate interactions).

Finally, leaders can help create a sense of security by protecting the group from forces that threaten to overwhelm members' abilities to give care to one another in the context of their work. Thus group leaders try to create relationships with organizational leaders that leave group members feeling both connected to and buffered from the larger organizational system. Effective group leaders enable the group to remain both autonomous from and related to those who wield power in the organization; the autonomy offers members the sense of a protective distance, the relatedness a sense of protection. When group members feel intruded upon by organizational leaders, their sense of autonomy collapses and leaves them unsure about the group's ability to protect its members; when group members feel ignored or abandoned by their organizational leadership, their sense of connection to the larger organization collapses and leaves them unsure about the group's political importance and power. An effective group leader works to create a relationship with his or her own leader that enables both of them to neither abandon nor intrude upon the groups for which they are responsible. In these terms, empowered groups are those in which members experience themselves collectively as able to provide for and protect one another in relation with powerful others who protect them from debilitating environmental conditions and provide access to important resources and information.

Implications for Managing the New Career

I have offered here a vision of temporary and more permanent groups serving as secure bases for their members, places to which they can retreat for caregiving during moments of confusion, threat, and insecurity. Translating this vision into reality across organizations and their various departments, functions, and subcultures demands that the organization and its group leaders hold dear the values of organizational caregiving, financially and/or morally. Financially, organizational caregiving (and the creation of secure bases) translates into organizational effectiveness, measured along a variety of indicators: lower rates of absence and turnover; less incidence of costly errors and lapses; higher customer or client satisfaction; more innovative ideas, products, and processes; the generation of skills among the workforce; and ultimately, higher profit margins. Morally, organizational caregiving can be understood as a way for people to treat one another that generates compassion, personal growth, and meaningful attachments, thus allowing for the creation of humane communities. Neither value precludes the other.

Organization and group leaders who subscribe to either of these two values are in a position to instigate or support the creation of secure bases for their members. Part of their task is educating themselves and others. Leaders can conduct experiments of sorts, testing the hypothesis that groups and departments whose members experience themselves as cared for, as having secure bases to which they can retreat when necessary, ultimately perform more effectively and profitably than those without. Publicizing the results of these experiments can create the wider cultural perception of organizational caregiving as a profitable way of doing business. The task then becomes creating systems that reinforce task-related caregiving behaviors. When pay raises and job promotions are based, for example, partly on the extent to which group members rate their leaders and one another as effective task-related caregivers, the creation of secure base relationships will increase dramatically. Such reward systems, as supported by systems of education, training, feedback, and communication, enable real change to occur in group and organization cultures. That change must fit, of course, the beliefs and values of leaders with formal authority.

An example of this sort of cultural movement is found in the classic case of Johnsonville Sausage, the manufacturing company owned and managed by Ralph Stayer (Stayer, 1990). Stayer noted that although the company was performing reasonably well financially, the lack of motivation apparent in the workforce was costly (in terms of low-quality product, extensive overtime, job absence, and costly processing errors) and did not bode well for strategic changes he planned in response to increased competition. Stayer instigated a series of changes that included, among others, the creation of teams across the company that were authorized to make key decisions about their work, figure out how to implement those decisions, and develop and implement appropriate systems for rewarding, training, hiring, and firing members. These teams were largely self-managing. They became settings to which members brought their confusions, dilemmas, and concerns and in which they received from one another support and other forms of organizational caregiving. Managerial jobs across the organization were redefined such that managers became educators, charged with the growth and development of those for whom they were responsible. Pay raises and promotions for managers and workers alike were hooked into the extent to which the workers learned new skills, both task and interpersonally related. Stayer's creation of what I call an organizational community—in which an "older generation" provides support for the growth and development of a "newer generation"—reflected his belief in the financial and moral benefits of organizational caregiving. He created an underlying belief and value system in which caregiving was central to his workers' (whom he called *members*) work identities.

Career Development Professionals

Career development professionals occupy roles through which they can help organization members learn the skills of providing and eliciting appropriate caregiving at work. Such skills are increasingly important to the construction of careers. As organization members assume greater responsibility for managing their own careers, they need others to help make sense of situations and career moves that seem confusing, disconcerting, or even threatening. Creating and sustaining such caregiving relationships at work is tied to organization members' abilities to manage their own careers as well as to their abilities to collaborate effectively with others in completing shared tasks and achieving shared goals.

Providing caregiving is a matter of performing the sorts of behaviors listed above that leave others feeling valued, valuable, and cared for in the context of their work role performances. These behaviors require both specific skills—such as active listening—and a more general stance, that of making oneself accessible to and empathic for others. Such skills may be acquired through training (particularly training that requires experiential learning, such as role plays). The caregiving stance is a matter of recognizing when others need various forms of support, for which they may ask directly or, as often occurs, indirectly, verbally (speaking sharply or not at all) and nonverbally (looking dejected). At such moments, organization members can become temporary attachment figures, making themselves accessible to others needing a secure base for momentary support. This is a mature act; the maturity involves finding and maintaining the appropriate boundaries between self and other: bringing oneself close enough to establish relatedness while maintaining enough distance to enable autonomy for both self and other. The alternatives are debilitating: a lack of relatedness engenders isolation; a lack of autonomy engenders the loss of self. Maintaining the appropriate boundary between self and other offers both relatedness and autonomy. Less mature acts involve people being unable to give care at all (through lack of ability, desire, or spirit) or seeking to give care too often (deskilling others).

Secure base relationships also involve skills of asking for caregiving when appropriate and receiving it when offered. It is a mature act to call for help and support only when it is needed and use can be made of it. Less mature acts involve people being unable to call for caregiving (attaching shame to such calls) or calling for caregiving too often (deskilling themselves). Organization members can learn to elicit caregiving when they need temporary support. Adults, unlike infants and many children, are able to ask directly for support, and they are able to use others as temporary attachment figures without remaining entrenched within the sorts of unidirectional dependency relations that characterize early parent-child relations. People can learn to ask for what they need from others, to distinguish appropriate and inappropriate situations, and to reflect on the patterns of their help-seeking behaviors, noting when it seems that they have asked too little or too much from others.

To support training efforts, career development professionals can institute feedback processes by which group members share their perceptions about the quantity and quality of their caregiving and care-receiving interactions, thus enabling them to refine their skills. A 360-degree feedback process, in which organization members receive feedback from co-workers ranging across functional and hierarchical roles, is ideal, particularly when related to performance appraisals. Career development professionals can help create systems that reward, formally and informally, the creation of attachment relations in organizations—for example, merit reviews based not simply on task performance but also on the nature of the relationships that group and department members create and sustain that demonstrably help them manage uncertainty and turbulence.

To the extent that such caregiving relationships are talked about at work—in organization leaders' verbal and written communications, company newsletters, and the like—they become woven into the culture. Such normalizing is important. It is often the case that organization members are supposed to take care of themselves and not appear "weak" by looking to others for support. Such norms undermine the extent to which people are able to form the connections necessary to create meaningful, secure attachments with those best able to empathize with and support their efforts. Creating norms that support caregiving relationships is partly a process of relating stories through newsletters, videos, presentations, and other types of sanctioned media. Career development professionals can perform the key role of inserting stories about effective acts of organizational caregiving into the organization's story-making (and thus meaning-making) machinery.

Conclusion

A paradox lies at the heart of the argument presented in this chapter. When organizations turn members loose in their internal marketplaces, requiring them to win, again and again, jobs on projects that add value to their organizations, they create certain working conditions: stress and uncertainty; a greater sense of competition, implicit or explicit, for desirable projects. As members are tested more rigorously, they are able to develop and draw more deeply on their skills and talents and are generally required to be more personally engaged in task performances. However, there is less time and energy for members to create supportive relationships with one another that would help them manage these conditions. Hence the paradox: organization members often feel too overwhelmed and anxious to create meaningful attachments with one another exactly when they need such attachments the most.

But to the extent that people understand that they are caught in this paradox, they are able to make conscious choices about the extent to which they create meaningful, secure attachments with one another. Facilitating this understanding is a matter of organization members speaking up about their experiences and other members relating to their experiences. Career development professionals can help create settings in which such conversations occur, in the context of training; interventions into groups and departments whose members are physically, emotionally, or intellectually withdrawing; and information sessions. Readings, cases, and exercises help ground such conversations. The point is to actually discuss personal experiences of the paradoxes of connection and disconnection. When the feeling of wanting but being unable to attach to one another is brought out in the open, people are more able to understand the choices they make about how to manage that paradox.

To the extent that organization members create meaningful attachments that they find helpful in managing their uncertainty, they will integrate those relationships into the self-management of their organizational careers. This means that organization members will increasingly use one another as informal support systems (and job-placement networks), sources of learning about themselves (through candid feedback), and work partners (as they develop and bid on organization projects together). Under the terms of the new contract, such self-management—the managing of oneself with the help of others—is not simply ideal but also essential.

References

Ainsworth, M.D.S. (1967). *Infancy in Uganda: Infant care and the growth of attachment.* Baltimore: Johns Hopkins University Press.

Ainsworth, M.D.S. (1990). Some considerations regarding theory and assessment relevant to attachments beyond infancy. In M. T. Greenberg, D. Cicchetti, & E. M. Cummings (Eds.), *Attachment in the preschool years.* Chicago: University of Chicago Press, 463–487.

Bass, B. M. (1990). *Bass and Stodgill's handbook of leadership* (3rd ed.). New York: Free Press.

Bowlby, J. (1973). Self-reliance and some conditions that promote it. *British Journal of Psychiatry, 130,* 201–210.

Bowlby, J. (1980). *Attachment and loss: Vol. 3. Loss, sadness and depression.* New York: Basic Books.

Bowlby, J. (1988). *The secure base.* New York: Basic Books.

Hakim, C. (1994). *We are all self-employed.* San Francisco: Berrett-Koehler.

Heard, D. (1982). Family systems and the attachment dynamic. *Journal of Family Therapy, 4,* 99–116.

Hirschhorn, L. (1990). Leaders and followers in a postindustrial age. *Journal of Applied Behavioral Science, 26,* 529–542.

House, J. S. (1981). *Work stress and social support.* Reading, MA: Addison-Wesley.

Kahn, W. A. (1990). Psychological conditions of personal engagement and disengagement at work. *Academy of Management Journal, 33(4),* 692–724.

Kahn, W. A. (1992). To be fully there: Psychological presence at work. *Human Relations, 45*(4), 321–349.

Kahn, W. A. (1993). Caring for the caregivers: Patterns of organizational caregiving. *Administrative Science Quarterly, 38*(4), 539–563.

Kahn, W. A. (1995). Organizational change and the provision of a secure base: Lessons from the field. *Human Relations, 48*(5), 489–514.

Kahn, W. A., & Kram, K. E. (1994). Authority at work: Internal models and their organizational consequences. *Academy of Management Review, 19*(1), 17–50.

Mayeroff, M. (1971). *On caring.* New York: HarperCollins.

Noddings, N. (1984). *Caring: A feminine approach to ethics and moral education.* Berkeley: University of California Press.

O'Reilly, B. (1994, June 13). The new deal. *Fortune,* 44–52.

Pines, A. M., & Maslach, C. (1978). Characteristics of staff burnout in mental health settings. *Hospital and Community Psychiatry, 29,* 233–237.

Shapiro, E. R., & Carr, A. W. (1991). *Lost in familiar places.* New Haven, CT: Yale University Press.

Stayer, R. (1990, November-December). How I learned to let my workers lead. *Harvard Business Review,* 2–11.

Weiss, R. S. (1982). Attachment in adult life. In C. Parkes & J. Stevenson-Hinde (Eds.), *The place of attachment in human behavior* (pp. 171–184). New York: Basic Books.

Chapter Seven

Growth-Enhancing Relationships Outside Work (GROWs)

Victoria A. Parker

Although Rashida took great pride in her work as an advertising copywriter, she lacked confidence in her efforts. She found that waiting for and receiving feedback on her written work made her extremely anxious. Thus, early in her career, she often asked her spouse to read through her work for major clients before turning it in to her superiors. While she knew that such writing coaching might be available from co-workers and superiors, Rashida felt uneasy seeking it, given her newcomer status in the organization.

Kevin had only met Rick a few times, in tennis matches arranged by their club, but he could already tell that Rick was a difficult person. In fact, he reminded Kevin of his boss in Information Resources, a very aggressive and slightly younger man who often made him feel he was not doing enough. In fact, Kevin could not understand why Rick continued to play him, especially since Kevin did not seem to match Rick's intensity level in the matches. When Kevin finally asked, Rick responded, "Because I want to see if I can

Note: I am grateful for the helpful comments of colleagues Tim Hall, Kathy Kram, and Kent Seibert on earlier drafts of this chapter, as well as for the comments of my at-home editor, Greg Estey.

get you to play harder. I know you'll be tough to beat if you do." Kevin wondered if his boss felt the same way.

In earlier chapters, we have developed the ideas that career development depends on personal development and that personal development depends on adaptability, self-learning, feedback, and other similar processes (see Introduction, this volume). If we are to take these notions seriously, it follows that interpersonal relationships both at work *and outside* work can influence career processes. Friends and family are often acknowledged as sources of useful contacts (for example, "My aunt's old friend Marion helped me get the first interview"). They are much less often publicly credited as important influences on ongoing career development. Yet, as the stories above begin to illustrate, there are many ways in which such influence might be felt.

Like Kevin and Rashida, many employees have come to depend on relationships extending far beyond the boundaries of particular organizations and fields to facilitate their continued development. Why is this so important? So far in this book, we have sketched a picture of the "new employment contract" as one that is likely to involve frequent changes of organization and career direction. In such a world, the development of growth-enhancing relationships within just one organization or just one career field may prove to be of limited value. Thus growth-enhancing relationships outside work (which I call "GROWs") that enable career development are not just an unappreciated resource; they are a resource that will become increasingly important as opportunities for organizationally determined careers become less available.

In this chapter, I will discuss traditional views of the connection between GROWs and careers and then describe an alternative view, one that allows for more types of influence from more types of relationships. I will go on to discuss several specific types of relationship influence on career. Of course, extraorganizational relationships may have both positive and negative influences, but this chapter will focus on the positive influences of such relationships because existing theory has often paid more attention to the potential dark side. I will also show how organizational and individual conditions affect the influence of GROWs and I will identify some of the potential difficulties in these relationships. Finally, in this chapter, we will see how individuals and organizations can benefit from GROWs.

Traditional Views of GROWs

Although the connection between relationships and psychological development has become well-established (for example, Miller, 1991; Chapter Four, this volume), the careers field to date has concerned itself primarily with intraorganizational issues (Arthur, 1994) such as mentoring relationships with others within a particular organization.

Relationships Undervalued

The predominant view has been that family relationships are sources of demands for time and energy that compete with career-related priorities in a zero-sum game (Evans and Bartolomé, 1984). The potential influence of nonfamily relationships on career processes has generally been ignored, given the overall invisibility of these sorts of connections (Chapter Eight, this volume). The possibility that we may learn things in personal relationships that contribute quite directly to personal *and* career growth has seldom been considered.

The need to look more closely for such contributions is shown by the ill effects on careers of the absence or de-emphasis of such relationships. Although the failure to attend to such relationships may be a career advantage in the short term, it can eventually yield patterns of behavior that are problematic for both career *and* personal growth (Kofodimos, 1990; Korman, 1988). Kofodimos (1993) found that executives who devalued intimacy both at work and at home tended to develop these dysfunctional patterns: resistance to others' input, failure to seek necessary help, loss of subordinates' motivation due to lack of delegation, overly demanding expectations, lack of empathy and compassion, and trouble forming comfortable working relationships. These bad effects on "on the job" behavior provide a strong argument for developing a new view of the role relationships with friends and family can play in personal and career development.

Social Support Theory

One important exception to the old and narrow view of the career impact of personal relationships is found in social support theory. Social support theory suggests that many types of relationships outside of work may be sources of informal social support for career development. At a very basic level, such support is crucial in keeping job-related stress and health problems to a minimum (House, 1981). The positive effects of social support on health derive in part from meeting basic human needs for security, social contact, and so forth. These positive effects may also cancel out or at least mitigate the negative impact work-related stress can have on health.

Social support can take the form of emotional support, appraisal support (providing information about how the individual is perceived), informational support, and instrumental support (House, 1981). As I suggested earlier, GROWs have long been seen as sources of instrumental and informational career support. More significant but less apparent are the opportunities they provide for appraisal support and emotional support, which tend to occur only in more intimate relationships but can lead to major changes in self-perception and interpersonal skills.

A New View of GROWs

Aside from a relatively small number of managers at an organization's core, organizations of the future will have increasingly fluid boundaries, adjusting staffing on a project-by-project basis (Handy, 1989). As a result, many individuals are likely to find that their work histories involve several organizations and possibly even multiple career fields. The related trend toward interorganizational ventures and networks of various sorts (Alter and Hage, 1993) is also likely to blur organizational boundaries and decrease the stability of working relationships.

Boundaryless Careers

Arthur (1994) found that such "boundaryless careers" are likely to increase due to decreasing job tenures and the increasing percentage of jobs located in small businesses. In such a scenario, relationships at the workplace are not likely to develop the stability and intimacy necessary for personal and career growth. Ties outside of any particular employing organization will become correspondingly more important in meeting those needs for stability and intimacy. In a boundaryless career, GROWs would become just as important as mentors, superiors, and peers within any particular organization, perhaps even more so because they would offer greater continuity.

The Importance of GROWs

As the social support theory discussed earlier illustrates, relationships outside work are integral to career processes throughout an individual's career for several reasons. The most fundamental is that they are opportunities for personal growth that may have many career-related implications. Kofodimos (1990) found that executives who have well-developed relationships outside of work are more likely to develop the empathy and compassion that will enable them to understand their co-workers and subordinates, offer encouragement and appreciation, seek advice when needed, delegate appropriately, and more.

Specific Effects of GROWs

So far, I have suggested some general ways in which career growth may be influenced by GROWs. In this section, we will see specific examples of how these influences may play themselves out.

Relationship Changes

A change in a particular relationship—whether it be an absence, a presence, or a change in level of intensity—may draw attention to career concerns. For example, empty-nesters may increase career involvement in response to new time or energy *or* may feel free to cut back on career involvement now that financial responsibilities are lessened. A caretaker for an ill family member may decrease career involvement in response to reduced time or energy *or* may find career issues more engaging because they are a respite from the emotionally draining work of caregiving. A single person's career may be influenced by a new involvement in a spiritual community; efforts to lead a life more consistent with that community's beliefs cause the person to question values underlying previous career-related decisions.

Relationship Influences on Values

A long-term relationship may influence the individual's values and opinions about careers and shape the direction of career growth. For example, graduating students' career assumptions and plans are often heavily influenced in interaction with their parents, who have been guiding the student toward at least a general standard of living—if not particular occupational aspirations—for twenty years. During career assessment activities, undergraduates often report that they are discarding certain career interests because their parents perceive them as "impractical" or "too risky."

Career/Relationship Overlap

A personal relationship may overlap a career. For instance, children, siblings, or spouses may turn an entrepreneur's solo venture into a family business; spouses may make contributions ranging from unacknowledged help with the books to coproprietorship; and elected officials may appoint friends to political jobs, leading to intertwined careers. In each of these cases, the original personal relationship is now overlaid with a professional relationship, and there may be very little separation between the two. Some individuals find this convergence between the personal and professional to be highly energizing and engaging, but others find it to be claustrophobic and inhibiting.

Relationship Influences on Self-Perception

Relationships may fundamentally alter individuals' perceptions of themselves and their abilities. Theories of adult development, particularly those focused on women's development, have increasingly emphasized the extent to which personal development is driven by close interpersonal relationships at all stages of the life cycle (Gilligan, 1982; Kegan, 1982; Miller, 1991). For example, a parent may learn from his relationship with his child that he cannot be in control and that he needs to let go in order for the child to learn, and then he finds that his approach to subordinates' learning has also changed. In other examples, therapeutic relationships (such as psychotherapy) could also lead to such insights, or the chance to try out new roles in relation to teammates on athletic teams or on volunteer committees may also lead to major changes in self-perception.

Relationship Difficulties

Difficulties in an extraorganizational relationship may provide the stimulus for personal growth that ends up having career-related implications. For instance, confronting a newly rebellious teenager may cause a parent to reconsider habitual ways of dealing with power conflicts, leading to new responses to power conflicts at work. An adult child in conflict with a parent may suddenly see ways in which conflicts at work are similar and thus be free to think about some new ways of handling such situations.

Such difficulties may even lead to a broad reevaluation of career and life priorities. For example, individuals experiencing the "career success and personal failure" syndrome described by Korman (1988) may realize via failures of personal relationships that a lifestyle oriented primarily toward external achievement at work is too costly. Such individuals may ultimately seek to develop a different orientation toward their work, one in which the work's intrinsic rewards become more important.

Defining Growth

Though we have been looking mainly at positive career influences, there is the potential in each of these categories for GROWs to both stimulate *and* impede growth and development. Thus there is great variety in not only the types of influential GROWs and the mechanisms by which they influence personal and career growth but also in the extent to which that influence is positive, which varies depending on the perspective of the observer. For example, is encouraging a friend to take six months off to realize her vision of sailing around the world helping her to achieve her dreams or to run away from her problems?

The Positive Influence of GROWs

We have looked at a variety of ways in which GROWs may influence career and personal growth. We now turn to the effect of individual and organizational factors on a person's openness to such influence. There are several factors at the individual level that determine the extent to which a person is involved in and influenced by relationships outside of work. These factors include the extent to which work and personal life are integrated or separated; the relative importance of various subidentities; the importance of and skill at learning from relationships; the availability of different types of relationships; and differences in career and life stage.

Connected Work-and-Life Roles and Values

Individuals differ in the extent to which each of their various life roles (for example, manager, daughter, neighbor) is salient and the extent to which those roles may conflict with each other. Lobel (1991) proposes that work and nonwork roles are likely to be equally salient and nonconflictual when the values associated with each role have a great deal of overlap. It seems reasonable to expect that a person whose work-and-life roles are governed by the same values would tend to have GROWs that influence their careers because the roles are not likely to be rigidly separated from one another; what is not clear is whether those consistent values facilitate *or* impede career growth.

On the other hand, Lobel (1991) also proposes that value differences between an individual's roles will lead either to increasing conflict between the roles or to conflict reduction via increasing separation of the roles. While the value differences may be situationally determined, it is the individual who determines whether the response will go toward increased role conflict or increased role separation. In the case of role separation, segmentation theories of work-life balance suggest that the two spheres can be held distinct (Zedeck, 1992). In a situation where an individual has successfully segmented his or her life roles, it is less likely that career growth would be influenced by a nonwork relationship because the individual is likely to be working hard at maintaining a separation between the different spheres. This segmentation would make experiences in one role seem unrelated to experiences in the other role(s).

Subidentity theory may also be helpful here (Hall, 1971, 1986). To the extent that an individual's career subidentity becomes more involving than other subidentities, it is likely that relationships at work will be given more time and emphasis than nonwork relationships, leading to a self-reinforcing cycle of increasing career involvement. This cycle may also be linked with increasing personal imbalance (Kofodimos, 1990). Thus the potential influence of nonwork relationships on career processes would be low and would decrease over time. If, however, nonwork subidentities are more involving and are given more emphasis, they will tend to be the locus of more important relationships, which are more likely to stimulate growth and have some influence on career processes.

Relationship Skills and Interests

Individuals vary in the extent to which they emphasize personal relationships. Individuals also vary in the extent to which they are skilled at developing and learning through relationships. Kofodimos (1990) found that individuals who have trouble with intimacy tend to focus on work relationships to the exclusion of others and that relationships at work tend to be much more superficial than those outside. Thus the extent to which GROWs might influence career growth for such individuals would be quite limited because the individuals are unlikely to be very engaged in such relationships—or if they are, they may lack the skills (such as active listening, openness to feedback) that would enable them to learn through those experiences.

Organizational Culture and Relationship Skills

Organizations vary in the extent to which emphasis is placed on relationship skills. Many organizations have taken strategic steps to increase the development of in-house relationships such as mentoring (Kram and Bragar, 1992). Individuals in such organizations are likely to develop better relationship skills and to place a higher value on such skills; this may make them more prone to develop growth-enhancing relationships both within and outside the organization. In other organizations, particularly those with cultures emphasizing strong individual performances, the development of stronger interpersonal skills is usually not a priority.

Availability of Relationships

Expatriate employees are the prototypical case of employees cut off from most sources of relationships *other than* their employing organizations if they choose not to develop local connections. This is also true of some military workers, indeed of workers in any organization that is tightly bounded from the external environment either by geography, secrecy requirements, or culture. In these cases, it may be difficult or even impossible for individuals to develop relationships outside of the work context and hence impossible for their personal and career growth to be influenced by such relationships. The lack of such GROWs may be one of the unrecognized impediments to personal and career growth in such organizations.

Time and Energy for Relationships

Research on the interrelationships between career stage and life stage suggests that the ambitious striving of the early career years may leave little energy for the development of family and other personal relationships but that individuals often become more open to cultivating such relationships later on in midlife (Voydanoff, 1985). However, this pattern may be more typical for men than for women. Many women, socialized into the importance of relationships and their potential for growth, typically emphasize them in the early career years and may only become more interested in separation and autonomy at midcareer (Gallos, 1989). Thus men's career processes may be more influenced by GROWs at midcareer and beyond, whereas women's career processes may tend to be more affected by such relationships during earlier career phases. Of course, there are many exceptions to this general pattern. Women who enter careers traditionally dominated by men, such as medicine or law, may tend to follow the typically male pattern and de-emphasize relationships during the early years. The importance of relationships in women's development at all phases (Miller, 1991) may mean that GROWs are more important to women at every stage, even after they become relatively de-emphasized.

Challenges and Benefits of Examining GROWs

Looking at the interactions between career processes and relationships outside of work can be tough, perhaps because acknowledging the influence of such interactions contradicts the prevalent image of career development as a rational, autonomous process. Indeed, looking at such relationship influences points instead to the way that career development is often shaped by seemingly random events in which individuals other than the main actor play large roles. The challenges presented by a closer look at the potential influence of GROWs are not insurmountable, though. There are ways to handle them and benefits to be gained by taking a closer look.

For Individuals

Relationships, especially with family members, are likely to have their own sets of challenges and problems that individuals may prefer to ignore or avoid through increased work involvement (Bartolomé, 1983; Korman, 1988). Troubled children whose needs interfere with career pressures, spouses trying to figure out their own career dynamics—in these instances and many more, relationships may appear to be a hindrance and thus avoided. Paradoxically, taking the time to systematically think about the positive impact of such relationships on one's development may provide some needed perspective on the relationship.

As Fletcher (1994) convincingly argues, personal relationships have been relegated to the private sphere *and* devalued as women's work, making it difficult for both women and men to attend to them while in their public, career roles. For men, emphasizing relationships and the necessary skills may seem not only unrelated to work but also unmasculine. For women, emphasizing relationships and the necessary skills may raise fears that they will be stereotyped as "soft" or negatively judged for placing value on personal connections outside the workplace. While these fears are real, individuals who do not go beyond them run the risk of missing out on valuable insights into themselves gained in the context of GROWs.

For Career Professionals

Career professionals may fear that looking at the growth potential of GROWs is a bit like opening Pandora's box: more may end up coming out than fits within the domain of career counseling. This may not be an unrealistic fear. The career professional may decide to be very clear at the outset regarding the boundary between career counseling and more extensive personal counseling and be prepared to make appropriate referrals, if necessary.

For Organizations

Facilitating activities that integrate career processes and personal relationships can be risky business for organizations, given large individual differences among employees in this arena. There is also the potential for such activities to become intrusive (Korman, 1988). Organizations must avoid inadvertently implying that more GROWs equals better or that such relationships should be cultivated strictly for instrumental reasons.

However, looking at GROWs as a potential resource for career growth may be a timely antidote to the tendency for organizations to view outside relationships strictly in terms of their costs (family leave, elder care benefits, release time for community service, and such). Thus, rather than seeing such extraorganizational involvements as legitimate but unfortunate distractions from career concerns, organizations can instead appreciate them as potential venues for growth and learning that can transfer into the job setting.

Tapping the Potential of GROWs

Given these difficulties, the reader may reasonably wonder, how can the implications of GROWs be addressed? Under the new employment contract discussed earlier and in other chapters in this volume, most individuals will not be able to expect that their career growth and development needs will be met within one organization. It is more likely that individuals will have to design careers that cross organizations and fields, and in order to do so, they will need to find ways of stimulating their own career and personal growth. Here are a few suggestions for how to capitalize on the contributions of GROWs.

1. *Career self-assessment and development activities should explicitly address and investigate GROWs for any individual in any career stage.* Individuals should be encouraged to look at the events and relationships that have stimulated personal growth and to examine how such changes may have influenced their career attitudes and behaviors. One mechanism for doing this would be to construct a relationship map on which an individual's GROWs could be depicted on a variety of different attributes, such as strength, function, and potential to contribute to growth. This retrospective approach may heighten appreciation of the importance of these relationships as well as make individuals more open to such learning.

During such a self-assessment activity, Rashida, whose case was described at the beginning of this chapter, came to realize how significant her spouse's writing coaching had been in developing her sense of confidence in her writing skills. She was also able to recognize that she had internalized much of his coaching and thus no longer needed it to the same extent. This led her to reflect on ways in which their relationship had been a source of growth for *his* career.

2. *Individuals who are in career transitions should be encouraged to consider the role of such relationships in helping them learn what they need to know about themselves in order to take next steps.* A good friend or spouse may help a person learn more about him- or herself and thus get out of a rut; a friend may have suggestions for other sources of helpful information or specific action recommendations; a relationship may be the arena for some confronting feedback that motivates the individual to make changes.

In Kevin's case, Rick's comments led him to see himself and his relationship with his boss in a new light; he later was able to confirm with his boss his new understanding that much of the apparently negative feedback he had received was actually just intended to spur him to an even higher performance level and was not at all an indication of poor performance.

The process of executive coaching described by Kaplan and colleagues (1991) is structured to ensure that extensive feedback, from both within and outside the individual's organization, reaches the executive, along with recommendations for specific behavioral changes. Although the resources required for full-blown executive coaching are not available for everyone who is in a career transition, the emphasis Kaplan and his associates place on looking at the full person in order to diagnose areas for development is an approach that could be more widely used.

The developmental sanctuaries described in Chapter Thirteen in this book may be a mechanism career development professionals can employ to facilitate such relationships. Freed from the pressures to be invulnerable that the workplace often seems to hold (Kaplan, 1991), individuals in such groups may be freer to seek, receive, and hear clear feedback. Such experiences may be particularly empowering for individuals who have previously looked to their employers for career development and growth and who are concerned about their abilities to handle these activities internally.

On the other hand, individuals with relatively small extraorganizational relationship networks may have difficulties, especially if they believe they have made sacrifices in this area in order to advance their careers. Thus interventions that address these issues must be coupled with appropriate support, specific suggestions on how to expand these networks, and the recognition that this is difficult work.

3. *It should be legitimate for all employees to make time for nonwork activities (and GROWs)*. In Chapter Eight, Mary Young focuses attention on one particular demographic group in order to make a broader argument that work-life balance is essential for everyone. The many potential career development implications of GROWs offer compelling support for the importance of developing such a balance. Individuals whose time and energy are inordinately devoted to their workplaces and workplace connections have little opportunity to develop GROWs, much less to learn from them. Organizations can help by making flexible working options available to all employees, regardless of their particular life situation. Some organizations are already doing just this (see Chapter Eight, this volume).

Conclusion

Growth-enhancing relationships outside work are unappreciated, underutilized resources that are increasingly important in the current career environment. Through personal change wrought in the context of a variety of interpersonal relationships, individuals can also develop their careers. This view challenges the prevalent assumption that career development happens only in the context of relationships at work, and it also provides powerful support for the necessity of maintaining a work-life balance in which there is room for many kinds of relationships.

References

Alter, C., & Hage, J. (1993). *Organizations working together.* Newbury Park, CA: Sage.

Arthur, M. B. (1994). The boundaryless career: A new perspective for organizational inquiry. *Journal of Organizational Behavior, 15,* 295–306.

Bartolomé, F. (1983). The work alibi when it's harder to go home. *Harvard Business Review, 61*(2), 67–74.

Evans, P., & Bartolomé, F. (1984). The changing pictures of the relationship between career and family. *Journal of Occupational Behavior, 5,* 9–21.

Fletcher, J. K. (1994). *Toward a theory of relational practice in organizations: A feminist reconstruction of "real" work.* Unpublished doctoral dissertation, Boston University.

Gallos, J. V. (1989). Exploring women's development: Implications for career theory, practice, and research. In M. B. Arthur, D. T. Hall, & B. S. Lawrence (Eds.), *Handbook of career theory* (pp. 110–132). Cambridge, England: Cambridge University Press.

Gilligan, C. (1982). *In a different voice.* Cambridge, MA: Harvard University Press.

Hall, D. T. (1971). A theoretical model of career subidentity development in organizational settings. *Organizational Behavior and Human Performance, 6,* 50–76.

Hall, D. T. (1986). Breaking career routines: Midcareer choice and identity development. In D. T. Hall & Associates, *Career development in organizations* (pp. 120–159). San Francisco: Jossey-Bass.

Handy, C. (1989). *The age of unreason.* Boston: Harvard Business School Press.

House, J. S. (1981). *Work stress and social support.* Reading, MA: Addison-Wesley.

Kaplan, R., with Drath, W. H., & Kofodimos, J. R. (1991). *Beyond ambition: How driven managers can lead better and live better.* San Francisco: Jossey-Bass.

Kegan, R. (1982). *The evolving self: Problem and process in human development.* Cambridge, MA: Harvard University Press.

Kofodimos, J. R. (1990). Why executives lose their balance. *Organizational Dynamics, 19*(1), 58–73.

Kofodimos, J. R. (1993). *Balancing act: How managers can integrate successful careers and fulfilling personal lives.* San Francisco: Jossey-Bass.

Korman, A. K. (1988). Career success and personal failure: Mid- to late-career feelings and events. In M. London & E. M. Mone (Eds.), *Career growth and human resource strategies* (pp. 81–94). New York: Quorum Books.

Kram, K. E., & Bragar, M. C. (1992). Development through mentoring: A strategic approach. In D. Montross & C. Shinkman (Eds.), *Career development: Theory and practice* (pp. 221–254). Springfield, IL: Thomas.

Lobel, S. A. (1991). Allocation of investment in work and family roles: Alternative theories and implications for research. *Academy of Management Review, 16*(3), 507–521.

Miller, J. B. (1991). The development of women's sense of self. In J. V. Jordan, A. G. Kaplan, J. B. Miller, I. P. Stiver, & J. L. Surrey (Eds.), *Women's growth in connection* (pp. 11–26). New York: Guilford Press.

Voydanoff, P. (1985). Work/family linkages over the life course. *Journal of Career Development, 12,* 23–32.

Zedeck, S. (1992). Introduction: Exploring the domain of work and family concerns. In S. Zedeck (Ed.), *Work, families, and organizations* (pp. 1–32). San Francisco: Jossey-Bass.

Chapter Eight

Career Issues for Single Adults Without Dependent Children

Mary Young

When I began my doctoral studies at Boston University, I also entered a hotbed of work-and-family issues. Not only were a number of faculty and doctoral students—many of whom have contributed to this book—studying the impact of work life on families and family life on employees and their organizations, but many of them were also struggling with these issues in their own lives. Birth announcements regularly appeared on the department office's door. Young children swarmed underfoot at twice-yearly departmental parties. Work-family balance, boundaries between home and job, and the split between public and private identity—these were intriguing intellectual topics as well as ongoing personal struggles for my colleagues. They were also significant issues for *me*, although I am divorced and have no kids. In fact, work-and-life issues were central concerns for everyone I knew, especially for people in their thirties and forties, regardless of their life status.

What surprised me most, however, was that here, in a place where so many people were thinking and talking about the inter-

Note: Thanks to Peter Stein, Tim Hall, Kathy Kram, Meryl Louis, Marion McCollom, Bradley Googins, James Hunt, Sharon Lobel, and Vicky Parker for comments and suggestions that have contributed to the development of this chapter.

action of work and personal life, everyone was calling it "work and family." The issues were who's going to cook dinner and who's going to drive the kids to school, whose career gets put on hold for a while and who gets to move ahead. Framed in those terms, "work and family" had nothing to do with me.

Yet my own struggles balancing life at work and life outside of work are replicated in the dozens of stories I have collected over the past five years. Here are just two.

Nancy is a forty-year old college administrator. Three years ago, she was "picked out of the chorus line" of junior staff people by a vice president who recognized her ability and drive. Challenged by her mentor to achieve more than she would have previously thought possible, Nancy flourished as never before. Her boss praised and rewarded her and piled on new challenges. Nancy soared. Wounded by divorce and disappointed in her midlife dating opportunities, she poured herself into a job that had no limits. There was always good reason to come in early, stay late, or bring work home. She lunched with colleagues and met work friends for dinner or a movie after work. Although she longed for a romantic relationship, it seemed increasingly difficult to find one. She felt stressed and tired at night and lonely on the weekend. But at work, she felt successful, needed, even loved.

When Jack moved to the midwest from New York City, he had no idea how often his life status would become an issue. When another executive's wife found out that Jack was single, "she became obsessed with finding a wife for me," he recalls. "It was a very difficult situation." Some of the awkwardness came from living in a community where it is just assumed that all adults are married or seriously looking. Not having kids or a spouse makes him "sort of a novelty act," Jack says. It also has more serious repercussions. "For married people, there's a wall between life inside and outside work. That doesn't happen for me." Nevertheless, he says, "I *do* have other things to go home to."

Single adults without dependent children, whom I call SAWDCs (pronounced "saw-ducks"), are not an insignificant minority, although their absence from the organizational literature might suggest that they are. In fact, SAWDCs comprise almost one-third of the workforce. Defined as men or women who are not currently in a long-term relationship and who do not have children under age eighteen, SAWDCs represented about 30.3 percent of the U.S. labor force in 1990, according to an analysis by the Center for Labor Market Studies at Northeastern University.

Overview

This chapter will attempt to redress the "disappearing" of SAWDCs in several ways. First, it will explore some of the societal and organizational forces that contribute to the absence of single adults from most career discussions. Next it will draw upon the experiences of Nancy, Jack, and other SAWDCs I have interviewed to suggest the particular issues SAWDCs face in managing their careers. Significantly, these experiences have implications not only for SAWDCs: they also speak to broader work-and-life issues that are relevant to all adults but that the rubric of work and family effectively obscures. Finally, I will suggest implications of these issues for career professionals and organizations.

Definition of SAWDCs

SAWDCs may be divorced, separated, or widowed. They may be among the 10 percent of adults who never marry, or they may simply have no partner or spouse at this point in their lives. Perhaps they are childless or their children are over the age of eighteen. SAWDCs may be heterosexual, lesbian, or gay. Although "SAWDC" is not a previously established demographic category, I will argue that examining SAWDCs' experience can add much to our understanding of work-life balance and of adulthood and careers.

Defined in this way, almost everyone will be a SAWDC sooner or later. In fact, many of us will be SAWDCs more than once in our careers, most likely when we first enter the workforce, perhaps again in middle adulthood, and then later in our career. Yet despite the fact that most of us have belonged or will belong to this category, SAWDCs are almost invisible in the literature on adult development (Erikson, 1963; Gould, 1980; Levinson, 1980) and work life (see, for example, Zedeck's review, 1992). The very fact that SAWDCs have so much greater presence in the workforce than they do in scholarship *about* the workforce is a clue to the cultural assumptions underlying both theory and practice, an idea that I will develop further.

Perceptions of SAWDCs

In order to understand the impact of life status on career, it is useful to take stock of popular assumptions regarding unmarried adults.

The sociology of singles is limited. "Little is known about singles except that they are unmarried," Kimmel summarizes dryly (1974, p. 218). Lucille Duberman suggests why this is the case: "Sociologists are as human and as culture-bound as anyone else and thus tend to ignore those segments of society that do not conform to our cultural norms. This obvious omission tells us something about our society and our discipline. Surely the oversight is not because sociologists are unaware that a sizable proportion of our population is unmarried. Rather, the neglect reflects our adherence to the ideal that everyone should marry and that, if he or she really wants to, anyone can" (Duberman, 1977, pp. 118–119). Sociologist Peter Stein agrees: the lumping together of so many distinctive statuses (never married, divorced, separated, widowed) into one residual category—single— is "testament to the imperialism of marriage" (Stein, 1978, p. 3).

Research has shown that singles are stereotyped as deviant (Adams, 1976; Austrom, 1984; Stein, 1989), and their marital status is attributed to immaturity, psychosexual conflicts, inability to commit, or homosexuality (Duberman, 1977). Unattached women may be viewed as a threat to married couples (Duberman, 1974), bachelors as "shirkers . . . willfully selfish persons" (Turner, 1970, cited in Davis and Strong, 1977). In 1955, less than 10 percent of Americans believed that unmarried people could be happy (Coontz, 1992, p. 25). Eighty percent of Americans surveyed in 1957 said that people who choose not to marry are "sick," "neurotic," and "immoral" (McLaughlin et al., 1988); 25 percent of Americans still held that view in 1977 (Coontz, 1992, p. 186). Even Anita Hill was subject to such stereotyping: during the 1991 Senate hearings on Clarence Thomas's nomination to the Supreme Court, Hill's credibility was challenged partly on the basis of her status as a single woman, she said. "In constructing an explanation for my marital status as a single, I became unmarriageable, or opposed to marriage, the fantasizing spinster, or the man-hater" (Hill, 1992).

In a meta-analysis of family structure stereotypes, Ganong, Coleman, and Mapes (1990) reviewed twenty-six studies published between 1978 and 1989 and concluded that married adults are perceived more positively than adults of other marital statuses and that adults who remain voluntarily childless are perceived less favorably than parents.

While marriage and parenting are assumed to be the normative adult roles, historian Stacey Coontz claims such assumptions have, in fact, ebbed and flowed over time. The "family values" that we label as traditional actually reached their current level of acceptance only after World War II. Before then, the centrality of marriage and parenthood had actually been *declining* for 150 years, "with only partial and temporary interruptions during the 1950s," says Coontz (1992, p. 187). The current trend for postponing marriage (from an average of age 20 for women in 1955 to age 23.6 in 1988, and from age 22.6 for men in 1955 to age 25.9 in 1988, according to the U.S. Bureau of the Census) must be reexamined, therefore, in a broader historical context. It is not a startling new development but rather a return to the way things were in the United States before World War I. People marry today at about the same age as they did in 1870, and the number of never-married people in the United States is proportionately smaller today than it was in 1900 (Coontz, 1992, p. 183).

Nevertheless, while our assumptions about what is normal are based on recent, rather than longer-term demographic trends, they persist. In laboratory experiments, psychologists Claire Etaugh and Lisa Birdoes found that undergraduates rated married men and women of any age as happier and more secure than unmarrieds. Divorced adults were viewed as less responsible and stable than marrieds and never-marrieds as less sociable. The authors conclude that "those who have attained the state considered most desirable in our society, i.e. marriage, are viewed most positively regardless of their age or sex" (Etaugh and Birdoes, 1991, p. 496). One key reason why career issues are tough for singles, then, stems from cultural assumptions about the single person's social status and particularly about the value of his or her various identities (for example, as friend, son or daughter, lover, volunteer) relative to the value of other people's roles as parent or partner.

Many people—particularly those who are married or who are under age thirty—discount both the stereotypes of singles and their impacts. But not only do these cultural assumptions affect relations between SAWDCs and non-SAWDCs, but single people may also internalize these beliefs about *themselves* (Ganong, Coleman, and Mapes, 1990). The consequences can be seen in the career dilemmas faced by SAWDCs such as Nancy and Jack, both in the workplace and in managing their lives outside of work.

SAWDCs in the Workplace

Few studies have focused on the relationship between life status—that is, whether one is single or partnered and the parent of a child under eighteen or a nonparent—and various workplace outcomes. However, previous research has shown a relationship between life status and hiring, compensation, performance evaluation, promotion, developmental relationships, work involvement, and satisfaction with work and life.

Hiring

Singleness appears to affect women's job chances differently than it does men's. Career consultants interviewed by the *New York Times* (Bradsher, 1989) said that single women have an advantage because they are perceived to be dedicated to their careers. Men, however, are expected to be married by the time they reach thirty or at least thirty-five. Employer preferences may vary depending on the industry. Professions that require long hours and extensive travel may favor unmarried men under age thirty. Investment banking and administrative and managerial jobs in many other fields prefer over-thirty, married men.

While half of the top executive women in one survey were single, less than one-tenth of the executive men were (Bradsher, 1990). This promarriage bias is strongest in regard to men at the top of the organization. Senior male executives are less than half as likely as other men their age to be single; they are also more likely to be married to their first wife.

Performance Evaluation

Russell and Rush (1987) studied the effects of fictitious employees' gender, marital status, and parental status on performance appraisals conducted by male and female undergraduates. Men's performance ratings were not affected by their parental or marital status. For women, however, marriage and family status were significant factors. Married mothers received the most favorable evaluations and the mildest penalties for poor performance. Single women, by contrast, received the harshest evaluations and consequences. To explain this effect, the researchers propose that married mothers were perceived to have an external, temporary reason for their poor performance (caring for their children). The low effort of single women, however, was attributed to chronic, internal factors (laziness). At first glance, Russell and Rush's data seem to conflict with the finding that half of female executives were single women. Perhaps this difference can be explained by looking at who is doing the evaluating, hiring, or promoting. The raters in the Russell and Rush study were undergraduates, whereas executive appointments are most likely to be made by senior men.

Promotions

The majority of companies responding to a 1974 study reported that only 20 percent of their management employees were single (Jacoby, 1974). More recent data suggest some change, but the impact of marital status on career advancement may be different for men than for women. A 1991 study by Korn/Ferry found that 93.5 percent of male, senior executives in a large corporation were married, as compared to 84.1 percent of men aged forty-five to sixty-four in the United States population at large (Bradsher, 1989). Korenman and Neumark (1991) found that married men had an 11 percent higher likelihood than single men of being promoted.

Compensation

Employees' marital and parental status also affects their earnings. Roskies and Carrier (1994) found that women without children reported working significantly more hours than their colleagues with children, yet both groups earned comparable pay. Schneer and Reitman (1993) surveyed MBA degree holders and, after controlling for age, hours, experience, employment gap, and field of responsibility, found that single women earned 12 percent less than their married counterparts. To explain this finding, they hypothesize that married women's careers benefit from the emotional and instrumental support of a spouse. For the male MBAs in Schneer and Reitman's study, the effect of life status was more complex: the earnings bonus came for married men with children and a wife who stayed at home. Single men and men in two-career couples with or without children had equal incomes. In another study, Korenman and Neumark (1991) report that both black and white men's earnings vary with marital status: they earn most if they are married; if they are divorced or separated, they earn more than if they had never been married. All three studies suggest that pay may be contingent on martial and family status and perhaps more so for women than for men. Life-status differences in compensation may simply be a secondary effect of the life-status bias in hiring, promotion, and performance appraisal that I have already mentioned. Pay differences may also stem from employers' perception that employees who have "a family to support" need larger incomes than those who do not.

Developmental Relationships

Although SAWDCs comprise almost one-third of the workforce, they remain a minority in most organizations. (Exceptions include the financial service firms, high-tech start-up companies, and other industries that employ a primarily young-and-hungry workforce.) Like religious or racial minorities, women in historically male occupations, and other nontraditional employees, SAWDCs face particular challenges in establishing mentoring and other developmental relationships. While this dynamic has been explored in regard to cross-gender and cross-race relationships (Kram and Hall, 1995), it has not been studied among people of different life status. Nevertheless, because such relationships are based in part on perceptions of similarity, which lead to mutual attraction and identification, it seems reasonable to expect that life-status differences may inhibit the development of mentoring relationships.

Moreover, I predict that the cultural values and assumptions about life status also operate within established mentoring relationships, affecting each party's perceptions and understanding of the other's work-and-life issues.

For example, it is hard for SAWDCs to exhibit what is important about their nonwork lives in framed photographs on their desktop. They have no stories to tell about their children's latest milestones. As one perceptive non-SAWDC told me, "It's not so much the *content* that's important about these conversations; it's the *function* they serve" in building rapport and establishing developmental relationships.

Work Investment

In a 1974 study, 60 percent of the major corporations surveyed reported that single executives tend to "make snap judgments" and 25 percent believe singles are "less stable" than married people (cited in Stein, 1976). Twenty years later, my own research suggests that singles are still regarded as less stable. As a result, they may also be perceived as less committed to their jobs than employees who are spouses or parents (Schneer and Reitman, 1993; Stein, 1976).

Interestingly, there is significant evidence to the contrary. Davis and Strong (1977) note that single men have a tendency to over-invest in work because that is often the primary source of their identity. Childless women (both married and single) work significantly longer hours and report higher work involvement than do women with children (Roskies and Carrier, 1994). Schwartz (1982) found that strong identification with the occupational role was a common coping strategy for unmarried men and women. Later in this chapter, I will suggest some of the workplace practices and the underlying assumptions and attitudes that influence SAWDCs to work more hours than employees with children.

Satisfaction with Work and Life

Austrom (1984) found that singles were significantly more likely than marrieds to view work as the major source of satisfaction in their life, although marrieds expressed a higher level of work satisfaction. This finding is consistent with Roskies and Carrier (1994), who found that social support is the most significant contributing factor to singles' emotional well-being and overall life satisfaction. Those who were satisfied with their lives in general were most likely to enjoy working for their present employer, find their job interesting, be involved in their work, and regard their job as the major source of satisfaction in their life (Austrom, 1984). This interaction of life work and nonwork leads us to examine another set of career issues that SAWDCs face: balancing work life and life outside of work.

Life Status, Equity Issues, and Work-Life Balance

In recent years, the gradual development of "work-family" programs and policies in organizations has given rise to a fledgling but highly visible countermovement. Though small in formal membership, the ChildFree Network has become a vocal champion for the equal rights of employees—both married and unmarried—without dependent children, a group that comprises about two-thirds of the U.S. workforce. Stories about the Childfree Network in the *New York Times* (Lafayette, 1994; Williams, 1994) and the *Wall Street Journal* (Grossman, 1993; Guyon, 1991) have featured interviews with childless employees, both married and unmarried, who feel they have been penalized in the workplace for not being parents. They receive fewer benefits and, in fact, think of themselves as subsidizing health care and other benefits awarded other employees' family members. Frequently, they are not entitled to flexible work arrangements or unpaid leaves for which employees with children do qualify. Furthermore, in many cases, the kinds of informal accommodations that an understanding supervisor may make to support an employee's nonwork demands are simply not offered to those without traditional families. Not only are singles expected to work longer hours, including evenings, weekends, and holidays, but they are also expected to be free to travel, transfer, or accept long-term training or work assignments in another location.

The equity issue has two sides. Many nonparents feel shortchanged by what they receive from the organization. They also feel they are expected to give back a disproportionate amount. It is individual co-workers, quite often, rather than the organization itself, who take up the slack during someone else's three-month maternity leave or when a frantic colleague has to leave at midday to pick up a sick child at day care. Thus work-family equity has at least two aspects for employees who fall outside traditional work-family programs: they feel penalized in terms of both what they are expected to give and what they do not get.

For these reasons, work-family programs are beginning to stir up a palpable backlash in some organizations. Resentment is likely to be particularly strong when formal policies support a narrow range of employees' nonwork needs—for example, offering day-care referrals and parental leave but not elder care, family emergency leave, or unpaid time away from the job for other reasons, such as taking a sabbatical or going to school.

The split between employees with and without children may also be exacerbated by *informal* practices that support parents but do not acknowledge the nonwork needs of other employees. My own research suggests that even in an organization which claims to have a consistent policy, informal practices regarding "who works when" vary among work groups (Young, 1994).

Data from pilot interviews also indicate that the relationship between an employee's life status and work time (that is, when and how much an employee works) is moderated by the life status of his or her supervisor and co-workers. For example, being the only SAWDC in an enclave of partnered parents will affect both your work time and your perceptions about its fairness. The more heterogeneous the life status of group members or the more similar an employee's life status is to that of the supervisor and co-workers, the less significant the relationship between life status and work time becomes (Young, 1994).

While the equity of work time and benefits may be an increasingly important issue in many organizations, it is not the only way in which being a SAWDC affects one's career.

SAWDCs' Struggle with Work and Nonwork

Taped to my computer is a tattered, photocopied quote, posted several years ago as a reminder to myself: "The challenge to develop, balance, and harmonize working and loving is with us every day, regardless of the presence or absence of a job or a loved one" (Rohrlich, 1980, pp. 231–232).

Here is an elemental truth that both SAWDCs and non-SAWDCs may forget: it is not necessary to have a spouse or children to experience the relentless tug-of-war between having and doing good work and living a good life outside of work. You do not need kids or even a partner to realize that overcommitment in one area inevitably takes its toll on the other.

Over the years, Nancy's career has become less satisfying as a sole source of emotional support, and she has put more energy into developing her life outside of work. She is an active member of her church, serves on several committees, and helps lead an outdoor activities group for high school students. She loves to cook and regularly hosts friends for dinner. She serves on her town's recycling committee.

Like Nancy, Larry is divorced. When he was married, he and his working wife split the domestic to-do list: trips to the dry cleaners, groceries, yard work, bill paying, car repairs, and remembering birthdays. Now it is all up to him. Although he can cover the essentials (in part, by hiring a cleaning person and yard service), a lot of other things now fall through the cracks: sending Christmas cards, keeping up with old friends who have moved away, hosting a neighborhood potluck. Larry still occasionally manages to meet a co-worker for pizza on the way home, but the regular routine of Sunday night suppers with friends or annual ski trips with former college classmates has fallen by the wayside. There is just not enough time for keeping in touch.

To people caught in the monumental challenges of juggling work and family—"family" meaning a partner and/or one or more children—SAWDCs' struggle to have a life outside of work may sound pretty inconsequential. In fact, on more than one occasion, someone has come right out and asked me, "So what's the problem?" when I mention my interest in SAWDCs' work-life balance.

The problem, as any SAWDC will tell you, is that it is *hard* to balance work and personal life for numerous reasons, some of which pertain to all employees and others that are particular to SAWDCs. For one thing, work time for U.S. workers has increased. In economist Juliet Schor's analysis, the average employed person in the United States is now on the job 163 more hours each year— the equivalent of an extra month of 40-hour work weeks—than in 1948 (Schor, 1991). Given the fixed number of days in the week and hours in the day, that means there is progressively less time for nonwork activities.

This change affects everyone in the workforce. But what makes this shift particularly difficult for SAWDCs is that their nonwork needs and responsibilities are less visible and less socially supported than those of working parents. We have already seen how, in both name and practice, many work-family programs exclude nonparents and nonmarried employees. But on a much more subtle level, such programs marginalize a long list of other nonwork roles and identities that may be important *not only* to SAWDCs but also to non-SAWDCs and to the communities in which they live. These other nonwork activities include community involvement; relationships with family members (most SAWDCs do, after all, have families) and others with whom SAWDCs form family-like connections, romances, recreational and leisure pursuits; and all of the day-to-day responsibilities of maintaining a life.

In fact, maintenance activities may demand more time of a single adult than they might of someone who has a spouse or partner. Being solely responsible for a household simply takes more time than it would if these responsibilities were shared. But that is not the only reason why singles need significant time outside of work. They are also solely responsible for doing whatever it takes to maintain a healthy social network—a social network that needs to be larger than it would if they had a built-in companion. In the past, both domestic and social responsibilities were delegated to the stay-at-home spouse (Kanter, 1977). Many male executives still have these traditional arrangements (Schneer and Reitman, 1993). But even if both spouses work, research has shown that women typically perform a disproportionate amount of the household jobs (Hochschild, 1989). This means that SAWDCs are disadvantaged in that they do not have either a spouse to share these responsibilities (the enlightened option) or a wife to take on additional duties (the traditional option).

This single-person penalty is particularly insidious because SAWDCs are perceived to have "fewer" responsibilities, thus more time; they may therefore be expected by supervisors to stay longer at work or by siblings to take greater responsibility for an aging parent. Ironically, however, singles are also perceived to need *less* time because their nonwork roles and responsibilities are less socially valued than those of married people or people with children. Dating, spending time with friends, keeping commitments to people who are not one's kin—all of these are regarded as less important. At the very least, they are viewed as discretionary activities, things you do only if there is time left over after work. My research suggests that SAWDCs may experience the least support for their life-outside-of-work when they are in a demographic minority—that is, when their supervisor and co-workers have traditional lives as partnered parents (Young, 1994).

While many workplaces marginalize SAWDCs' needs, the relational approach to career development supports them. It neither explicitly values one kind of relationship over others, nor does it suggest that SAWDCs necessarily have either less need or less opportunity for connection at work or outside of work.

In fact, as research (Allen and Pickett, 1987; Austrom, 1984; Roskies and Carrier, 1994; Stein, 1978) shows, "discretionary" activities are essential for singles' well-being. Thus it is not simply "nice" to have the time to pursue hobbies, maintain a social network, or nurture close emotional ties with people who are not one's partner or children—it is a fundamental requirement for a single person's mental health and, by extension, physical well-being. Moreover, the consequences of not maintaining an adequate life outside of work are potential problems not only for the individual SAWDC but also for organizations in terms of health care costs, employee performance and productivity, job satisfaction, and commitment. In Nancy's case, severe back problems brought on by overwork forced her to miss weeks of work recovering from back surgery. The consequences of SAWDCs' work-life imbalance also affect friends, families, and communities.

Beyond Work and Family

Until now, I have argued that SAWDCs need a balance between work and personal life and also need organizational help in achieving it. I have argued that achieving a satisfying work and personal life balance benefits not only the individual SAWDC but also his or her organization, friends, family, and community. Now I would like to take one giant step further. In my view, many of these arguments can be made for all adults, not just for those without children or a partner. I believe the language of "work and family" does a disservice to us all—to non-SAWDCs as well as SAWDCs—by unnecessarily restricting the range of identities, roles, and activities we recognize as important in adult life. At some points (early in one's career, for example, or during the first few years of parenthood), work and parent-to-partner roles may require virtually 100 percent of one's time. Other roles—friend, cousin, community volunteer, mentor, hobbyist, neighbor, YM/WCA board member, uncle or aunt, amateur actor or chorus singer—may get pushed so far down on the list that there is no time left for them. Yet over the longer course of adulthood, we all benefit from experiencing a broad range of roles. (This is particularly true today: not only do children grow up and leave home, spouses die, and marriages end but also careers in organizations are increasingly unstable.) We need to strive for mastery in some areas and in others simply to play. As Chapters Five and Seven in this volume assert, we need to nurture and be nurtured at home, at work, and in our community. We need to experience that our entire identity is not solely dependent upon either work *or* family. Thus, while the focus of this chapter is on SAWDCs' career issues, my concern—that the term *work and family* is handicapping because it frames the issues much too narrowly—is one that extends to all adults, regardless of their partner or parent status.

The Challenges for SAWDCs

So far, this chapter has identified factors that make it difficult for SAWDCs to achieve a balance between work and life and suggested consequences for individuals and organizations. Before proposing how career-development practitioners can address these problems, I want to suggest some deeper causes. This next section examines the underlying cultural, organizational, and institutional factors that work against the broadening of "work and family" to "work and life."

Cultural Assumptions About Individual Achievement

Sociologist Rosabeth Moss Kanter was one of the earliest organizational writers to examine work-and-family issues. One of her most important contributions was to identify what she called "the myth of individual achievement," which obscures the contributions of "family as helper" (Kanter, 1977, p. 15). Kanter's discussion focuses on formal or informal participation by the spouse (usually the wife) and even the children. For example, an executive's family members may attend social functions that are a component of the executive's job or forge social ties with an associate's family, all of which benefit the executive's career. SAWDCs' ability to perform or even to qualify for such a job may be limited for lack of a family. The myth of individual achievement also overlooks the family's contributions in the form of emotional support. The built-in coaching, sympathy, cheering on, and buffering that many spouses and families provide are invisible but crucial forms of career support that SAWDCs may lack or may garner only if they maintain a diverse network of friends and family.

The myth of individual achievement coupled with our cultural assumptions about "normal" adult roles, which I addressed earlier, present special career challenges for SAWDCs. What makes them particularly difficult is that these challenges are seldom recognized or discussed.

Organizational Culture

These same cultural assumptions affect organizations as well as individuals, which is the second reason why career issues may be especially tough for SAWDCs. The field of work and family has enshrined a pantheon of corporate success stories, such as the annual winners of *Working Woman* magazine's Best Companies award. It is not uncommon to discover that the company's support for working parents grew out of the CEO's personal awakening. If leaders must have a personal encounter with work-and-family conflicts—either their own or their grown children's—to become advocates for a more "family-friendly" corporate culture, then the prospects that leaders will through personal experience become advocates for work-life balance seem slim.

As already seen, the bias against hiring or promoting unmarried men over thirty reduces their chances for becoming top decision makers. The paucity of unmarried men in top positions increases the likelihood that work-life balance will continue to be seen primarily as an issue for working parents, particularly mothers. Although a much larger percentage of executive women than executive men may be unmarried or not have children (Bradsher, 1990), most of them have risen by meeting traditional expectations about how long and how hard they work rather than by questioning these practices (Kofodimos, 1995).

Moreover, many professional service firms in fields such as law and accounting are characterized by an "up or out" culture. Everyone knows that working seventy or eighty hours a week is the only way to move ahead. Employees who want to survive do not buck the system, and only those who become partners can expect to remain in the firm after age thirty-five. Recently, some firms have begun establishing multiple career paths to allow for greater flexibility. Significantly, however, these programs are aimed at women who want to take time out to have a family. The culture of most firms that operate on the basis of billable hours, like the culture of many professions, does not support work-life balance across the board for every employee.

But it is not just executives and professionals who encounter balance troubles in the workplace. Critical theorists argue that all employees' nonwork needs are intrinsically antithetical to the organization's short-term interests. Organizations make concessions to nonwork because they have to, particularly with the growth of two-career families, not because they have suddenly grown more altruistic or magnanimous. However, they limit these concessions as much as possible by defining them as "work-and-family" issues rather than as work-life issues that affect the quality of life for *all* employees. Most organizations continue to reward personnel who maintain a solid boundary between work and personal life. They provide numerous incentives for overwork (Kofodimos, 1995). They rely on "face time" (the number of hours one is physically visible in the workplace, as opposed to not working or working at home or on the road) as a measure of employee commitment. They downsize and restructure the organization, which leaves fewer employees shouldering more of the work, hoping to be rewarded with job security. As anyone knows who has been lured or pressured into working more than he or she honestly wants to, organizations exercise many kinds of rewards and punishment to encourage employees' investment in work.

Institutional Forces

In the face of cultural and other organizational inducements, it takes a counterforce at least as powerful to free employees from the lure of overwork. For many, that counterforce comes from having a long-term, heterosexual relationship or having children. Getting married and/or having kids not only gives you an important nonwork role, but it also sanctions these roles by means of long-established institutions—marriage and the family. Here then is a third factor that blocks the expansion of "work and family" to encompass "work and life."

Because SAWDCs are not represented by any institution, there is no counterpart to work or family that can champion their needs. Hence, at the institutional custody battle for employees' time and loyalty, SAWDCs are not even seated at the table. Moreover, the demographic diversity of SAWDCs—young unmarrieds; divorced, separated, widowed, or never married adults from early- to mid- to late-career; childless couples or those whose kids have flown the nest—mitigates against their identification with each other as a common group. I submit that it is only when some new development, such as work-family programs, introduces a tangible injustice does SAWDC-ness become salient as a group identity.

These factors—cultural assumptions about career as an individual achievement, corporate and professional cultures, and the absence of institutional support for SAWDCs—exert a significant but often unrecognized influence on individual lives.

Implications for Career Professionals

The preceding sections have shown that life status has significant impacts on both the work and nonwork aspects of career. SAWDCs, their supervisors and co-workers, and even their families and friends, may unconsciously give greater legitimacy to parent and spouse roles than to SAWDCs' nonwork roles. Organizations, in turn, support SAWDCs' overinvestment in work by holding different expectations for SAWDC employees and by elaborate systems of rewards and punishment. Although it is uncommon, in my experience, to hear employees who are in the establishment stage of their careers—that is, who are in their twenties—complain about life-status inequities, such inequities become more apparent and more painful for older SAWDCs.

The potential for overinvestment in work has at least two major consequences for SAWDCs. The first is that it makes them more vulnerable to job insecurity under the new career contract. Although SAWDCs may not have the extra mouths to feed and bodies to clothe that employees with kids do, and although they are (arguably) more mobile, they may also lose more when they lose their job. For many single adults, work is their central life role, the principal social arena, the primary source of emotional support.

A second consequence of SAWDCs' potential overinvestment in work—and, more than likely, an antecedent as well—is that it becomes more difficult for them to experience what I call the "nonwork aha!" Although not mentioned per se in any established career theory, the nonwork aha! is represented in many models nonetheless. It is the realization that work is not the be-all-and-end-all. In my experience, this realization often hits people once they start having or wanting a family of their own. But for those who do not become parents, whether by choice or chance, this midlife wake-up call may take longer. For Nancy, it came when her chronic back problems sent her to the hospital for three weeks and for the first time she took a step back to reevaluate her life. Jack's great awakening came in his mid fifties, after years as a fast-track and permanently jet-lagged consultant, and settled in his brain like an endless chorus of "Is That All There Is?" by Peggy Lee. SAWDCs are just as likely as non-SAWDCs to realize that work may not be everything. But this realization may come later or at greater emotional cost to them if they feel they have made a bad bargain in their career.

Because there is a propensity among SAWDCs to overinvest in work and because it may have serious consequences, career professionals can serve as a significant countervailing influence in several ways:

  • *By examining their own assumptions regarding life status and career.* All of us, as products of our culture, carry around many of the values and beliefs identified in this chapter. The first step for career-development practitioners is to become more aware of their own attitudes and assumptions about life status and career.

  • *By surfacing the client's underlying attitudes and assumptions about life status and career.* One way to begin this process is to explore the client's feelings about the way his or her work and non-work activities are divided. What factors support the division? What factors work against changing it?

- *By helping the client see the influence of culture and social institutions.* It is important for SAWDCs to recognize that they are not solely responsible for their work-life attitudes, feelings, and behaviors; these are reinforced by families, friends, organizations, and society at large. It is also helpful for SAWDCs to learn they are not alone or imagining things if they feel their nonwork lives are marginalized. Support groups and seminars for SAWDCs—such as those that many companies already offer for new parents or soon-to-retirees—can provide insight, group affiliation, and new social bonds. (See Chapter Five in this volume for more on using groups to promote self-reflection and self-transformation.)

- *By validating the importance of work-life balance.* One obvious step is to encourage SAWDCs to develop a well-rounded life: to play as well as work; to pursue mastery in some spheres but to enjoy remaining an amateur in others; to develop and nurture relationships with people other than co-workers and not to undervalue those relationships simply because they are not traditional family.

Balancing is important for everyone, and it makes particular sense in an era when lifelong devotion to one's career or organization is at best a risky proposition. But simply encouraging SAWDCs to be well-rounded is a superficial intervention. To treat the symptoms without also acknowledging that implicit attitudes and cultural assumptions affect how SAWDCs perceive themselves and are perceived by others is to do a serious disservice. These must be made explicit and discussible before individuals or organizations can truly change.

What Organizations Can Do

- *Expand the policy focus from work-family to work-life.* Since the expansion of corporate work-family programs in the 1980s (Gallinsky and Stein, 1990), a growing number of companies have broadened their programs to work-life (Williams, 1994). Some firms have changed more about their programs than the labels (Williams, 1994; Grossman, 1993). Kodak permits employees to take a leave from work "for a compelling personal experience" in addition to more traditional reasons like education or family hardship. Corning allows childless employees time away from the job to do volunteer work. Hewlett-Packard's flexible working arrangements are available to all employees, regardless of their personal circumstances, as are flexible work hours at Spiegel Inc. Quaker Oats gives childless employees an annual credit of $300 to offset their lower health care costs. The Life Cycle Approach is a "diversity-friendly" benefits program offered to companies by Segal Associates. Employees and employers pay into a "savings" account from which they can withdraw (within limits) for dependent care, home buying, tuition, or legal services (Jenner, 1994).

- *Remove career penalties for work-life balance.* Formal policies are one thing. Actual practices in the day-to-day, late-night-to-late-night work group are another matter. Research has shown that employees entitled to work-family benefits such as flextime or parental leave often do not take advantage of these programs for fear of hurting their careers. In a work culture where new parents feel it unwise to take time off from work, childless employees may feel even less safe opting for flexibility.

- *Educate managers about SAWDCs' work-life needs.* In a variation on the theme "Everyone's equal but some are more equal than others," supervisors and co-workers may assess some folks' personal-life needs as more deserving than others. To address such tendencies, Corning has not only changed its formal policies, it also trains managers to apply work-life guidelines even-handedly to all employees (Grossman, 1993).

- *Offer flexibility to all.* Corporate training is unlikely to eradicate the everyday privileges ascribed to the adult roles of parent and spouse because the granting of such privileges is deeply ingrained in our culture (Ganong, Coleman, and Mapes, 1990). Nor can formal work-life policies explicitly address every life-status variation and need. We have already seen that formal policies granting special consideration to some but not others lead to friction among life-status groups. A more promising approach is to permit all employees flexible work arrangements, as Hewlett-Packard does. Under such a program, life-status differences among employees become less divisive than they have become in other companies' work-family programs. Everyone benefits equally across the life course, whether their need is for parental leave, full-time education, travel, elder care, personal odyssey, or a dry run of retirement.

The greatest obstacle, of course, is that until organizations accept that flexibility is a good business strategy (Jenner, 1994), they will continue to reproduce the larger culture's values. Furthermore, if singles themselves subscribe to these values, even unconsciously, then they will never "push back" against the status quo to assert their right to work-life balance.

References

Adams, M. (1976). *Single blessedness.* New York: Basic Books.

Allen, K. R., & Pickett, R. S. (1987). Forgotten streams in the family life course: Utilization of qualitative retrospective interviews in the analysis of lifelong single women's family careers. *Journal of Marriage and the Family, 49,* 517–526.

Austrom, D. R. (1984). *The consequences of being single.* New York: Peter Lang.

Bradsher, K. (1989, December 13). Wedded for success. *New York Times,* C1.

Coontz, S. (1992). *The way we never were: American families and the nostalgia trap.* New York: Basic Books.

Davis, A. G., & Strong, P. M. (1977). Working without a net: The bachelor as a social problem. *Sociological Review, 25*(1), 108–129.

Duberman, L. (1977). *Marriage and other alternatives.* New York: Praeger.

Erikson, E. H. (1963). *Childhood and society* (2nd ed.). New York: W.W. Norton.

Etaugh, C., & Birdoes, L. N. (1991). Effects of age, sex, and marital status on person perception. *Perceptual and Motor Skills, 72,* 491–497.

Galinsky, E., & Stein, P. J. (1990). The impact of human resource policies on employees. *Journal of Family Issues, 11*(4), 368–383.

Ganong, L. H., Coleman, M., & Mapes, D. (1990). A meta-analytic review of family structure stereotypes. *Journal of Marriage and the Family, 52*(2), 287–296.

Googins, B. K. (1990). *Work/family conflicts.* New York: Auburn House.

Gould, R. (1981). Transformational tasks in adulthood. In S. Greenspan & D. Pollock (Eds.), *The course of life: Psychoanalytic contributions toward understanding personality development* (pp. 55–89). Washington, DC: U.S. Department of Health.

Grossman, L. (1993, June 21). What about us? *Wall Street Journal,* p. R8.

Guyon, J. (1991, October 23). Inequality in granting child-care benefits makes workers seethe. *Wall Street Journal*, p. 1.

Hill, A. (1992, October 16). *Race, gender and power in America.* Speech at Georgetown University Law Center conference, Washington, D.C. (Reuter Transcript Report).

Hochschild, A. (1989). *The second shift.* New York: Avon Books.

Jenner, L. (1994, March). Issues and options for childless employees. *HR Focus*, 22–23.

Kanter, R. M. (1977). *Work and family in the U.S.: A critical review and an agenda for research and policy.* Newbury Park, CA: Sage.

Kimmel, D. (1974). *Adulthood and aging.* New York: Wiley.

Kofodimos, J. R. (1995). *Beyond work-family programs.* Greensboro, NC: Center for Creative Leadership.

Korenman, S., & Neumark, D. (1991). Does marriage really make men more productive? *Journal of Human Resources, 26,* 283–307.

Kram, K. E., & Hall, D. T. (1995). Mentoring in a context of diversity and turbulence. In S. Lobel & E. E. Kossek (Eds.), *Human resource strategies for managing diversity.* London, England: Blackwell.

Lafayette, L. (1994, October 16). Fair play for the childless worker. *New York Times*, p. 11.

Levinson, D. J. (1980). Toward a conception of the adult life course. In N. Smelser & E. Erikson (Eds.), *Themes of love and work in adulthood* (pp. 265–281). Cambridge, MA: Harvard University Press.

McLaughlin, S. D., Melber, B. D., Billy, J.O.G., Zimmerle, D. M., Winges, L. D., & Johnson, T. R. (1988). *The changing lives of American women.* Chapel Hill: University of North Carolina Press.

Parker, V., & Hall, D. T. (1992). Expanding the domain of family and work issues. In S. Zedeck (Ed.), *Work, families, and organizations* (pp. 432–451). San Francisco: Jossey-Bass.

Rohrlich, J. B. (1980). *Work and love: The crucial balance.* New York: Summit Books.

Roskies, E., & Carrier, S. (1994). Marriage and children for professional women: Asset or liability? In G. P. Keita & J. J. Hurrell, Jr. (Eds.), *Job stress in a changing workplace* (pp. 269–282). Washington, DC: American Psychological Association.

Russell, J. E., & Rush, M. C. (1987). The effects of sex and marital/parental status on performance evaluations and attributions. *Sex Roles, 17*(3/4), 221–236.

Schneer, J. A., & Reitman, F. (1993). Effects of alternate family structures on career paths. *Academy of Management Journal, 36*(4), 830–843.

Schor, J. (1991). *The overworked American: The unexpected decline of leisure.* New York: Basic Books.

Schwartz, M. A. (1982). *The career strategies of the never married.* Paper presented at an American Sociological Association meeting, San Francisco, CA.

Stein, P. J. (1976). *Single.* Englewood Cliffs, NJ: Prentice Hall.

Stein, P. J. (1978). Lifestyles and life chances of the never-married. *Marriage and Family Review, 1*(4), 1–11.

Stein, P. J. (1989). Lifestyle diversity: Remaining single. In J. Henslin (Ed.), *Marriage and family in a changing society* (pp. 62–72). New York: Free Press.

Turner, R. (1970). *Family interaction.* New York: Wiley.

Williams, L. (1994, October 12). Childless employees demanding equity in corporate world. *New York Times,* p. 1.

Young, M. B. (1994). *Life status, work time, and the perceived fairness of who works when.* Unpublished doctoral dissertation proposal, Boston University School of Management.

Zedeck, S. (1992). Exploring the domain of work and family concerns. In S. Zedeck (Ed.), *Work, families, and organizations* (pp. 1–32). San Francisco: Jossey-Bass.

What Should I Do About It?

Now that we have, we hope, some new conceptual tools for promoting development in the new career environment, in Part Three we turn to ideas for career interventions: what should we do about career development?

We start from the perspective of the individual, with Chapter Nine describing how communities and individuals (particularly enlightened leaders) can create safe havens or personal zones for reflection and marshaling resources. There is much value here for professionals such as coaches and counselors who work with individual clients, and for organizational consultants this chapter raises possibilities for creating organizationally supported safe havens.

In Chapter Ten, Kent Seibert presents personal reflection as an aid to individual career growth. Experience is the best teacher, he believes, if you can learn from it. Seibert identifies specific steps we can take to use reflection to enhance experience-based learning. In Chapter Eleven, Barbara Walker shows us how relationships with people one sees as different can be a particularly powerful source of learning. As she indicates, many of the competencies developed in diversity work (self-reflection, dialogue, creating safety for learning, and so on) are the same career competencies demanded by today's environment. Thus diversity work equals personal development, which equals career development.

One particular group seen as different by many employees is older workers. Ironically, most of us—if we are fortunate!—will become members of this "different" group eventually. Chapter Twelve describes the unique issues facing the older worker and presents practical ideas for promoting career development in late career. (Of course, "late career" will be getting later and later as we move into the 21st century, as life spans and career spans lengthen.)

Chapters Thirteen and Fourteen present very specific suggestions for the career professional. Jane and Bill Hodgetts, two such practitioners themselves, describe the ways they create career support groups, or developmental sanctuaries, in the midst of the work environment. They present a series of issues and questions for career professionals to consider as they seek ways to provide such sanctuaries amid the realities of their clients' own work environments. Our hunch is that in years to come we will see a rich variety of structures to give people some kind of personal space to step back, with supportive colleagues, to reflect and to gain perspective and renewal. Chapter Fourteen discusses how new approaches like the Hodgetts's are creating a new role for the career practitioner. Like the new employee, the new career professional is becoming more protean: self-driven, results-oriented, ad hoc, and focused on psychological success and opportunities for just-in-time, reality-based learning.

Finally, in Chapter Fifteen, the editor gets the last word: to reflect on the ideas in this book and to speculate about using relational and work-based resources for growth in the service of a life worth living.

Chapter Nine

Creating Safe Havens at Work

Meryl Reis Louis

The new world of work is in truth many different worlds, all seemingly turbulent and uncertain, where change is perhaps the only predictable characteristic. For some professionals, the work world is one of continued employment in the high-intensity, smaller core (Handy, 1989) of the reengineered firm (Hammer and Champy, 1993). For others, it is a portfolio of interwoven projects, a patchwork of contracts, activities, involvements, what Mirvis and Hall call the "boundaryless career" (1994). For still others, it is a simultaneous involvement in multiple long-term ventures requiring wise husbanding and allocation of oneself as a fixed and limited resource. Finally, for some who face a lack of appropriate paid work, the experience may be of scrambling to make ends meet while searching for a place to use oneself in the world.

For most professionals, then, regardless of venue, the current world of work is a world of more to do than can be done in the time available and of complex tasks requiring multiple and diverse sets of hands and eyes and minds. It is a world in which the work

Note: For their helpful comments on drafts of this manuscript, I wish to thank Tony Athos, Lloyd Baird, Jean Bartunek, Margaret Benefiel, Dick Broholm, Michael Brown, Dave DeLong, Frank Friedlander, Connie Gersick, Tim Hall, Deborah Kolb, Barbara Mahon, Joanne Martin, Debra Meyerson, Mary Shotwell, David Specht, Lee Sproull, and Caroline Whitbeck.

is done by people who come together across traditional organizational boundaries in cross-functional teams, multidisciplinary task forces, partnerships, and interorganizational alliances (Kanter, 1989)—temporary systems that house today's more challenging projects (Bennis and Slater, 1968). Working in these increasingly flat, flexible, and diverse arrangements means coping with unclear authority structures and diffuse reporting relationships. In other words, we professionals—whether we work in industry, education, health care, government, or another sector—work in what feels like storm-tossed seas. Long past are the purposefully flowing though turbulent permanent white waters Peter Vaill described as recently as 1989. At least then the banks of the river were stable and the basic direction of flow was clear!

The Need for New Skills

We have seen that an individual's effectiveness in the new world of work depends on a greatly expanded set of skills. People continue to need an array of well-honed technical, professional, and managerial skills. But now they need to be skilled as well at planning, developing, and managing their own careers. They also need to be able to operate as entrepreneurs to generate projects on which they will work: to sell, staff, and garner resources to undertake those projects, whether or not they are working within a particular firm or as a consultant or contractor teaming with representatives of one or more firms (Kanter, 1989; Handy, 1989).

Beyond these entrepreneurial and career management skills is yet another domain to be mastered. The rush and press of today's work environments can strip once-rewarding tasks of their meaning or unseat our sense of connection to what we once found meaningful even as they drain us of energy and perspective. Thus the need for skill at creating "safe havens," settings in which we may be restored. The word *haven* is defined as a sheltered harbor, a place of refuge or rest, a sanctuary (*American Heritage Dictionary*, 1976). The phrase *safe haven*, though redundant linguistically, is meaningful experientially. It conveys a well-bounded place of safety, whether in one's mind or in physical space, within what seems an unsafe or threatening environment.

For our purposes, then, safe havens are protected spaces created in the midst of stressful environments. They are trustworthy places in which various kinds of work—personal and organizational—can be done. Safe havens can be created in two contexts: among individuals and collectively as people work together in groups. In either context, safe havens serve as islands of calm in the stormy seas of our work and life environments, places in which we can do the work of coming to terms with our increasingly stressful and challenging lives. As such, they restore perspective and replenish energies, elements vitally important to individual and collective effectiveness on the job. In this way, moments spent in safe havens enable and sustain individual efforts and in turn contribute to organizational ends.

In Chapter Six of this volume, Bill Kahn discusses secure base relationships. These can be understood as interpersonally anchored safe havens of an especially personal nature. They are characterized by a greater measure of personal feedback, disclosure, and connection than that required to do the task. In contrast, individual-level safe havens arise out of a particular quality of relationship with oneself—a quality of active self-respecting. Also, interactions in collective safe havens are likely to be much less personal in nature than would be found in secure base relationships.

We will see, in this chapter, how individual and collective safe havens serve us, what they feel like, and conditions that foster and hinder their emergence. To illustrate these points, I will be speaking quite personally. The form of exposition differs somewhat in the two sections following from my sense of the differences in what safe havens are like and how to support them in the different contexts. I note this to normalize what has become a pattern in readers' responses and in recognition of the fact that fundamental to safe haven experiences is an attentiveness to one's own response—crediting its legitimacy without necessarily discrediting another's experience.

Varied Forms of Individual Safe Havens

Individual safe havens may take many different forms and serve different functions. They include, for example, a time reserved to sit quietly without directing my attention to a task, a moment of silence I may give myself before I speak, the space I allow between my words now that I have learned to slow down. Music is as much the spacing of silence as it is the playing of a sequence of notes.

Consider an example. A safe haven may consist of "nothing more" than a moment of silence I give myself before I speak. "Nothing more" is in quotes because we tend to think of a moment as something small and insignificant. In the context of this example, it means a great deal—a moment in which to collect my thoughts, to settle myself, to take a calming breath, perhaps to come to attention, noticing the state of my audience. In addition, "nothing more" is in quotes because it sounds like something easy to accomplish. In truth, however, taking that moment of silence requires a great deal of me, as I must break with both my habit and the culture of my work setting, which encourage me to speak quickly and allow for little silence between speakers.

Individual safe havens may serve as an antidote to the adverse effects of one's immediate work environment. One person's safe haven may be still and quiet in contrast to the turbulence and press of the work environment, whereas another's might be active and stimulating against the backdrop of the too familiar, no longer challenging job. Individual safe havens may also be thought of as the space of one's well-centered or focused self, an internal state out of which one acts and strives in the world. Whether as antidote, protected space out of which developmental work may be undertaken, or centered place, time spent in that state is strengthening, restorative.

This space of renewal and perspective can be reached as well by means that are other than still and quiet. Runners, distance swimmers, musicians, and others "lose" themselves in their respective activities and may be restored in similar ways. What the still and quiet forms offer is a ready availability anytime, anyplace. For instance, I have a friend who regularly enters a space of safe haven while hanging onto a strap on the metro as he commutes to work, arriving refreshed. Although outwardly present in his confined space, jostled by the stopping and starting of the train and the comings and goings of fellow passengers, he empties his mind of deliberate thought or attentiveness, resting and attending instead to what may arise from within. In this sense, the act of moving toward safe haven has much in common with and may in fact be reached by meditation, prayer, focusing, and a host of other processes. What I mean to call attention to here is the space created through these processes, and the feasibility and desirability of attaining that space, rather than any one means of attaining it.

From these examples we can see that safe havens may be created with and for myself while I am in the presence of others or alone. (Safe havens may be created as well with a group of people, as we will discuss later.) We can also see that safe havens may take place in real time; they can occur when I am on-line doing a task (as in the example of the moment of silence before speaking), in the space within my message, in my presence in speaking and my openness to what is unfolding in the setting itself. They may take place in time-outs while at work, such as a few minutes of quiet before a meeting, or off-line when I am not attending to specific tasks. In addition, safe havens are found in significant downtimes such as retreats and sabbaticals (Louis, 1996). Thus safe havens vary along many dimensions, including their location, duration, frequency, focus, means of reaching them, whether others are present, and if so whether the safe haven is an individual or collective experience.

Given all this variability, what then do safe havens have in common? What work is done in creating them, by whatever means and toward whatever ends? Two features link these divergent situations. In creating a safe haven, I very firmly create boundaries to keep out the world, and I remain open to what will unfold within that protected space. I think of an individual safe haven and the way I create it as consisting of two interior movements or inner foci. The first is *an opening up* of a space as if holding back the press of the immediate environment, and the second is *an opening into* an attentiveness, of letting thoughts dissipate to be replaced by a listening state. These interior movements may occur in the blink of an eye or over a considerably longer period of time.

Effects of Individual Safe Havens

What happens when one opens up a space in the midst of the ongoing stream of events and activities, and opens into an attentiveness? For me, it is the convening of a stillness. My breath eases; sometimes

I realize I have been holding it. My emotions may be quieted or stirred, depending on which represents relief from my predominant and now burdensome state. An image, phrase, or question may rise within me that is relevant to the task at hand or that points to a more fundamental task to be addressed. I may hear myself asking for help, seeking guidance, expressing concern for a friend. I am in a reflective pose, but one not focused on a particular problem.

Whether I return from this space energized or calmed, it is with a renewed sense of direction, perspective, and/or the courage to seek further. I have touched "home"—this space of safety within that seems tailor-made to nurture me in my current condition. I venture forth as after a good night's sleep, sometimes with a hearty appetite for challenge, and at other times with my grasp loosened on what now seems less important. While for now my experience is of returning to safe haven periodically, others may carry on their daily activities from within such a place of inner calm.

An Experiential Definition of Individual Safe Havens

My experience of these interior movements is sometimes manifest in my body in a way that communicates clearly to some but not to others. I imagine holding my arms out at shoulder height, curving them slightly to describe the outlines of a very large circle. I am aware of the tension in the outer edge of my arms, especially my upper arms, and focus on that tension. That tension is me holding back the press of my immediate world. Pushing against my arms is the barrage of information, task demands, and deadlines that for the moment I am holding back. I occasionally want to thrust an elbow at some particularly intrusive demand, some deadline rudely pushing against me. For a brief moment, I may have to hold back as well a skeptic's raised eyebrow or cynical question that rises within me. I feel how it feels in the outer part of my arms to hold back the press of the world. This is the work of the first interior movement of creating a safe haven: opening up a space. After a brief time, I find myself attending to what remains, to what is possible in the wide circle my arms describe. With a gentle breath I rest myself in that space and am still a moment. My arms create a nurturing space within the circle they describe. I feel it in the gentle touch on the inner face of my arms. They almost float, so light is their press upon the me held in the circle. In experiencing this space of safety and self-nurturance, I am invited into an openness and attentiveness to a larger life force, my better self, the second interior movement in creating safe havens.

I am sometimes left with a slightly amused appreciation of some irony or unlikely but intrusive connection. It seems as though a coincidence or paradox has been revealed, as if I had found the hidden seam in a Möbius strip as it folds back onto itself; for me, the Möbius strip is the visual representation of the ironic. But regardless of the particular images or awarenesses that may be present with me on returning from my space of safe haven, the level of tension within me has receded. I feel refreshed and have regained a measure of perspective.

Foundations of Individual Safe Havens

Skill in creating safe havens is a matter of cultivating a set of practices, of supporting my intentions with a discipline. In this sense it is very much a matter of forming new habits. In turn, the inclination to create safe havens grows out of particular attitudes we hold toward ourselves without which the effort is empty and seldom sustained or truly enlivening. In cultivating these practices, we may create a sense of safety for ourselves even in the face of what we experience as unsafe environments.

What then are these attitudes? What attitudes about myself provide a basis or rationale out of which I undertake to create safe havens? They are expressed in the following statements.

"I am not alone in this venture. It is not all up to me."

"I recognize that there are greater forces at work though I don't really understand them."

"I am nothing without my good word and am committed to telling what is true for me, even when it is inconvenient or seems risky."

"I am as worthy of my own respect as is any stranger I might meet."

These statements reflect qualities of humility, openness, integrity (that is, honesty with courage), and self-respect. Although they may sound simple, they are quite difficult for many of us to take to heart, and speakers often stumble with emotion when reading them aloud slowly and sincerely. I invite you to try it. Personally, I find it particularly difficult to hold myself as both "only human" and worthy of respect. I find it difficult to stay centered in the notion that it is *not* all up to me, falling prey to what Parker Palmer astutely refers to as functional atheism (1992)—that is, acting out of the belief that it *is* all up to me, I am alone, and it is within my control.

Fundamentally, creating a safe haven evidences cultivation of a particular relationship with myself. For that moment or hour, I hold myself in an internal environment of respectfulness, attentiveness, and kindness. As I enter into a safe haven, I am behaving toward myself in a way that says that "I am worthy and I am [only] human." If this thought is transferred to an interpersonal context, we would recognize it as characteristic of any truly healing relationship.

The safe haven I experience involves another relationship as well. It entails a relationship with a life force beyond my human consciousness or ego. This life force may be seen as the collective unconscious, intuition, the human spirit, the spirit, God. It is again an acknowledgement of some force larger than my will (May, 1983). As I enter the space of safe haven, I open myself to what I may be given from this source, and I may enter seeking insight or guidance on particular matters.

Finally, depending on the situation, a safe haven may involve being in relationship with others as with oneself, in a respectful and kind manner.

The Use of Queries

I have found that the use of a particular form of question, a query, helps me return to center. My use of the term *query* stems from the Quaker tradition (Louis, 1994). In the query form of a question, there is no evaluation. Queries take the form of "Do I (or we) . . . ?" or "Am I . . . ?" rather than "To what extent have I . . . ?" or "How well did I . . . ?" A query is an invitation to be my better self at this time. There is no reference to a particular past or a conditional future. I can use queries to call me back to being whom I wish to be. They are a no-fault form of trying. I imagine having one or more of them affixed to my bathroom mirror to wake up to in the morning. They express my current aspirations for myself, giving me a form in which to express my values without flogging myself.

By way of illustration and as a segue into the next section, here are sample queries particularly relevant to creating conditions that support collective safe havens. They are adapted from an article that focuses on the relevance of Quaker practices for organizational renewal (Louis, 1994). Queries are listed here with supporting queries that describe what I must *do* to support how I want to *be* in my life roles.

- *Am I patient and genuinely present in my dealings with others?* Do I refrain from overscheduling myself, maintaining the boundaries necessary for me to be on time, to be patient and present in my interactions and activities?

- *Am I open to the benefits of a moment of silence to restore myself during and around the edges of a task?* Do I open up the space in my week to be quiet and attentive to an inner voice?

- *Do I invite others to be fully present when I am the convener or facilitator of a group?* Do I monitor the boundaries of our time together, beginning and ending a meeting's work on time? At the beginning of a meeting, do I give people a chance to arrive physically and mentally, to set aside business they have recently left and prepare for the present session? During a session, do I encourage a pace of discussion that allows us to take in and consider what has been said, to listen before forming responses?

- *Do I create opportunities for all to share responsibility for the task?* Do I recognize that shared responsibility may foster skill development, sense of ownership, and connection among us? Do I recognize that a sense of community fosters task accomplishment and the way the task is accomplished influences the sense of community that arises?

- *Do I seek to strengthen the ties among people working together, recognizing that we can tolerate a greater measure of difference on issues in the context of a reservoir of respect and acceptance and that out of difference can come innovation?*

These queries may be most pertinent to managers, assuming as they do that the speaker has a relatively high level of autonomy in dealings with others at work. In contrast, queries for the "managed" and those experiencing deliberate oppression, inadvertent chaos, and/or powerlessness in the workplace might include the following:

- *Do I speak what is true for me even in the face of pressure to do otherwise?* Do I seek guidance from within and beyond myself on how to proceed when I am facing a dilemma? Do I seek the courage to stand publicly behind what I feel led to support?
- *Do I test my assumptions about the unalterability of what I experience as dysfunctional practices on the part of those in power?* Do I support the efforts of those in power to improve their effectiveness as designers and directors of the organization's work?

In summary, two points about queries should be underscored. The key is first to craft queries appropriate to the situation that one is experiencing and second to monitor the match between one's current set of queries and the value-based challenges one experiences at work.

Related Phenomena

What I am describing as a safe haven experience is related to various other phenomena. It can be seen in psychodynamic terms as a type of holding environment (Shapiro and Carr, 1991; Heifetz, 1994), a term that has been adapted from early childhood development research and is used as well to describe therapist-patient relationships. "For a child, the holding environment serves as a containing vessel for the developmental steps, problems, crises, and stresses of growing up. Within the parental hold, the child's growth can be protected and guided" (Heifetz, 1994, p. 104). Heifetz has extended the use of the term to refer to "any relationship in which one party has the power to hold the attention of another party and facilitate adaptive work" (1994, pp. 104–105). In this sense, genuine healing relationships of all kinds represent holding environments. As distinct from the explicitly interpersonal nature of secure base relationships discussed by Kahn, here we are talking about the possibility of holding environments created within an individual rather than between two or more people. The "relationship" is with oneself and perhaps with a larger life force rather than necessarily with another human being. A safe haven at the individual level is one in which I cultivate an attentiveness to an inner voice that I have not consciously created. Gerald May's use (1983) of the term *willingness,* in contrast to *willfulness,* captures well this phenomenon. In willingness, one is open to guidance from a source beyond human will. This may be familiar to some readers as *discernment*, a term used in certain spiritual traditions.

As we shall see in the next section, another critical skill in the new, more turbulent world of work is the capacity to foster and maintain a collective safe haven experience.

Collective Safe Havens

Something akin to the individual safe haven experience is produced on occasion among a group of people working together. Collective safe havens are places where groups of people make and subsequently find the civility to work together in settings bounded enough to hold at bay the turbulence beyond the door. For some, the experience of a collective safe haven may satisfy the need for individual safe haven.

In the face of collective safe haven, a group is enabled in doing its work and members feel individually and collectively enriched and enlivened through their work together. The potential for this lies in the way a group comes together and works together. As we will see, a group's members, designer, and leader influence the extent to which the group's potential as a safe haven is realized and preserved, as do a variety of conditions under which the group convenes.

The work of creating collective safe havens parallels the work we saw at the individual level. In particular, the members of a group create and maintain adequate boundaries between the group and its larger environment, and they maintain an atmosphere within those boundaries of self-respect and respect for one another. The terms *enclave* and *ethos* are useful for identifying and distinguishing among the two tasks: *enclave* calls attention to the external boundary work, and *ethos* points to what goes on within those boundaries. More formally, an enclave is defined as "any distinctly bounded area enclosed within a larger area" (*American Heritage Dictionary*, 1976). Thus, in becoming a safe haven, a group does the work of making itself into an enclave. Ethos refers to the "disposition, character, or attitude peculiar to a group that distinguishes it from other groups; the fundamental values or spirit; mores" (*American Heritage Dictionary*, 1976).

In becoming a collective safe haven, a group cultivates an ethos of respect in the way group members hold the task and treat one another (and themselves) as they do the group's work. Although personal relationships may develop among some members of a group working on a common task, they are not a necessary condition for the emergence of a safe haven experience.

The situation that prompted my interest in safe havens in group contexts is a useful illustration. From this and other case situations, we can see ways in which members, leaders, and arrangers of working groups can help or hinder the creation of collective safe havens.

A Case Illustration

A few years ago at work, I rotated onto a cross-functional committee charged with reviewing the cases of faculty coming up for tenure in the School of Management, preparing reports and recommendations to go to the university-wide committee, and presenting the year's cases to our colleagues in the school. The work of the Appointments, Promotion, and Tenure (APT) committee had strategic import for the school, the departments, and the individuals whose cases we reviewed. The seven of us worked under nearly impossible deadlines in highly political waters to evaluate the work of people in fields foreign to our own. Thus the situation itself reinforced humility and a sense of needing the expertise of one another.

Our first task was to choose someone to chair the committee. We chose George, more because he was willing and experienced than through any more reasoned process. In truth, no one really wanted the job. George's behavior along with conditions under which we came together were pivotal in our developing into an enclave, a well-bounded working group. First, a look at how it felt.

The Feel of a Collective Safe Haven

As we worked together, I noticed that I was checking my usual urgency at the door. My habit of doing several things at once—of keeping one eye on the tasks remaining on my various to-do lists—stopped kicking in after a few meetings. The pressures on us from colleagues with a stake in the outcome stopped at the door as well. With time, I became aware that I and the others were very present to one another and to the task. Terms in which I have made sense of this are that the group had achieved strong psychological boundaries (McCollom, 1990; Alderfer, 1980).

There was as well a sense of the integrity of our time and space together. With only very occasional exceptions, meetings started and ended on time with all members being present for the duration of our meetings. Exceptions were cause for concern, as when one member's mother became quite ill. It was entirely clear who was and who was not a member as well as the basis and duration of membership.

Nor were we interrupted in our work. Our meeting room was in a different building from any of our offices and was separated from the outer hallway by a door, a small corridor, and another door. There were no disruptions or distractions as we worked: no phones rang, no one walked by or came in with messages during our sessions. Thus our temporal and spatial boundaries were strong as well (McCollom, 1990). In this sense, then, we were a distinct and very well-bounded group functioning within a larger group. We were an enclave well sheltered during our deliberations from the turbulence beyond the door.

We met in a conference room with a rectangular table that was neither too big nor too small for the size of our group. Unlike Goldilocks in the bears' house, ours was an environment that fit us. I wonder if we weigh enough the trade-offs entailed in tolerating the inadequate rather than fine-tuning the fit of an environment to its inhabitants.

A gentle deliberateness grew among us, both toward our task and toward one another. We did not rush ourselves or each other. Occasional laughter punctuated our work. There was a lightness but not in the sense of telling jokes or ridiculing anything or anyone—just easy, joined laughter. There was a sense of having an opportunity to reflect together in the midst of doing the task, a sense that it was legitimate to call attention to assumptions, to the larger issues, to broader perspectives. I came to feel a sense of respite when we were in the room together, a sense of expansiveness—as if we had been given additional resources and time.

I am aware as I write this that the phrase "a sense of" is repeated often in this description. And I am hard pressed to replace it with something that as accurately captures what I experienced and how I felt about it. So I will leave what is perhaps an annoyingly repetitive construction in order to convey the message concerning what I experienced there in the room, about the distinctive character of our way of being as a group—its ethos, that is.

Within a few weeks, I came to feel that same sense of expansiveness, almost peacefulness, when I was doing APT work between meetings of the committee. A few weeks after that, I found myself looking—in curiosity at first and later with longing—to see if this pattern of working together was present in other groups in which I was then participating. There was, it seemed to me, a detectable carry-over or residual effect on other contemporaneous work-related settings. I was left to wonder whether there would as well be a carry-forward to future group experiences and what would keep the effect from fading once I had left the group in which it had been fostered.

Organizational Arrangements

Under conditions where a group is well-bounded, there is an opportunity for an ethos to develop in which the group's members experience safety within its boundaries. A set of conditions associated with the charter, setting, membership, and leadership of the APT committee aided us in opening up a secure space in which to work in becoming an enclave and, within that enclave, in establishing the particular ethos of respect, openness, humility, and integrity fundamental to a safe haven experience. An awareness of such conditions can be an aid for those structuring a work group or those serving as members or leaders of it.

First, we came together as a group with some continuing members, who carried pieces of knowledge about the task process, and some new members, including our chair. By virtue of including newcomers, all were not yet socialized into a tradition and could therefore recognize and raise questions about traditional ways of working (Louis, 1980).

It is easier to start fresh than to try to make over an existing group with well-established though not entirely functional habits and culture. Also, there are advantages and disadvantages, depending on the particular task the group faces, of being composed of all new members versus a mix of new and old. The key is having the freedom to negotiate afresh how members will work together. This is unlikely to happen in cases where only a very small minority of the members are new and the leadership is not rotated. At the same time, where a group is to tackle a task with a history, there are clear advantages to having some continuing members who carry intelligence so the group does not have to remap resources, hazards, and so on. It is a delicate balance. In the case of the APT committee, the balance of old and new members, about half and half, seemed about right. The procedure of electing committee members with staggered three-year terms seemed to fit well the needs of this recurring organizational task.

Second, we had the advantage of being composed of people from various parts of the larger organization. No two of us were from the same department. Familiarity can be a curse in high-pressure environments. As Kahn has noted in Chapter Six, regression and projection are particular hazards when we are stressed and work in situations in which we lack adequate caregiving relationships or secure bases. I have observed, however, that even highly stressed individuals given to anxiety tend to "keep it together" in front of organizational strangers, while they may direct regression and projections toward persons in their organizational family groups. But this should be no surprise. Didn't our families put on a good face for company? Why shouldn't we do the same at work when our early family dynamics are triggered under stress in organizational settings?

The implication is that it is easier when members come from different parts of the larger organization to coax a group into good habits. In contrast, when all members of a new group are drawn from the same larger group (as when a committee is formed within a department to handle a task), it is likely that the habits of the larger group will be replicated in the new group. Unless the larger group has good group habits and its members have some consciousness about them, the larger group's bad habits will infect the new group. In addition, we tend to be polite to strangers or when we do not know the local rules or customs. When new, when in doubt, when dealing with strangers or those in higher authority, we tend to take literally such instructions as starting times of meetings. It conveys respect, among other things. In such situations, it is easier to establish the respectful treatment of oneself and one another's time, as well as the integrity of the task and the group's boundaries—all of which is fundamental to the development of a collective safe haven experience.

The third condition under which the APT committee convened that affected the development of a safe haven was that we had a compelling task to do. Our shared perception of the importance of the work itself, its visibility and consequences for the organization and individuals, focused our attention; it put this work higher on our personal priority lists. Fourth, there were some natural boundaries around our work (for example, its confidentiality and the press of the school's eyes on us). These conditions reinforced the sense that our presence at meetings was not optional.

Thus we found ourselves in a group with some newcomers and some oldtimers, all of whom were organizational strangers. And we had a compelling task to do that carried with it some natural organizational boundaries. But what of the leader's role in shaping boundaries and what happens within them?

A Leader's Effect

George set a tone for us out of which a sense of a protected work space, an enclave, emerged. We became aware of ourselves as a group and of the boundaries separating us from the rest of the school. His way of being as well as his behavior toward us and the task shaped considerably the norms of our group, though he never seemed to behave in order to produce a particular effect on us.

For instance, the way George listened seemed to infect us. I wished to transplant it liberally across my other committee settings. He listened as if nothing mattered but the speaker and what he or she was saying at that very moment. Yet his listening style was neither penetrating nor intense. It's funny that I should notice such differences in how I might be listened to. But, then, it's not at all funny—the difference was striking, both in how I felt under this gaze and its effects on members' contributions and emergent relationships. There seemed to me a luxuriousness, an abundance, in his attentiveness to each speaker in turn. When listened to in this way, I came to feel deeply respected. I recall thinking, Is what I am saying *that* important? Perhaps I should listen more deeply to myself! In the moment, I was amused and surprised. Had I been listened to so sloppily elsewhere that there should be such a contrast? I found myself wondering. I became more careful in the time I took. I chose perhaps more carefully when to speak, questioned just a little more deeply why I was about to add something. Not surprisingly, under George's tutelage we came to listen to one another deeply and to respond thoughtfully.

Not only was George very present to the task at hand, but he usually planned agendas for us that could be accomplished in the time allotted. A task was not to be pushed through simply to have it done, and so on occasion we held over an item to be continued at our next meeting. He seemed quite comfortable with that, although I was conditioned to expect a combination of exasperation and failure.

There was a comfortable matter-of-factness in the care George signaled us, through his example, to take about each aspect of the work. On reflection, I realize his very manner was a reminder of how hurried activity, a rushed or too full agenda, or slipshod work can affect the quality of a product.

No doubt a quiet style such as George's is not the only way. But in this situation, the quiet departed substantially from the tone and pace of work in other groupings in the same organization. The difference was appreciated, producing a restful effect. Further, in numerous ways good group facilitation has much in common with the production of a collective safe haven. It is in fact an important condition in producing safe havens.

Diffusion of Leader's Style

All were included, and after a time, quieter members began to contribute more often, including themselves more in the work carried out in the room. People were recognized for their expertise and sought out by others as sounding boards on technical, organizational, and editorial matters. Due credit was given. Help given outside meetings was acknowledged during meetings. Appreciation was generously expressed, though never to flatter or in an obsequious manner.

Impediments to Collective Safe Havens

In contrast with the previous section, here we consider both what may prevent collective safe havens from forming as well as what may undermine them once formed. Unchecked violation of norms of civility and respect destroy the group's essential sense of safety (Peck, 1993; Putnam, 1993). Checked, an occasional violation can in fact strengthen the group. It provides new evidence that feeling safe is warranted. However, even a single unchecked violation is damaging in a well-established group and may disrupt inalterably the development of norms of civility in a newly forming group.

Sarcasm, ridicule, snideness, barbed questions, or exaggerated disbelief in response to another's comments represent such violations. Evidence that norms of civility and respect have been violated are visible and audible in the reflexive in-breath of shock, the turned-away faces (as if having been slapped), the downturned eyes around the table, even an occasional flushing of the one toward whom the behavior was directed and in some cases among others present. These signal a turning point in the group's life and a testing ground for the leader. Will we be protected? Have we the capacity to protect ourselves?

Public courage (McDermott, 1992) is required to gently but firmly stop the process and respond to the violation. For example, it may be appropriate to take the floor by asking for a moment to collect oneself before speaking. It is likely others present could use a moment to regain their balance as well. Anyone in the room who was aware of the violation and was psychologically present (Kahn, 1992) is likely to also have experienced some degree of empathic shame at the remark or behavior—as a witness or in kinship with the person to whom it was directed. After a silence, the one who stopped the process must question the appropriateness of the offending behavior and do so in a way that does not provoke defensiveness but rather invites the offender to redress the error, apologize if warranted, and be made whole again as a member of the group. Adult-to-adult confrontation with concern for group process, not parent-child scolding, is called for here. If the leader fails to act on the group's behalf, another member needs to step in. Where no one does, surely the group's capacities for candor, caring, and trust have been diminished, for they are the products of the safety produced in collective safe havens.

Cynicism unchecked, particularly in a newly forming group, drives potentially available members to go underground emotionally. It sends the signal that noncynics are chumps to continue believing what is clearly unrealistic, impossible, passé, or in some other way naïve. Cynicism checked by another member or the leader and curtailed by the offending member can again strengthen a group. In a sense, the group's potential as a safe haven is formed out of the hopefulness and faith its members advance the group; the cynic pours cold water on the sparks of hope.

Oppression by a leader or other dominant member has similar effects. Unchecked oppression represents a condition under which, over time, the lights go out in members' eyes. Hope dies. Initiative and voice are squelched. Adolescent energies erupt at breaks from the tyrant's presence. Lethargy or the fomenting of rebellion replaces creative energy focused on the group's task. Wresting the group from oppression leads to temporary euphoria, but it takes much energy to reconquer the territory from counter-dependence to maturity. Any new leader rising to power in the aftermath of such rebellion would be wise to help the group incorporate and affirm positive features of the former oppressor or risk having the group forever hamstrung by its history with this authority. The parallel to individual development during adolescence should be obvious.

The physical environment represents an impediment if it occasions interruptions and disruptions or in other ways is not appropriate to the group's needs. Holding meetings in areas where people walk by or conversations can be overheard is distracting and signals that our conversations in the group are not privileged or private. Having a small group meet in a large room—particularly if the seating configuration pushes people to speak to one another across a large distance—generates anxiety rather than containing it. Add to that a high-stress context, membership of those present in the same organizational family, a large hole in the middle of the room around which people sit, into which they speak, and across which they look at one another, and you have the ingredients for disaster, not a safe haven. Anxiety unchecked precipitates regression and projections, particularly among members of the same organizational family.

A paternalistic style on the part of a convener or leader represents an impediment to the formation of a safe haven. Paternalism fosters dependence rather than interdependence. In addition, it is usually associated with a selective rather than open flow of information among members, further undermining the development of a sense of safety.

Similarly, the presence of exclusive subgroups—groupings where some but not all members from the larger group have had a chance to select into the smaller group—can syphon off energy and commitment to the larger group and its collective task. For instance, when individuals meet their interpersonal needs in and form attachments to a subgroup, they are less likely to expend energy (and take risks) in the larger group to maintain the norms of civility fundamental to the production of a collective safe haven. Members of the subgroup may be more tolerant of damaging behavior in the larger group. There may be more gossip outside of meetings of the larger group but less real-time involvement in shaping and maintaining a respectful, attentive ethos during meetings of the whole. Thus a number of conditions and events can undermine the maintenance of collective safe haven. How then can human resource professionals support individuals and collectives in creating and harnessing the benefits of safe havens at work?

Implications for Human Resource Professionals

What we have seen is that the new world of work is an inherently (too) stressful environment. It is one in which energy, perspective, and meaning take a beating in the daily crush of our schedules and commitments. I have suggested that among the skills professionals will need to thrive in these environments is the self-awareness to sense when they need to refresh themselves and the ability to create safe havens in which to do so. By unpacking moments from my own experience, I have tried to let the reader see one set of ways in which this may be done. There is no magic in my particular process. What matters is attending to your own needs and creating processes that work for you. It will help if we talk with one another about what works for us and if we make it legitimate not only to list our obligations but also to share the toll they take. From that base, we may be able to create more easily and more frequently restorative spaces around the edges of work. We may as well be able to create within task settings, individually and collectively, adequately bounded civil and hospitable settings in which the work gets done and along the way we regain perspective, renew our energies, and can once again feel flowing through us a sense of meaning and purpose in our professional work.

The role of the human resource professional in this process is at least three-fold. First, HR professionals can help facilitate a general awareness of the conditions within which we work. They can help us come to alternative and more useful interpretations of our work environments. In particular, they may help us learn from those in settings in which stress and turbulence is not new. For instance, social workers who treat burnout, stress, and ambiguity as a normal part of the job find it easier to act to take care of themselves when they feel the warning signs of stress (Meyerson, 1994).

Normalizing the experience—that is, coming to appreciate we are not alone in experiencing a shared situation in a particular way (for instance, as abusive)—is an important beginning as it may help us channel energies toward that which we can do something about rather than trying to tame a river. Out of normalizing can come conversation in which commiseration gives way to sharing coping strategies.

Second, HR professionals can help us learn to read ourselves, to listen more closely to our own needs so that we can become sensitive to the need to move into a safe haven. From there we may be encouraged not to wait until we are near burnout, but may engage in preventive work. Along with this, HR professionals can expose people to a variety of ways to find and make safe havens. Some Japanese firms provide instruction in using time away from work and are locking out employees to make them take that time. Their experiences might be a good resource.

A third avenue for HR professionals is to help prepare people to participate in working groups and teams. That preparation should entail training for membership. Included in this preparation should be inculcation of an appreciation (perhaps through work with case examples), supported with skill practice and coaching in a set of competencies. These include the following:

Recognizing what contributes to and what impedes the formation and maintenance of adequate boundaries

Recognizing the impact of member behaviors on the ethos of the group, what enhances and what undermines the civility and safety of a group

Practice designing and intervening in groups to structure and restore boundaries

Practice in sowing an ethos of civility and intervening with members to restore it

Adults can learn much by watching with focused attention noteworthy behaviors of individuals in action. This is true whether the domain of learning is managerial, technical, interpersonal, and so on. The person who is masterful at running a meeting is a resource to all who witness her performance, if the witnesses care to notice and reflect on the skilled performance before them. What it takes is focused attention, a particular kind of noticing. The HR professional can help us harness such adult learning processes, enhancing the learning resources available throughout work settings.

May we come to attend with self-respect and humility to our needs for a moment of quiet amidst the fray. That respectful and humble attending is the foundation out of which safe havens can be developed. May we learn to create trustworthy pockets of calm, whether as individuals or members of groups, out of which we may be restored in energy and perspective, rediscovering the meaning a task has for us and a deeper connectedness to ourselves, to one another, and to a larger life force. Thus we may reap the benefits of creating safe havens at work.

References

Alderfer, C. P. (1980). Consulting to underbounded systems. In C. P. Alderfer & C. L. Cooper (Eds.), *Advances in experiential social processes* (Vol. 2, pp. 267–295). New York: Wiley.

American Heritage Dictionary. (1976). Boston: Houghton Mifflin.

Bennis, W. G., & Slater, P. (1968). *The temporary society.* New York: Harper-Business.

Hammer, M., & Champy, J. (1993). *Reengineering the corporation: A manifesto for business revolution.* New York: HarperCollins.

Handy, C. (1989). *The age of unreason.* Boston: Harvard Business School Press.

Heifetz, R. A. (1994). *Leadership without easy answers.* Cambridge, MA: Harvard University Press.

Kahn, W. A. (1992). To be fully there: Psychological presence at work. *Human Relations, 45*(4), 321–349.

Kanter, R. M. (1989). *When giants learn to dance.* New York: Simon & Schuster.

Louis, M. R. (1980). Surprise and sense-making: What newcomers experience in entering unfamiliar organizational settings. *Administrative Science Quarterly, 25,* 226–251.

Louis, M. R. (1994). In the manner of Friends: Learnings from Quaker practice for organizational renewal. *Journal of Organizational Change Management, 7*(1), 42–60.

Louis, M. R. (1996). A sabbatical journey: Toward personal and professional renewal. In P. Frost & S. Jackson (Eds.), *Rhythms of academic life.* Newbury Park, CA: Sage.

May, G. G. (1983). *Will and spirit: A contemplative psychology.* New York: HarperCollins.

McCollom, M. (1990). Group formation: Boundaries, leadership, and culture. In J. Gillette & M. McCollom (Eds.), *Groups in context: A new perspective on group dynamics.* Reading, MA: Addison-Wesley, 34–48.

McDermott, B. (1992). Discussed in a course on the spiritual exercises of St. Ignatius, Weston School of Theology, Cambridge, MA.

Meyerson, D. E. (1994). Interpretations of stress in institutions: The cultural production of ambiguity and burnout. *Administrative Science Quarterly, 39,* 628–653.

Mirvis, P. H., & Hall, D. T. (1994). Psychological success and the boundaryless career. *Journal of Organizational Behavior, 15,* 365–380.

Palmer, P. J. (1992). Leading from within: Reflections on spirituality and leadership. In J. Conger (Ed.), *Learning to lead.* San Francisco: Jossey-Bass.

Peck, S. (1993). *A world waiting to be born.* New York: Bantam Books.

Putnam, R. D. (1993). *Making democracy work: Civic traditions in modern Italy.* Princeton, NJ: Princeton University Press.

Shapiro, E. R., & Carr, A. W. (1991). *Lost in familiar places.* New Haven, CT: Yale University Press.

Vaill, P. B. (1989). *Managing as a performing art: New ideas for a world of chaotic change.* San Francisco: Jossey-Bass.

Chapter Ten

Experience Is the Best Teacher, If You Can Learn from It

Real-Time Reflection and Development

Kent W. Seibert

Steve Fuller works in sales for a large consumer products manufacturer. His company, SofTouch, is a leading producer of skin care products. As a regional sales manager, Steve has received several awards for his successful sales efforts in this highly competitive industry. Based on his previous track record of success, Steve was transferred to the company's new venture start-up division, which is informally called SOP (SofTouch Oral Products). SOP's mission is to develop and sell products in a brand new area for SofTouch: oral hygiene. The first new product, an all-natural toothpaste, has been developed and test marketed with success. As part of SofTouch's assignment management program, Steve was asked to join SOP for a two-year developmental assignment as its national sales director. This assignment provides Steve with several learning opportunities: understanding a new product, creating a national sales force from scratch, and helping build SOP from an idea to a viable new division of SofTouch.

To learn as much as he can from this experience, Steve needs to be reflective. According to conventional views of reflection, Steve will only do some reflecting if he is encouraged to by a career practitioner. This is best accomplished by scheduling some time at the conclusion of Steve's two years (and perhaps once during the assignment) when Steve can be guided through a formal review of the experience, including identifying important lessons learned. Although there is clear value in this "after-the-fact" review of experience, it is no longer adequate in the world of the new career contract.

Pausing only occasionally for serious reflection is a dangerous way to approach the world of work today. The days when it was acceptable or even desirable to "check your brain at the door" of your employer have evaporated in the heat produced by the emergence of the new career contract. As Victoria Marsick (1990, p. 23) has noted, "It used to be that businesses thrived on the unexamined, almost mindless repetition of a proven formula. Today, workers at all levels are called upon to think differently and more deeply about themselves, their work, and their relationship to the organization." The turbulent, uncertain world of the new career contract demands no less.

The Need for Mindful, Reflective Learning

The increasing need to engage oneself mentally in one's work is nowhere more important than in the area of learning and development. While conscious cognition has always been important to career learning and development, today it is indispensable. If there will be any security in the new contract, it will come from confidence in one's ability to regularly grow and change by learning new things. What those new "things" are will be less important than the ability to learn them because the things will change but the need to learn will remain constant.

What will this learning and development look like? Since it will have to be responsive to ongoing change, it will need to transcend traditional education and training approaches. While such formal approaches are usually well designed and well intentioned, they also tend to be inflexible and unresponsive. Created to serve the stable world of the past, they are less useful in the "nanosecond nineties" (Peters, 1992). In contrast, development strategies that build on naturally occurring work experiences are more flexible and responsive and thus are better suited to current conditions (Seibert, Hall, and Kram, 1995). Learning from experience is the cornerstone of such strategies.

It is axiomatic that we learn from experience . . . or is it? Contrary to popular belief, we do *not* learn directly from experience. Experience merely provides raw data. This data is rich with potential for learning, but it is not the learning. It is only after we attribute meaning to an experience—that is, when we interpret the raw data of the experience—that learning can result. Thus we learn from the meaning we give to experience, not from experience itself, and we give meaning to experience by reflecting on it (Kolb, 1984; Mezirow, 1991).

Reflection has long been integral to discussions of experiential learning. It is just now beginning to be recognized by companies such as AT&T and PepsiCo as a "new" skill for operating in today's fast-moving economy (Sherman, 1994). Put simply, as it is defined here, reflection involves deciding what is happening in an experience, what it means, and what to do about it. This includes reflecting about oneself as well as others and their needs. Indeed, the ability to see beyond oneself and to become aware of how one can serve others is becoming increasingly important.

It is through reflection that learning is extracted from experience—be that a particularly challenging assignment or a stimulating relationship with a mentor or peer. Relationships are uniquely related to reflection. On the one hand, they are a rich source of raw data for reflection, as in the case of having a particularly effective boss one seeks to emulate or even a poor boss one reflects on in order to learn how not to behave. On the other hand, relationships also serve as a vehicle through which a person engages in reflection. A relationship based on interdependence, mutuality, and reciprocity (see Chapter Four, this volume) is ripe for fruitful reflection. Whether the relationship is with a formal coach or a trusted colleague or even with a friend or spouse (see Chapter Seven, this volume), articulating one's thoughts to someone else is a powerful means of reflection.

Despite the centrality of reflection to learning from experience, negative perceptions of it are common. It is often viewed as a form of contemplation, well suited to a monk or scholar but impractical if not irrelevant to a manager or professional. Again quoting Marsick (1990, p. 23), "Workplaces are not typically associated with reflection or critical self-reflection, ideas that are often considered 'soft' and somewhat irrelevant to the hard-nosed, bottom-line, results-oriented world of business. In the workplace, reflection of any type has been considered a luxury, something that takes place only in the ivory towers of academe, and by its very nature somewhat unrelated to 'real life.' "

The discussion of reflection presented in this chapter is based on the preliminary findings of an exploratory study of managerial reflection at a major manufacturing firm (Seibert, 1996). It will be shown that much of common thinking about the role of reflection in the workplace is based on an overly narrow and thus limiting view of what reflection actually entails. An alternative perspective of reflection presented here will demonstrate the usefulness of reflection to managing careers in the new contract. Before turning to this perspective, I will review current views of reflection.

Existing Views of Reflection in Theory and Practice

The most well-developed theoretical perspectives of reflection are summarized in Exhibit 10.1. All these theoretical perspectives share in common the belief that reflection is a mental activity involving gathering and then processing data from an experience in order to make sense of it and decide what to do with it.

In the realm of practice, reflection is just now beginning to be incorporated into planned development activities in business. Some management development programs have begun to include reflection as an explicit objective (Marsick, 1990; Sherman, 1994). Robinson and Wick's description (1992) of programs designed to facilitate managers' on-the-job learning at two companies illustrates how reflection is getting incorporated into formal development efforts. According to these researchers, the three basic elements of learning from experience are planning prior to the experience, action learning during the experience, and structured reflection opportunities ("time-outs") after the experience. The guiding principle for programs such as these is that experience provides only the *opportunity* for learning to occur. In order for learning to actually happen, the manager must extract from experience the lessons

**Exhibit 10.1. Summary of Major
Theoretical Views of Reflection.**

Lewin (1951)	*Reflection:* Reinforces learned behavior and leads to new or higher-level abstractions
Kolb (1984)	*Reflective Observation:* Careful observation and description to understand situations and their meaning
Mezirow (1991)	*Content Reflection:* Thinking about what one perceives, feels, thinks, or does. *Process Reflection:* Thinking about how one goes about perceiving, feeling, thinking, or doing *Premise Reflection:* Becoming aware of and then critiquing the meaning one gives to experiences
Marsick (1988)	*Reflectivity:* Thinking directed at understanding oneself
Schön (1987, 1983)	*Reflection-in-Action:* Thinking about what one is doing while one is doing it *Reflection-on-Action:* Thinking back on an experience after the fact

it provides. Guiding managers through a formal, structured process of reflection is presented as the primary way to do this. This is generally done by "creating a resting place" for learners (Boyd and Fales, 1983, p. 10) in order to "step back and ponder one's experience " (Hutchings and Wutzdorff, 1988, p. 15). In practice, then, reflection tends to get framed rather narrowly as identifying "lessons learned" or as "pondering or reviewing" an experience in one's mind after the fact.

To date, the richness of reflection as a theoretical construct has been diluted in its application to managerial learning. Also, the use of words like *resting place* and *pondering* to describe reflection reinforce the perception that it is a contemplative activity far removed from the real demands of organizational life. The characteristics of this commonly held view of reflection are summarized in the left-hand column of Exhibit 10.2. The right-hand column illustrates each characteristic by presenting the thoughts of a hypo-

Exhibit 10.2. The Conventional View of Reflection.

Characteristic	The Career Practitioner's View
Passive	"There must be something we can do to get people to sit still long enough to do some thinking."
Contrived	"Let's design a reflection workshop."
After the Fact	"We'll schedule people to attend the month after their assignment has ended."
Time Consuming	"It'll take at least two hours."
Narrow	"We'll have people list the new job tasks they can perform."
Context Independent	"We'll make sure there are no interruptions by doing this off-site."

thetical career practitioner who is considering incorporating a formal approach to reflection in her organization's assignment management system. Designing a two-hour, off-site workshop and requiring people to attend exemplifies this view. It is based on the assumption that managers will reflect only if they are forced to. This positions reflection as a contrived activity the responsibility for which lies with the career practitioner.

The picture of reflection painted by the characteristics listed in Exhibit 10.2 is based on the way reflection is typically translated into practice in the business world by those working to promote learning from experience. Some aspects of the picture are commendable (such as getting people to stop for a moment after an experience to identify key learnings). But overall, the picture is a limiting one, especially in the dynamic world of the new career contract.

An Alternative View: Real-Time Reflection

If the new career contract requires learning from experience and if that requires reflection, then what type of reflection is most conducive to learning within the climate of the new contract? Based on research with managers in the competitive consumer products industry (Seibert, 1996), I believe "real-time" reflection is an

answer. Exhibit 10.3 (left-hand column) shows how the characteristics of real-time reflection correspond to the conventional view
of reflection. Exhibit 10.3 also continues the example begun in
Exhibit 10.2, except that now the thoughts of a hypothetical person undergoing a developmental job experience are used to illustrate real-time reflection.

By returning to Steve Fuller, who was introduced at the beginning of this chapter, we can see how a manager in a challenging
learning situation naturally engages in reflection in real time.

Real-time reflection is Steve's responsibility, not some career
practitioner's. True, to be most effective he will need the input and
support of other people, but it will be driven by Steve himself. It
begins naturally the moment Steve starts his new job. Confronted
with a host of things with which he is unfamiliar, he cannot help
but begin to reflect on them. He responds in the experience by
forming in his mind a host of questions intended to help him get
a grasp of the situation (and on another level he may also begin to
question why he let himself get into this situation in the first place!).
In Steve's case, these can be questions such as, who will be the
ultimate consumer of natural toothpaste? Can these consumers be
reached through the same distribution channels we currently use
for our skin care products?

To answer questions such as these, Steve did a lot of traveling
his first few months on the job. He visited as many markets and as
many customers (drugstores and so on) as he could. He viewed
what he was doing as getting the "m.o." of various markets. Much
of the thinking he did here was stimulated by interactions with
other people. He met with store managers to understand their
pricing policies, how their stores were laid out, and how toothpaste
was displayed. With these new insights, he would return to head-
quarters to share the information with his boss and with SOP's two
marketing specialists. These discussions, including occasional dis-
agreements, eventually sharpened Steve's understanding of the key
issues involved in marketing a new type of toothpaste.

Steve found that some of his best reflecting was done in the
context of meetings. Having to present and then defend his ideas
to others forced him to think issues through thoroughly before
going into a meeting. Being required to write trip reports also pro-

Exhibit 10.3. Current Reality: Real-Time Reflection.

Characteristic	The Developing Person's View
Active	"This experience is mentally stimulating. What's the most productive way to do that thinking?"
Natural	"I can't help but ask, what's going on here? What does it all mean?"
During the Experience	"How can I reflect throughout this experience to identify key issues and learning opportunities?"
Brief	"What 'windows of opportunity' are there in my workday to reflect? While I'm waiting for a meeting to begin?"
Broad	"What am I learning about this job, this organization, my co-workers, myself? How do I feel about all this?"
Context Connected	"What regular work activities promote reflecting? Writing progress reports? Preparing presentations?"

vided a natural opportunity to reflect on critical issues identified in the field. These reports were usually written on the flight home. Since he traveled so much, his days in the office were often filled with back-to-back meetings. This left little free time to mentally process the results of meetings. Steve found that the brief time he spent walking from one meeting to the next could be used productively to identify and catalogue key issues.

Steve quickly found that to be successful in his new role required that he learn not just the technical aspects of his job, such as the major competitors in various markets, but also a host of non-technical things as well. As a venture start-up, SOP had a very different culture than SofTouch. Things were more informal and people were expected to take risks, which was discouraged at Sof-Touch. Reflecting on this led Steve to also reflect on himself as he became aware of his own discomfort with ambiguous, high-risk situations. This broad reflection also included Steve's reflecting on his boss, who was hired from outside SofTouch, and on the two marketers. Their styles were more confrontational than what Steve was used to. He respected their ability to speak their minds, but he still had not figured out when they were giving just a personal opinion versus offering their professional judgment.

Steve's story, which is based on the experiences of an actual manager faced with a similar challenge, illustrates most of the characteristics of real-time reflection. As Steve demonstrates, to engage in real-time reflection is to actively process new experiences on the fly. It is to confront challenge with a spirit of enthusiastic inquiry.

Characteristics of Real-Time Reflection

Although reflection can be thought of as the opposite of the action component of learning from experience, it is not a passive activity but rather an active mental process. The current dynamic business environment is best responded to with natural learning strategies (such as developmental job assignments), which themselves are best accomplished through active reflection. Akin to "mindfulness" (Langer, 1989), this type of reflection refers to a state of conscious involvement with experience. This requires deliberately bringing one's thinking to the level of conscious awareness. It means approaching learning situations not only with a desire to "get your hands around the situation" but also with an equally strong desire to "get your head into the situation." This type of reflection was common among the managers I interviewed.

In this environment, reflection becomes a natural, adaptive response. Instead of being seen as something that is alien to the action orientation of managers, thus requiring contrived activities in order to produce it, reflection is viewed as the normal response to managing ongoing turbulence and change through continuous learning. What is different today is that success is accomplished not by mastering the routine (for example, mass production), which once mastered can be managed mindlessly. Instead, success comes by leveraging the novel (for example, finding new applications for evolving technologies), which requires ongoing, mindful learning.

As technology and society continue to change at a faster and faster pace, so reflection cannot occur only retrospectively at the conclusion of learning experiences; rather it needs to happen during the experience. If the conventional view of reflection emphasizes debriefing at the conclusion of an experience, real-time reflection stresses "inbriefing" throughout a learning experience. Thus the reflection happens in real time, in the midst of the experience, while it is possible for the thinking to have an immediate impact on the experience. Although debriefing is still seen as necessary and important, alone it is inadequate because it ignores the opportunity for midcourse learning and adjustment. In contrast to a one-time review of an experience, inbriefing involves continuous review throughout the experience.

This type of reflection does not and indeed cannot take large amounts of time; it is ongoing and highly concentrated. When reflection becomes a mental discipline occurring naturally throughout an experience, it is able to quickly focus on what is important because relevant data have been collected and processed all along.

However, just because real-time reflection is brief in duration does not mean it is superficial. On the contrary, it is broad. The rationalistic, task orientation of the conventional approach to promoting reflection means that thinking is focused narrowly on job tasks, duties, and responsibilities. Real-time reflection focuses thinking as broadly as possible. Thus interpersonal relationships, the things in the organization that help or hinder job performance, one's own feelings, and technical tasks themselves all become legitimate fodder for reflection. Furthermore, there is recognition that emotions play an important role in reflecting on learning experiences. People who reflect in real time understand that they bring all of themselves—their hearts as well as their minds—to their efforts to ascribe meaning to their experiences.

Real-time reflection not only looks at individuals holistically but also sees them as connected to a larger organizational system in important ways. An accurate view of reflection thus recognizes its connection to context. The current climate of most organizations exerts certain pressures that can make it difficult for people in learning situations to think. This creates the conventional view that meaningful reflection can only occur by separating people from their normal work environments. However, this same environment also provides conditions that are conducive to reflection. Real-time reflection seeks to capitalize on those conditions. The need to regularly respond to change, to function more as a member of a team, and to manage oneself all encourage reflection *if* a person recognizes the need for increased cognitive engagement at work as an opportunity to reflect.

According to a real-time perspective, reflection is most productive when used to ride the winds of change rather than to seek shelter from them. In fact, not only does a real-time view recognize the importance of organizational context to reflection but it acknowledges that reflection transcends traditional organizational boundaries as well. Thus it is often away from work, when commuting, exercising, conversing with family and friends, that some of the most meaningful reflection happens. This was especially true for the managers I studied (Seibert, 1996).

This alternative picture of reflection recaptures some of the richness of reflection as it has been presented as a theoretical construct. It also transcends existing theoretical notions by suggesting several additional dimensions of reflection. Most importantly, it relates reflection to the world of the new career contract and shows the importance of real-time reflection to operating in that world.

It is not coincidental that each characteristic of real-time reflection in Exhibit 10.3 is illustrated by a question. In a world of constant change, the ability to ask good questions is at least as important as the ability to produce answers. Real-time reflection at its core is a process of intentional inquiry. It is also more than coincidence that real-time reflection is best illustrated by the thoughts of a person experiencing a developmental challenge rather than those of career practitioners. Practitioners have a role to play in facilitating real-time reflection in the environment of the new contract, but real-time reflection ultimately emanates directly from the learner (Seibert, 1996).

One characteristic of real-time reflection is especially critical for success in the new contract. The idea that one should reflect broadly, particularly that self-reflection is essential, deserves further attention.

Self-Reflection and Other-Reflection

The foundation of self-understanding is holding an accurate perception of oneself. This is the premise of the recent emphasis on

360-degree feedback, which provides developmental feedback to people based on observations of their superiors, peers, and subordinates (O'Reilly, 1994). When this form of reflection is applied to the self, it is often thought of as the act of viewing oneself in a mirror, of seeing one's reflection. This connotation probably comes from the Latin root for reflection, *reflectere,* which means to bend back. If accurate perception is the beginning of self-understanding, then the idea of the need to get a clear picture of oneself through a mirror is a useful one. Indeed, accurate self-perception is foundational to meta-learning—learning how to learn—which is seen as an essential response to living with constant change (Hall, 1986).

Of course, simply gaining a clear picture of oneself in a mirror is a first step. But it then becomes necessary to compare that image with some external standard. One can only determine the acceptability of one's image by comparing it to something beyond oneself. In the old career contract, the external standard was set by the organization with which one had a long-term commitment. Whether defined by a set of developmental competencies or expressed implicitly through norms about the kinds of managers that "get ahead," the organization set the standard for making comparisons. As the long-term commitment between employers and employees is severed, the organization is no longer the source of the external standard. What then becomes the new source of the standard?

Without an external standard, self-reflection could degenerate into narcissism. The danger is in becoming self- absorbed and in searching for security entirely within oneself. While self-understanding is necessary, it is not sufficient for success in the world of the new contract. An alternative source of the standard is proposed here: the needs of other people. This requires a commitment to other-directedness. Paradoxically, security in the new contract comes from worrying less about oneself and more about the needs of others.

This will not be a natural response for most people. The natural response to the demands, if not threats, of the new career contract is to become defensive and to turn inward. However, this reaction is ultimately self-defeating. The turtle that hunkers down in its shell may be protected, but it is also paralyzed. Investing oneself in identifying others' needs and then positioning oneself to be able to meet those needs can provide an ongoing sense of security because there are always unmet needs requiring attention. Thus others' needs become our opportunities. In addition to examining one's own image in the mirror, then, it is necessary to look *through* the mirror, as one looks through a window, to the world beyond oneself with all its attendant needs. This enables one to focus one's sight not only inward through self-reflection but also outward through other-reflection.

The Career as Service

At the heart of other-reflection as it relates to the new contract is the notion of the career as service. This idea certainly contrasts with the Machiavellian atmosphere resulting from the upward mobility focus of the old career contract. Even though the notion of career as service may appear somewhat radical today, it is not a new idea. The Latin word *vocatio* (the root of *vocation*) means to be summoned or called to a particular type of work, especially to religious service. In centuries past, when a distinction was generally not made between the sacred and the secular, most people, even those not engaged full-time in religious service, viewed their work as a form of service. Over time, the association of *vocation* with a call to service has faded so that the word today is defined as an occupation or profession. In many circles, the word *career* rather than *vocation* has come to be more commonly associated with people's work lives. The word *career,* originally meaning a path or course and implying rapid forward movement, is even further removed from the idea of work as service. Perhaps the time has come to revisit earlier conceptions of work.

Interestingly, such reviews are being made today in the name of adaptation to the future. This is evident in the current emphasis on both customer service and servant leadership. From *In Search of Excellence*'s (Peters and Waterman, 1982) core principle of staying "close to the customer" to the total customer satisfaction of total quality management (Sashkin and Kiser, 1993) to the succeeding through service to others of *Samurai Selling* (Laughlin, Sage, and Bockmon, 1993), business has recognized that a key to profitability is not to fool customers into buying but to provide them with products that meet genuine needs and to build lasting relationships by providing top-notch service. In short, the advice is to construct one's relationship with customers on the cornerstone of service. In addition, in arguing for "service over self-interest," Block (1993) has combined customer service with leadership. He claims that in an organization structured according to stewardship rather than patriarchy, service is everything. Customers are served by workers who in turn are served by bosses.

Service is best provided in the context of a relationship. It is impossible to serve and remain independent of others. Meaningful service is based upon interdependence. This principle is effectively demonstrated in Chapter Six, this volume.

Examples of Integrating Self- and Other-Reflection

The goal of self-reflection is to obtain an accurate perception of myself. The goal of other-reflection is to develop a clear picture of others' needs in order to assess how I could serve in meeting those needs. Self-reflection leads to self-knowledge. Other-reflection leads to service. Both are central elements for operating within the new career contract. For many people, framing reflection as helping one know oneself and serve others produces an image of workers in a local homeless shelter. That image is valid but incomplete. The high-pressure world of business also provides ample examples. Consider the following. Marc Andreessen recognized the help nontechnical people need to navigate the Internet (Losee, 1994). Drawing on his own considerable computer know-how, he created the Mosaic software and offered it free on the Internet. Within a year, a million people were using it, and Andreessen helped found a software start-up.

Leveraging self- and other-reflection into viable career options does not mean one has to start one's own business. Michael Iem has found plenty of needs requiring attention during his tenure at Tandem Computers (Richman, 1994). Shortly after joining the company as a junior staff analyst, he became aware of the market trend away from mainframe computers to networks that linked workstations and personal computers. Iem defined a need that, transcending individual needs, applied to the company itself: unless Tandem responded to the trend, its products would become obsolete. He then drew on his persuasive and industrial engineering skills to address the need. He had to convince Tandem managers that their old emphasis on mainframes was no longer appropriate and then develop a system using new technology. After demonstrating that his new system would actually work, he spent four years showing it off to customers and company sales personnel before the new network applications were fully accepted. Although he has no formal job title and no office at Tandem, he has developed a reputation as an invaluable problem solver, or "need fulfiller," to use a term consistent with other-reflection.

Despite these examples, identifying and meeting others' needs does not, of course, require an aptitude for high-tech wizardry. The key is to determine how something one enjoys and does well can be done in the service of others, as Christopher Birch has done (Smith, 1994). Recognizing that more than just the very affluent would like to be able to enjoy occasional sailboat cruising, Birch came up with the idea of a floating time-share. Combining experience repairing pleasure craft with a degree in geography, he now sells customers a boat for eight blocks of time of three consecutive days in the summer out of Boston harbor, plus a week in the Bahamas in the winter. Clearly, the individuals just described have a keen awareness of their own interests and capabilities. But they also demonstrate an ability to move beyond themselves and discover others' needs that they have the capability of fulfilling. In matching their capabilities to others' needs, they are engaging in self- and other-reflection of the broadest degree. Furthermore, in reflecting in this real-time way, they are responding adaptively to the requirements of the new career contract.

Practical Recommendations

The career as service perspective of the new contract implies that the role of career practitioners should be to serve others by identifying and meeting their needs. This is not that different in principle from the way many career practitioners currently view their role. But it can be quite different in practice if it results in meeting people's needs where the people actually are, which is in the midst of the current turbulence and uncertainty—rather than through inflexible, packaged programs. In terms of supporting learning, this means giving primary attention to supporting real-time reflection. How does one do this? Specifically, career practitioners should encourage managers to do the following:

- *Embrace intentional inquiry.* Being curious and regularly asking questions is the heart of reflection. Do not be content with obvious explanations. Ask why repeatedly to try to get at core causes. Make few assumptions and test the validity of those you do make. Explore how and why you are feeling the way you are. Examine the way your values and beliefs affect not only the answers you arrive at but the questions you ask. Do not take things for granted. You asked deep questions as a child. Recapture that desire to really know.

- *Recognize and harness natural thinking abilities.* As mentioned earlier in this chapter, it is hard not to be actively engaged mentally in work in today's business climate. Stop and take notice of when you reflect naturally. Explore what stimulates your most productive thinking. Perhaps it is when you encounter something that takes you by surprise or when you are faced with a particularly sticky problem. Capitalize on those times when you are already thinking to push your thinking deeper. In short, integrate deliberate reflection into your normal thought process.

- *Inbrief.* To wait to reflect after significant experiences is to miss important learning. Equally as important as debriefing after the fact is reflecting regularly throughout. This is especially important in dynamic environments where things change often and quickly become out of date. To do this, build reflection into regular job duties such as writing progress reports or performance reviews.

- *Identify brief windows of opportunity for reflection.* The day is full of these both at and away from work: in the shower, while doing housework, commuting and traveling, during lunch, when kept waiting (on the phone, for a meeting, in an airport), as well as in many unproductive meetings. All of us can do more than one thing at once. The energy meaningful reflection requires is most easily expended when you are engaged in a relatively mindless activity like driving or mowing the lawn.

- *Build relationships with "reflectors."* A core theme of this book is a relational approach to careers. Reflection often happens best in a relationship with a reflector, someone to whom you can talk openly about your experiences. The important role peers and coaches can play in facilitating reflection has recently been documented

(Daudelin, 1994). In order to make our ideas explicit to someone else, we are forced to make them explicit to ourselves. This is one key advantage of reflecting in relationships, as is the emotional support relationships provide, which is crucial for working through the tough, emotionally laden issues that are a part of most challenging developmental experiences. Having reflectors and being one yourself for other people are powerful tools for supporting real-time reflection. (This is also another example of the role of colearner relationships [Chapter Six, this volume] in fostering career development.)

Career practitioners should also work to promote conditions in their organization that enable real-time reflection. This can be done by helping the organization to do the following:

- *Reject the myth that we "learn from experience" and accept the reality that we "learn by reflecting on experience."* Simply understanding and acting on this truth can be extremely powerful for unleashing the learning potential of individual job experiences as well as organizational events.

- *Develop a language for talking about reflection that fits the organization's culture.* Since it deals with what and how we think, reflection is by its very nature abstract. Being intangible makes it no less real or important, but it can make it difficult to work with, especially in the nuts and bolts world of business. Creating a way to talk about reflection and its many facets can make it more tangible and thus more useable. Having a language for talking about reflection is also important because reflection is at its core about dialogue—dialogue with oneself or with others—and dialogue obviously takes place through the use of language. Terms such as *active* and *inbriefing* were used here to describe important aspects of reflection. You may find that replacing *active* with *dynamic* or *action-oriented,* for example, works better in your organization. Indeed, you may even find that the terms *thinking* or *processing* are more readily understood than *reflecting* in your work environment. The point is to develop a way to discuss things that heretofore probably did not get talked about.

- *Encourage bosses to recognize and promote their people's real-time reflection.* The active support of reflection by those in authority is critical to providing a work environment conducive to reflection. Bosses should be educated about real-time reflection and evaluated on their efforts to promote its use by subordinates.

- *Build reflection into regular work activities.* Position reflection in the organization as a normal part of doing business, not as some supplemental and therefore optional activity. This can be done by making reflection an explicit part of, for example, strategic planning, problem solving, status update meetings, and discussions with customers. In this way, reflection moves from being "nice" to do to being "necessary" to do.

As Marcus Aurelius wrote in *Meditations,* "Our life is what our thoughts make it." If anything, this is more true today than it was when it was first written centuries ago. Although the new career contract, which itself is still evolving, elicits anxiety, it need not create fear. Indeed, like a challenging job experience, its emergence is just the type of thing that can lead to meaningful growth and development if it is met head-on with real-time reflection.

References

Block, P. (1993). *Stewardship: Choosing service over self-interest.* San Francisco: Berrett-Koehler.

Boyd, E. M., & Fales, A. W. (1983). Reflective learning: The key to learning from experience. *Journal of Humanistic Psychology, 23*(2), 99–117.

Daudelin, M. W. (1994). Learning from experience through reflection. (Doctoral dissertation, Boston University, 1994). *Dissertation Abstracts International, 54*(12A), 4331.

Hall, D. T. (1986). Career development in organizations: Where do we go from here? In D. T. Hall & Associates, *Career development in organizations* (pp. 332–352). San Francisco: Jossey-Bass.

Hutchings, P., & Wutzdorff, A. (Eds.). (1988). *Knowing and doing: Learning through experience.* San Francisco: Jossey-Bass.

Kolb, D. A. (1984). *Experiential learning: Experience as the source of learning and development.* Englewood Cliffs, NJ: Prentice Hall.

Langer, E. J. (1989). *Mindfulness.* Reading, MA: Addison-Wesley.

Laughlin, C., Sage, K., & Bockmon, M. (1993). *Samurai selling: The ancient art of service in sales.* New York: St. Martin's Press.

Lewin, K. (1951). *Field research in social sciences.* New York: HarperCollins.

Losee, S. (1994, July 11). *Fortune* checks out 25 cool companies. *Fortune,* 116–144.

Marsick, V. J. (1988). Learning in the workplace: The case for reflectivity and critical reflectivity. *Adult Education Quarterly, 38*(4), 187–198.

Marsick, V. J. (1990). Action learning and reflection in the workplace. In J. Mezirow & Associates, *Fostering critical reflection in adulthood: A guide to transformative and emancipatory learning* (pp. 23–46). San Francisco: Jossey-Bass.

Mezirow, J. (1991). *Transformative dimensions of adult learning.* San Francisco: Jossey-Bass.

O'Reilly, B. (1994, October 17). 360° feedback can change your life. *Fortune*, 93–100.

Peters, T. J. (1992). *Liberation management: Necessary disorganization for the nanosecond nineties.* New York: Knopf.

Peters, T. J., & Waterman, R. H. (1982). *In search of excellence: Lessons from America's best-run companies.* New York: HarperCollins.

Richman, L. S. (1994, May 16). How to get ahead in America. *Fortune*, 46–54.

Robinson, G. S., & Wick, C. W. (1992). Executive development that makes a business difference. *Human Resource Planning, 15*(1), 63–76.

Sashkin, M., & Kiser, K. J. (1993). *Putting total quality management to work.* San Francisco: Berrett-Koehler.

Schön, D. A. (1983). *The reflective practitioner.* New York: Basic Books.

Schön, D. A. (1987). *Educating the reflective practitioner: Toward a new design for teaching and learning in the professions.* San Francisco: Jossey-Bass.

Seibert, K. W. (1996). *The nature of managerial reflection in learning from developmental job experiences in organizations.* Doctoral dissertation, Boston University.

Seibert, K. W., Hall, D. T., & Kram, K. E. (1995). Strengthening the weak link in strategic executive development: Integrating individual development and global business strategy. *Human Resource Management, 34*(4), 549–567.

Sherman, S. (1994, August 22). Leaders learn to heed the voice within. *Fortune*, 92–110.

Smith, L. (1994, May 16). Landing that first real job. *Fortune*, 58–60.

Chapter Eleven

The Value of Diversity in Career Self-Development

Barbara A. Walker

The new career contract raises a broad range of personal growth and self-development issues. Being responsible for one's own career requires developing and strengthening all kinds of personal abilities, skills, and competencies, such as a sense of self-direction and self-reliance, the ability to think through issues traditionally resolved by management, as well as the ability to connect on one's own with co-workers in order to solve problems and get the right things done. In other words, personal development becomes the employee's most important career development tool.

Personal and Organizational Development

The work of learning to value differences plays a key role in personal development and facilitates career development. In such work, we purposefully focus on differences in order to help employees learn how to use them as a major asset to their personal growth and to company productivity. Some companies call this work *diversity,* a term often used quite narrowly in today's society to refer to affirmative action. In this chapter, I use both terms—*valuing differences* and *diversity*—broadly to describe an all-inclusive philosophy that goes beyond the traditional issues of numbers, representation, and culture. Valuing differences not only focuses on race, gender, ethnicity, color, age, physical ability and disability, and sexual orientation, it also addresses all the ways people use differences to divide and exclude one another—income, education, occupation, religion, class, physical size, geography, politics, family and marital status, and so on.

The work of valuing differences challenges employees to view differences as assets and not simply as liabilities to be tolerated or overcome. Viewing differences as assets does not come easily to human nature. People find it easier to deny or ignore the tension and discomfort created by differences. They suggest that they would work better if they put their differences to the side and focus only on what they have in common. But as an old adage points out, "There may not be many differences among us, but what little there are are important." The differences among people often mean that they do not share the same view of what people hold in common. Some people cling to their difference as an expression of their identity and of their individual worth; their difference makes them unique. Focusing only on what people have in common can make people, particularly those who already feel marginalized by society, feel excluded and even more devalued.

The differences in people's perspectives, values, and cultures bring richness, depth, and insight into the workplace. Those differences become critical agents of learning, self-discovery, and the work of building productive relationships in the workplace.

Learning to value differences is the heart of the self-development work that is so essential to exploring and charting new career paths as well as honing the critical skills, competencies, and mind-set needed for career success. Diversity work is also an integral piece of organizational development work; it creates a continuous learning environment that encourages and supports employee career self-development.

In effect, valuing differences work is two career development strategies in one—personal development and organizational development. Diversity work and career self-development make a perfect fit.

Personal Abilities Essential to New Career Skills

To view them simplistically, the core tasks involved in the work of learning to value differences are (1) learning about people regarded as different, (2) learning about oneself, and (3) learning how to work with different people differently. As Table 11.1 indicates, when people undertake this work, they develop a broad range of personal abilities essential to all kinds of endeavors— including career self-development: learning how to learn, self-discovery, effective communication, building interdependent relationships, and coping.

Learning How to Learn

Learning to value differences enhances one's ability to learn in general. The work itself amounts to a focus on learning how to learn. One of the primary goals of the work is helping people learn how to open themselves up to learning from people they regard as different from themselves.

The honest and candid exploration of stereotypes and assumptions about people and their differences—no matter what the difference—is always highly emotional work. The ability to grow and learn is often constrained by a self-referent point of view: seeing one's own way as the right way and the norm by which to measure all others. Locked into an either/or approach to problem solving, people become threatened by deviations from their perceptions of the norm (Lorde, 1984). When people talk openly about their differences, they often feel uncomfortable and look for ways to exit or even sabotage the work. They fear that the differences of others mean that they themselves must change.

People learn best when they feel safe. Nowhere is this more evident than in diversity work. They feel most safe when they can count on each other to "hang in," to stay engaged in the learning process no matter how divergent their perspectives (Walker and Hanson, 1992).

Keeping people safe in order to manage the emotion and complexity of dealing with differences is also a way of helping people learn how to deal with change. Like diversity, the work of change is emotional, complex, and highly charged. Raising one's comfort level with change is an essential step in developing adaptability and reshaping the way people think about their careers.

In a safe environment—where they can be themselves and yet hang in with others—people learn how to talk and listen to one another, and they develop a high level of comfort entering dialogues

Table 11.1. Abilities Developed by Learning to Value Differences.

Personal and Career Abilities Developed	Core Tasks		
	Learning About Oneself	Learning About Others	Learning How to Work with Others
Learning How to Learn	✓	✓	✓
Self-reflection			
Keeping people safe			
Dialogue work			
Adaptability			
Self-Discovery	✓	✓	✓
Self-reflection			
Self-assessment			
Interdependent Relationships	✓	✓	✓
Teamwork			
Authenticity			
Trust			
Mentoring			
Effective Communication	✓	✓	✓
Inclusion			
Recognizing styles			
Coping	✓	✓	✓
Flexibility			
Being peers			
Goodwill			
Taking risks			

with people they regard as different. As participants hear each other's stories and tell their own stories, their learning and insights deepen.

In this process, participants learn the value of self-reflection. They not only learn how to draw meaning from their experiences but they also reflect on how they learn. They develop a sense of themselves as students of differences—in other words, as learners (Walker, 1986). This sense of identity as a learner leads to even deeper explorations and learnings and facilitates career development. Learners develop a high level of comfort level "trying on" the perspectives of others to see whether or not they fit. They are able to make rapid shifts as they incorporate new learnings and perspectives in ways of seeing and critically thinking about things.

In effect, in the past, employers' long-term commitment to job security helped some people stay safe. The new employment contract means that employees must find other ways to feel safe. Learning how to tap into a wide range of new sources of learning, such as learning about differences, can become a new anchor to career security.

Self-Discovery

Learning how to work with people regarded as different leads people into reflecting on the nature of their relationships with others. It also provides an unusual opportunity in the workplace to wrestle with basic identity questions, such as one's willingness and capacity to take risks, to be vulnerable, to share power, and to learn from others. In other words, learning to value differences is self-discovery. In this self-reflection process, people discover who they are, particularly in relationship to who they *say* they are. They discover who they want to be and get a handle on the work they must do to get there.

Such was the case with one of my colleagues who had returned to the corporate office after a long assignment in Europe. Often when people who had taken European assignments returned to the United States, they would find that they had missed out on the personal development work done by their U.S. colleagues. My colleague—a young man viewed as a high performer on a fast track—returned just after his U.S. colleagues had spent substantial time working on gender issues. He got in hot water almost immediately by constantly referring to the women in his organization as "girls." It was such an ingrained habit that no matter how often he was asked to change his language, it seemed he could not do it. His manager and colleagues wanted him to succeed in his new job, but they could not overlook his sexist language. Recognizing that he needed immediate help, his manager asked him to talk with the organization's diversity specialist. As they talked, he discovered that a key point of his resistance sprang from his own image of himself as a whiz kid, a kind of "boy wonder." When he realized that his self-identity supported his sexist language, he appeared to let go of his sexist labels quite easily.

In diversity work, as one learns how to question others, one also learns how to question oneself. The ability to do honest self-assessment—that is, to look at oneself in order to understand one's own processes and style and to recognize one's impact on others—is an essential task in developing a career path. For example, personality preference profiles such as Myers-Briggs and the Kiersey Sorter help people recognize whether they bring a process orientation or a task orientation to the way they work with colleagues. Such assessments have been extremely helpful in diversity work and can bring significant insights to the work of constructing a career.

Building Interdependent Relationships

Learning how to work with people well is clearly important personal development work. All too often training programs that profess to help people learn how to work with others are grounded in a concept of sameness—that is, learning how to work with people like themselves. Moreover, in some cases, learning how to work well with others is in reality a code for assimilation: learning how to take on the norms and behaviors of the dominant group in the organization.

Diversity work helps employees tap into the strengths that spring from the differences in their backgrounds, values, and perspectives. When people realize how much they can learn from and through one another's differences, they begin valuing each other. When they feel valued, they connect in ways that enable them to work together interdependently and synergistically. Recently, I worked with a group of all-white, all-male top executives. They were amazed when they examined their shared assumption that they were far more alike than not. They discovered significant differences that stimulated them to develop more meaningful and productive relationships with one another.

In interdependent relationships, employees are willing to share power and deepen their investment in becoming authentic with one another. Authenticity is important particularly when developing relationships across differences because it is the key to trust. The more people can trust others or at least predict their behavior with some accuracy, the more willing they are to depend on them (Walker, 1991).

When people become interdependent, there is less emphasis on having the correct answers up front. People accept their own vulnerability as well as the vulnerabilities of others and depend upon one another to generate potential solutions to problems. They learn how to follow as well as lead, to become members of teams. It also enables them to develop meaningful mentoring relationships, which is an important source of feedback as well as caring in the career development process (Kram and Hall, 1994).

Effective Communication

Building interdependent relationships in the workplace requires effective communication, just as it does in all important relationships. Yet communication is probably one of the most complex and difficult tasks of all, especially among people with very different backgrounds, values, and interests.

Clearly, vast cultural differences among employees, such as language proficiencies and accents, can affect their ability to make important connections and work well with one another. Diversity work encourages employees to develop their language skills, such as learning one another's language, reducing heavy accents, and developing effective presentation techniques.

But the fundamental aid to communication is one's mind-set. A valuing differences mind-set recognizes that communicating effectively with all kinds of people depends on an ability to recognize divergent perspectives and the willingness to remember that different people communicate differently. For example, one learns to recognize and deal with the substance behind people's perspectives, not just their style of communication. My own experiences have shown me that one of the most important communication tools is the willingness to reach out and make a genuine effort to communicate, whatever the differences in languages or accents. Many years ago, I was asked to make a diversity presentation to a group of international managers at a Fortune 500 company. Upon my arrival, I was greeted by a staff person who was very excited about the company's diversity work and who wanted me to make a good impression. As I was about to enter the room where the managers were waiting, she confided, "There are two managers from Japan over in the corner. Don't worry about them. They don't speak English well so all they do is sleep through all the presentations."

Although I wanted to make a good impression, it was my job to proactively role-model valuing differences skills and mind-set. During the question and answer period, I asked the managers from Japan to give their opinions on an issue we were discussing. When I could not understand what they were saying because of our language barrier, I asked them to slow down and help me understand. Encouraged to join in, they participated fully in the discussion that followed; it was clear that they were pleased to have been included. Needless to say, they did not sleep during my session, and according to the evaluations I made a good impression.

In valuing differences terms, communication is not simply a matter of technical skills but also a willingness to be vulnerable, to take risks, and to have the courage to reach out and include people who are different. When co-workers go out of their way to talk and listen to one another, they hear important nuances and grasp information that may be critically important as they make career decisions.

Coping

Valuing differences work is most often done in a spirit of optimism and hope. Learning to value differences helps people develop a mind-set of trust and constructive goodwill that enables them to deal effectively with the most complex and difficult problems. At the same time, the valuing differences mind-set enables people to accept the realities of organizational life, to hold on to what they view as positive while maintaining some healthy skepticism.

Perhaps the greatest challenge in the valuing differences work is learning how to deal effectively with people who refuse to accept or even recognize another person's difference. Whenever I make this point in my workshops, asking, "When you learn to value differences, how do you deal with the differences of the people who don't value you?" I hear an audible gasp. Everyone recognizes this question as a reality of life.

When people learn to value differences, they incorporate an accepting awareness of dilemmas and change, of complexities and ambiguities. They develop a flexible mind-set that permits a shift in ways of thinking about things and enables them to let go of an either-or approach to problem solving. They can admit mistakes and maintain personal comfort even when they are vulnerable.

With a valuing differences mind-set and safe and supportive relationships, people can develop effective strategies when they run into the maze of adversities, obstacles, and dilemmas that get in the way of career goals. For example, the ability to treat all co-workers as peers, including managers and executives, enables employees to raise important questions about company direction as well as practices and values that affect their interests. When employees can challenge the organization constructively and strategically, they can help bring about the changes they seek.

Activities That Support Career Self-Development

An organization-wide diversity initiative serves career development in innumerable ways. In addition to nurturing a learning environment and enhancing teamwork, diversity work builds flexibility into the organization itself; that is, the organization learns to pay attention to the complexity of people's needs—as individuals and as members of divergent identity groups. A philosophy of flexibility enables the organization to address a variety of competing interests and commitments equitably (Hall and Parker, 1993).

Small-Group Dialogues

One of the most effective and exciting ways to do the work of learning to value differences is small-group dialogue (Walker and Hanson, 1992). Dialogue groups are personal growth mini-labs in which seven to nine people meet regularly in order to learn about the issues created by their differences. People often recognize that the honest, in-depth exploration of differences cannot be done in isolation. It must be done with others and in most cases with people one perceives as different. Small-group dialogues represent a disciplined approach to thinking critically about the issues raised by differences (Walker, 1986).

In these dialogues, employees undertake—whether implicitly or explicitly—four distinct pieces of work: (1) erasing their stereotypes, (2) probing for the differences in the assumptions of others, (3) raising their own levels of personal empowerment by "de-victimizing," and (4) proactively building authentic and significant relationships with people they regard as different.

Dialogue participants learn to recognize and resist stereotypes, not only about people but also about work and the way they believe things ought to be. They develop comfort taking risks, talking openly and candidly in order to test the differences in their assumptions and perspectives. They try on one another's perspectives in order to gain insight into where others may be coming from. Through dialogue, participants learn how to communicate genuine acceptance of one another, a powerful factor in freeing the other person to truly stretch toward his or her potential. When people believe that they have been heard and accepted for who they are, they feel valued and open themselves up to the work of stripping away their negative assumptions and stereotypes.

These small-group dialogues give participants an unusual opportunity to develop a portfolio of experiences with people they believe are different, experiences that they may not ordinarily have outside of their diversity work. Participants discover the value of taking the time to reflect, to question, to listen and rethink issues (Howard and Howard, 1985). One dialogue group participant reported back to the group that their dialogue work had helped him develop critical insights on how his children learned and developed their perspectives on the world around them. He said that his children always did their homework in front of the television. It was not that they "watched" TV; it merely kept them company as they worked. One day when he came home from work, he realized that the program on TV was about prison. He noticed that the only prisoners' faces shown were those of young black men. It hit him, he said, that although he believed that he had taught his children not to be racist, their ideas and perspectives about race were being shaped by those images. That night, he began talking with his children on a regular basis about race.

People can hear and learn from one another only when they feel safe. In dialogue group work, participants make an up-front commitment to keep each other safe by hanging in with one another even when their perspectives and values are highly divergent. When they know that they can count on each other to stay engaged in the dialogue, participants feel safe to take risks, asking questions and expressing their fears. Participants also feel safe when they realize that although everyone brings some expertise into the dialogue, the emphasis is on learning, not teaching. As participants learn the lesson of how critically important it is to keep people safe, they infuse it into their interactions outside dialogue groups.

Small-group dialogues are a powerful form of personal development, providing access to different perspectives and ideas about new ways to approach all kinds of complex and difficult problems. They create innumerable and often exciting opportunities to critically think about a wide range of issues and to fully develop the personal abilities that make the difference in how one deals with life's issues. A network of dialogue groups across an organization lays a solid personal development foundation for sorting through the issues involved in career self-development.

At Digital Equipment Corporation, widely recognized in the 1980s as a leading pioneer of diversity work, a companywide network of dialogue groups became the engine of personal development and learning for its employees. When Digital conducted a study of the factors involved in leadership development, many of the participants reported that their dialogue group work was a significant factor in such development. It may be noteworthy that in 1979 when the very first dialogue group began, it contained three women and six men. At that point, two of the men were already vice presidents. The group met regularly for five years. By 1991, all the other participants had reached vice president or equivalent positions in their respective organizations.

Other Activities

Companies can sponsor a variety of diversity activities in order to build and maintain an environment that supports learning and career self-development. Even though some activities address a narrow set of diversity issues—for example, sexual harassment training or disability awareness training—they support growth and personal change. Other activities that help people shift their ways of approaching career development include win-win/conflict resolution training, efficacy-type programs for targeted groups, empowerment workshops, mentoring and coaching programs, celebrating differences events, and intercultural communication.

In a sense, diversity work is its own catch-22. On one hand, valuing people and their differences implies a strong ethic about the way people should be treated. However, by definition, diversity work cannot impose strict definitions and exacting standards on others about the ways in which the work must be done.

Organizational work intended to support career self-development, just as diversity work, must develop processes that honor different stages of personal growth as well as different learning styles and preferences. The bottom line is that organizational support of personal growth and career self-development must be flexible and done in ways that enable individuals to go forward at their own pace.

In a learning environment where people feel safe, employees—including those who would prefer to hold onto the old-fashioned notions of career development—can accept and even welcome the encouragement and the pushing so essential to their stretching and growing under the new employment contract.

References

Hall, D. T., & Parker, V. A. (1993). The role of workplace flexibility in managing diversity. *Organizational Dynamics, 22*(1), 5–18.

Howard, A., & Howard, W. (1985). *Exploring the road less traveled.* New York: Simon & Schuster.

Kram, K. E., & Hall, D. T. (in press). Mentoring in a context of diversity and turbulence. In S. Lobel & E. E. Kossek (Eds.), *Human resource strategies for managing diversity.* London, England: Blackwell.

Lorde, A. (1984). *Sister outsider.* Boston: Crossing Press.

Walker, B. A. (1986). *Leading dialogue groups: Leading dialogues about race, sex and all kinds of differences.* Unpublished manuscript.

Walker, B. A. (1991). Valuing differences: The concept and a model. In M. A. Smith & S. J. Johnson (Eds.), *Valuing differences in the workplace* (pp. 7–17). Alexandria, VA: American Society for Training and Development.

Walker, B. A., & Hanson, W. C. (1992). Valuing differences at Digital Equipment Corporation. In S. Jackson & Associates (Eds.), *Diversity in the workplace: Human resource initiatives*. New York: Guilford Press.

Chapter Twelve

Career Development for the Older Worker

Philip H. Mirvis
Douglas T. Hall

Over the past decade and a half, constant corporate restructuring and downsizing, the outsourcing of jobs to foreign countries, heightened job demands, longer hours, and reductions in health and pension benefits have taken a toll on working people of all ages but especially those over age fifty-five. The Laborforce 2000 survey (Mirvis, 1993) of over four hundred North American employers found that proportionately more older workers lost their jobs via corporate cutbacks over the five-year study period for two reasons. First, firms that made the greatest reductions in force—mature companies in heavier industries—employed a far larger share of workers over age fifty-five than other firms in the study. Second, favored downsizing measures, such as closing a plant or eliminating a layer of management, targeted the kinds of jobs and positions held by more mature workers and in the case of early retirement programs were aimed squarely at the longer tenure, older employee.

To make matters worse, a myriad of anecdotal evidence, backed up by rulings in several age-discrimination cases, indicates that some businesses singled out older workers in their downsizings (Anand, 1992). Deemed unfit for faster-paced jobs, unsuitable for retraining, and too expensive to keep on the payroll, older workers were equated with "deadwood" in downsizing firms such as CIGNA, where a top executive was quoted in a trade publication saying his firm would rather keep "up-and-comers" than "someone over fifty." Expressing their vulnerability and outrage over their treatment, employees dubbed the downsizing "RAPE" (Retire Aged Personnel Early) and called redeployment reviews "SCREW" (Survey of Capabilities of Retired Early Workers).

Attitudes Toward Older Workers

Companies faced with the choice between early retiring older workers or retraining and redeploying them have favored the former method (Barth, McNaught, and Rizzi, 1993). Immediate payroll savings are part of their calculus. The more significant factor, however, is expected return on investment: many companies do not expect to recoup the benefits of investing in older workers who, compared to early- or midcareer employees, have fewer remaining years of employment.

Employers have demonstrated a consistent bias toward younger versus older workers when it comes to training investments. The Bureau of Labor Statistics found that in 1983 and again in 1991, training increased up to age forty-four in the U.S. labor force, then tailed off substantially (Carnevale and Carnevale, 1994). The Laborforce 2000 study, in turn, found companies nearly twice as likely to spend "a lot of money" training a younger worker (thirty-five and under) versus an older one (fifty-one and over) (see Table 12.1).

The combination of employers' bias in favor of younger workers and the lack of training and retraining for older workers creates a vicious cycle of consequences. First, it results in a gradual erosion of older workers' value to the company relative to younger ones and encourages employers to believe that older workers are most expendable during corporate cutbacks. Then, to compound their problems, the failure to enhance their job skills prevents older workers from switching jobs and companies and makes it more difficult for them to reenter the labor force after a layoff or retirement.

Another variant of the cost-effectiveness argument against keeping older workers is that they simply cannot learn the skills needed to master today's jobs and are too inflexible to adapt to new assignments. Granted, most surveys find that employers give their older workers high marks on performance, loyalty, attendance, and even their job skills. There is nonetheless a perception that you "can't teach an old dog new tricks."

Table 12.1. Corporate Investments in Training.

Worker Age Group	Percentage of Companies	
	Investing Lots	Investing Little
35 and younger	29	21
Midcareer (36–50)	26	23
Older (51 and older)	17	34

Source: Barth, McNaught, and Rizzi, 1993, p. 168.

The Laborforce 2000 survey also found older workers rated better than the "average employee" in terms of attitudes, turnover, and such (see Table 12.2). At the same time, they were worse in terms of their health care costs, flexibility, and suitability for training (see Table 12.3). This echoes data collected in 1985 by the American Association of Retired Persons (1989) from a sample of four hundred human resource directors, which showed that only 10 percent were of the opinion that older workers are comfortable with new technologies.

Stereotypes about older workers' abilities to learn add to the vicious cycle that limits their training in organizations. Plainly, many employers are neither offering older workers as much training nor using age-appropriate training methodologies. Furthermore, older workers, anxious about their own learning abilities and uncomfortable with classroom instruction, may not appear to be as "ready" to participate in training and can have trouble mastering the material as quickly as younger workers. The consequence, in either case, is that prejudices and fears about the older worker's trainability and adaptability are reinforced.

The Human Toll

What happens to older workers who leave their companies through a layoff, plant closing, delayering, or early retirement? The bottom line is that they are out of work longer, suffer a greater earnings loss, and are less likely to be reemployed (Rix, 1995). Corporate banter reveals the human toll of downsizing: the layoff roster is

Table 12.2. Perceived Strengths of Older Workers.

	Percentage of Companies Rating Older Workers as Better than "the Average Employee"	
Criteria	All Companies	Companies with 30 Percent or More of Workforce Age 50 or Older
Work attitudes	57	64
Turnover	76	74
Absenteeism	66	60
Job skills	48	45

Source: Barth, McNaught, and Rizzi, 1993.

Table 12.3. Perceived Weaknesses of Older Workers.

	Percentage of Companies Rating "the Average Employee" as Better than Older Workers	
Criteria	All Companies	Companies with 30 Percent or More of Workforce Age 50 or Older
Health care costs	64	79
Flexibility in accepting new assignments	57	62
Suitability for training	37	50

Source: Barth, McNaught, and Rizzi, 1993, p. 163.

referred to as a "casualties list" in many companies and to-be-laid-off employees are called the "walking wounded." There is a toll among the "survivors" too. The working conditions of older people who continue to work in corporations have deteriorated during the past decade and a half. Pressures to work harder have mounted as companies strive to be globally competitive and get more for less from their downsized workforce. Meanwhile, most American companies have cut back on health benefits (sometimes pointing the finger at the higher health care premiums of older workers) and many have reduced pensions and retirement health care coverage or plan to do so in the future.

The rise of cynicism in the less stable and secure, more fractious and competitive workplace has been amply documented in national surveys of the workforce overall (Mirvis and Kanter, 1992). Yet during the past ten years, mistrust of employers and of work peers has risen most sharply among heretofore trusting older workers. Many people age fifty-five and over entered the workforce with the idea of a lifetime career with one employer. Experience mattered and maturity was valued in companies in the "good old days." Today, by comparison, many of these older workers feel devalued at work and face an uncertain future on the job and in their lives (see Table 12.4). It is not surprising, then, that cynicism about life and the American future has increased sharply among older working people, and that compared to just ten years ago, many more feel pessimistic and alienated.

Future Trends

Employment prospects look even more chancy for older workers over the next several decades. By the year 2005, as the baby boom generation matures, persons age fifty-five and older are projected to number nearly 30 percent of the working-age population in the United States and by 2020 almost 40 percent. From the 1960s though the mid 1980s, American men sought earlier and earlier retirement. However, a host of factors—including longer life expectancy, better health, and desires to continue working—suggest that more older Americans will want to stay in the labor force longer in the future. Given their rising health care costs, smaller amounts of savings and housing wealth, and the fact that prospective retirees are likely to have children at home or in college, it is also likely that many older

Table 12.4. Negative Worker Attitudes in the Workforce.

	Percentage of Workers Reporting Negative Attitudes	
Negative Attitudes	Age 49 and Younger	Age 50 old Older
Cynical about people	48	56
Alienated in society	19	30
Insecure on job	21	27

Source: Mirvis and Kanter, 1992, pp. 45–68.

Americans will have to stay in the labor force in order to pay their bills. If so, then those age fifty-five and older who are employed in the year 2020 could exceed substantially the projected 20 percent.

There is some hope that continued growth in small business and in the service sector could translate into new work opportunities for older people. Firms such as Days Inn of America and B&Q, p.l.c., a British housewares chain, have made employing older workers a centerpiece of their staffing strategy and have found them to be more productive and less likely to turn over than younger staff. Granted, these employers are not offering high-wage jobs to older workers. They do, however, provide flexible hours, which is a priority for older people who want to work part-time and can make do on lower rates of pay.

Still there is imbalance between supply and demand. Extrapolating from a Louis Harris & Associates survey of older Americans, one estimate is that there are 5.4 million people older people who are "willing and able" to work but are unable to find a job (Barth and McNaught, 1991). Of these older Americans, 38 percent are between the ages of fifty-five and sixty-four; 41 percent between ages sixty-five and seventy-four; and 21 percent age seventy-five or more. They match their working contemporaries in education levels, professional and technical skills, and self-reported health and fitness. Assuming no dramatic growth in small- and midsize service businesses, no changes in their willingness to hire older workers, and no changes in employment practices in larger corporations, the numbers of older Americans able to work but unable to find jobs could increase substantially as boomers age over the next decades.

Opportunities in the New Organization

The foregoing suggest that a major issue facing aging workers is the aging corporation. Businesses as well as government agencies and non-profits have all been forced, through severe crises, to acknowledge that their large, centralized, hierarchical organizational structures are simply too slow and too out of touch with customers and markets to adapt successfully to fast-changing, globally and technologically competitive environments. Accordingly, Charles Handy (1989) configures the organization of tomorrow in the form of a shamrock with three leaves, as described in Chapter Three in this volume. The first leaf, and the most important for continuity and organizational survival, contains a core staff of managers, technicians, and professionals. These are highly skilled individuals who are expected to make a major commitment to the organization and derive a lot of their sense of identity from it. The second leaf is contractors, specialized people and firms, often outside the organization, who serve a variety of needs, including supply, distribution, and routine control functions. Their work is not part of the essential core technology and competence of the firm and can usually be done better, faster, and cheaper by someone else in a smaller, more specialized, and autonomous position. The third leaf is the contingent labor force. These are part-timers and temporary workers who provide a "buffer" to the core workforce of a firm. This model provides an antidote to corporate aging. It means companies will undergo more or less continuous reshaping and restructuring and that employees of all ages will face more job movement in, out, and around its boundaries. The question at hand is, what might help aging workers adapt to this work environment?

Aging and Adaptability

One way to help people develop over the course of this type of career is to keep them moving through a number of career cycles rather than trying to prolong the maintenance stage of their career (Hall and Mirvis, 1994). A career path in the shamrock-type of organization, for instance, might have people work in core areas for a time, take a job in a supplier company or consulting firm, work as an individual contractor on selected projects, and then return to the fold as a senior core contributor and mentor.

Nevertheless, many employers today have doubts about the adaptability of their older workers. Interestingly, there is no physiological and scant psychological evidence that aging is in any way related to personal adaptability and resistance to change (Sterns and McDaniel, 1994). However, two factors may account for this perception of older people currently in the workforce. First, surveys by the Yankelovich Partners (1994) confirm that people of the "GI generation" (people the age of World War II veterans)—representing the oldest segment of the workforce during the past ten years—are comparatively low in their desires for novelty and change and most comfortable with the status quo. They are also more risk-averse than other generations and primarily oriented toward financial stability and security. Not surprisingly, they are also uncomfortable with new technologies. What is important to note about these findings is that they are not a function of the age of this generation: this age cohort has held similar attitudes about change over some twenty-five years of measurement by pollsters.

By contrast, members of the "silent generation" (those who came of age in the 1950s and make up the lion's share of the older worker population today) and "baby boomers" (who will be the great bloc of older workers in 2010) are progressively more apt to seek out novelty, take risks, be somewhat more comfortable with financial uncertainty, and make use of advanced technologies. Stereotyped attitudes about the inflexibility of older workers may well dissipate as the baby boomers in particular move further along in their careers.

A second factor contributing to resistance to change among today's older workers concerns their prior success following the "straight and narrow" career path. Research finds that early adult success reinforces a stable pattern of expectations and behavior (Hall, 1976). Many workers fifty-five and over entered the labor force with the expectation of a lifetime job with one employer. Their recipe for success—conformity, playing by the rules, and counting on their employer to "do what's right by them"—generally proved effective, at least until the traditional employment compact broke down.

Baby boomers, tomorrow's older workers, have had a different set of generational experiences. By now, the young, "new-breed" workforce of the late 1960s and 1970s is moving into midlife. Surveys in their early career years found many seeking out interesting and challenging work. This quest seemed to hold through the 1980s as the "new achievers" moved around organizations or else moved out to entrepreneurial ventures. Today, Maccoby (1988) finds that many boomers fit into the character type he calls the self-developer. This type seeks out knowledge but strives to balance mastery with play and family life. Looking ahead, aging boomers who have followed the self-development script will have had a history of capitalizing on the flexibility offered by the new career.

Aging and Trainability

Business is waking up to the economic payoff of providing more training and development opportunities for its people. Motorola spends $120 million on employee education; Arthur Andersen's training budget, 6.4 percent of revenues, is equal to that of Purdue University; and Saturn requires one hundred hours per year of formal learning for each management and union employee (Davis and Botkin, 1994). The result? Substantial gains in market share, productivity, and product quality respectively. What kinds of training is being offered today? In addition to technical skill training, the Laborforce 2000 survey found leading companies developing the interpersonal, communication, and problem-solving skills of employees—three skill areas deemed even more important for tomorrow's jobs. Another survey of U.S. firms with one hundred or more employees found 56 percent offering personal growth training to their employees (Gordon, 1988). It is not hard to imagine these firms making seminars on "flexible" career management part of their training portfolio in the future.

Amidst this cornucopia of training and development, the evidence is clear that older workers are getting the leavings (Lillard and Tan, 1992). Certainly, stereotypes about the interests and trainability of older workers are a factor explaining this training "gap" (Branco and Williamson, 1982). One common stereotype, for instance, is that older workers are not particularly interested in training. This is sharply contradicted by a Louis Harris & Associates (1991) study that estimated 4.6 million workers age fifty-five to sixty-four would consider taking classes to improve their employment opportunities or job skills. More pervasive and pernicious is the view that older workers are poor learners.

On this point, a wealth of evidence disputes the notion that older workers cannot learn new tricks. Study after study affirms that there is far more variability in skill acquisition and retention within age groups than, say, between younger and older workers (Cascio, 1994). Meta-analyses of the full portfolio of scientific studies in this area do suggest, however, that it takes older workers somewhat longer than younger ones, on average, to master more complex skills. They also work more slowly when applying these skills to high-technology jobs. The tradeoff here is that they tend to be more accurate than those who have a faster learning curve.

The research supporting these conclusions has its critics, and several studies find older workers quite trainable in high-tech skills (Hogarth and Barth, 1991). Indeed, two-thirds of the firms surveyed in the Laborforce 2000 study found their older workers to be comfortable learning new skills and technologies. Part of the problem may be related to the way companies go about training their older workers. Studies find that older people are not as comfortable with classroom-type skill training and have more trouble digesting written instructional material (Gist, Rosen, and Schwoerer, 1988). Some also become anxious about performing poorly on tests, which hampers their digestion of information. Yet when it comes to in-house training, the great majority (83 percent) of companies surveyed do not vary training methods to allow for the different age levels of the employees being trained, thus making no adjustments for the learning styles of older employees who have been out of classrooms for many years.

There is lots of practical advice available and a few notable examples of corporate training and retraining programs that have been tailored to the learning styles of older workers. But these latter programs are still the exception rather than the rule. We expect stereotypes about the learning abilities of older workers to lessen, however, as training programs aimed at older workers increase and prove their worth—conclusions supported by surveys of corporations and studies of the payoff of training older workers.

Flexible Employment

With more of this kind of training, development, and varied experience over the life course, the case can be made that older workers will provide just the kind of flexible resource companies need in the future.

The Shamrock Organization

Already, the more able and adaptable of today's older workforce are finding employment options in flexible firms. For instance, forty thousand older workers staff the growing segment of part-timers in the front-line service workforce at McDonald's, and a majority of those employed in the telephone sales offices of the Home Shopping Network are onetime retirees. Specialized recruiting and training efforts, dubbed the McMaster and Prime Timer programs in these two companies, in turn help these "working retirees" to make the transition to a new industry and work situation. Financial service firms such as Aetna, Prudential, and GEICO rehire their own retirees for part-time and temporary posts. The practice is becoming commonplace: over three-fourths of the firms surveyed in the Laborforce 2000 study "hire back" retired employees to work as part-time and seasonal help or as consultants.

Older workers also find opportunities on the second leaf of companies. The Texas Refinery and the Northwest Pipeline corporations, for instance, employ older workers as "independent contractors" in customer sales and service. Looking ahead, there will be more instances where older managers and workers buy out a unit of a large company and shape their business around contracts with their former firm. The organization-specific knowledge of these former employees will likely reduce the high coordination costs that hamper so many external vendor relationships, and, in return, keeping their former employer as a major customer ensures them a steady cash flow. Such local buyouts are becoming increasingly common in firms such as IBM, Honeywell, and others. Finally, there will, of course, continue to be opportunities for older workers in the core work areas of companies. Established competencies in design, development, and manufacture, for instance, are near irreplaceable. This is one reason why the Aerospace Corporation in Los Angeles employs 105 workers over age sixty-five in its laboratories and production facilities and why Graphic Controls in Buffalo has more than 100 skilled workers in its twenty-five years–plus employment club. Longer tenure employees also provide companies with continuity in vendor, distributor, and customer relationships and something akin to "institutional memory" in forecasting and planning.

New Employment Possibilities

In turn, many older workers will possess the skills and "learnabil-ity" to fill jobs in growth segments of the "postindustrial" economy. Employers today give mature workers high marks for their techni-cal skills and their pride in craft. They seem well suited, then, for employment as technicians—estimated to represent a fifth of total employment in the United States within a decade. Naturally, some updating of their skills may be needed for technical work in the future. Union Pacific Railroad and Northern Telecom, to cite two exemplars, reaped significant increases in productivity from upgrading the skills of their aging workforces and transitioning skilled blue-collar workers into higher-order technical jobs.

Other strengths of older workers are their positive attitudes and good work habits. This makes them ideal candidates for direct customer service and support jobs. Wal-Mart, as an example, employs an army of older workers as "greeters" in their stores and Avis rental car lots are staffed by corporate retirees. These are ways too that the experience of older workers adds unique value to a business. Indeed, the importance of having mature people around to mentor newcomers, socialize outside vendors in organizational morays, and embody important traditions of the corporate culture will increase in the "temporariness" of tomorrow's organization.

There also seems to be a good "fit" today between the increas-ing amount of part-time work in companies and the interests of older workers. On the employer's side, a 1992 study by the Society for Human Resource Management reported that more than 80 percent of companies who aggressively recruited and hired older workers found them to be more amenable than younger ones to working part-time (American Association of Retired Persons, 1993). As for workers, Louis Harris & Associates' survey (1991) of older Americans found that a substantial number of men (31 per-cent) and women (36 percent) employed full-time would prefer part-time work. By comparison, fewer older men (17 percent) and women (19 percent) who currently work part-time would prefer full-time employment.

Finally, chronological age will work in favor of some older workers in tomorrow's economy. The consumer marketplace will of course be aging along with the workforce and present new opportunities for older workers to be involved in the design, manufacture, and sale of products aimed at the elderly. For example, William Wasch, a corporate early retiree, has started a firm that "adapts" homes to the needs of the aged or disabled. His home is a showcase of new products targeted to this growing marketplace.

In sum, there will likely be a variety of flexible employment options open to older workers who want to work part-time or as contractors and new roles opening up in the core work of larger companies and small businesses that will fit their skills and needs. In addition, some of the flexible work options companies have available are particularly well suited to aging employees.

Flexible Work Options

Innovations in the scheduling and locale of work could also increase the "fit" between older workers and organizations. There will come a time when, say, financial service firms will rely on "telecommuters" to process transactions or conduct analyses. Who better to do this at-home work than electronically enabled older workers? Wells Fargo is experimenting with such a program. Tele-sales and -service opportunities are expected to grow dramatically in the near future. Several of the "Baby Bells," including U.S. West and Ameritech, have "electronic commerce" ventures that employ older workers otherwise slated for early retirement.

Job sharing is another flexible option well suited to older workers. Levi Strauss & Co. and many other "family-friendly" companies give employees the option to job share. Do these family-friendly options help older workers? Polaroid specifically focused this option on its older workers, giving them the chance to share jobs rather than undergo across-the-board layoffs following business downturns in the late 1980s and early 1990s. Interestingly, the American Management Association (1994) finds growing interest in this strategy among employers who have been through two or more downsizings and seen the consequences for morale.

One of the most important and beneficial of the flexible options suited to older workers involves the chance to participate in a "phased retirement" program. One in three companies surveyed in the Laborforce 2000 survey currently offer workers over age fifty-five the chance to transfer to less demanding jobs, in terms of hours and duties, for less compensation, and one in five have a formal program of phased retirement. Another 10 to 20 percent expect to offer these flexible options to older workers in the near future. Certainly, there is pressing need for this: a Louis Harris & Associates (1989) survey found that nearly three million workers, aged fifty to sixty-four, would work somewhat longer than they had planned if offered a job with fewer hours and responsibilities, even at a lower rate of pay.

Although phased retirement and alternative career paths may be cast as "benefits" for older employees, the option of moving able workers to more time-bound assignments, where the work is not calibrated to make or break a career, also serves the strategic interests of a business. Many older workers bring a shorter time horizon to job assignments than younger workers: they are more likely to be looking for something with a duration of, say, three to five years and to be less concerned about the impact of the assignment on their résumés or chances for a promotion. As such, they are good candidates for the sorts of work projects and temporary assignments that will constitute important work in the "de-jobbed" organization of tomorrow.

Competitive Advantage

An increase in the sheer number of older people in the workforce in the future, as baby boomers age, will likely heighten corporate attention to the issues of an aging workforce and lead to more responsiveness to older workers' needs. This is one favored explanation for why companies have become more aggressive in responding to the needs of working women. We think that consciousness raising about the advantages of having older people in the corporate workforce is also in order.

Age Equals Diversity

The resources to be found in a diverse workforce can be an area of great potential for gaining a competitive edge in the employee talent pool. The argument has been made, for example, that as diversity in the workforce mirrors diversity in a firm's customer base, the firm undertakes "internal" market research and builds customer preferences into its products and services. Already companies find that older Americans are worthy of their own special products and marketing efforts. We would argue that increasing the number of older workers in the design, manufacture, and testing of consumer products and surely in service delivery would be one means of ensuring that products and services will suit the tastes and fit the needs of the rapidly growing market segment of older consumers.

In addition, there is interesting evidence that groups composed of diverse individuals generate more creative ideas than more homogeneous groups and often engage in more cooperative rather than competitive behavior (Cox, Lobel, and McLeod, 1991; McLeod and Lobel, 1992). Age diversity is another means of stimulating ideas and fostering cooperation in corporations dependent on responding innovatively and smoothly to changes in the business environment.

There can be yet another natural advantage provided by older workers. More and more companies are finding that the glass ceiling is an unnecessary correlate of ageism in corporate life: it exists because of the assumption that people must reach a certain executive level by a certain age, say, forty and because of the fact that many employees, often women, take a slower advancement path in order to combine family and career, which does not get them to the target level by the target age. Of course, the very idea of an age-based career ceiling can become a self-fulfilling prophesy: older workers will naturally reduce their effort and commitment to development when further advancement is seen as futile. Recognition that older workers add value, by contrast, would send a very different message to employees about what they have to contribute at later career stages. With assumptions related to employee age being reevaluated, we are seeing that it is possible for people to perform very successfully in senior positions long after what had been viewed as the upper age limit. Further consciousness raising about the benefits of age diversity might shatter the glass ceiling altogether.

Socially Useful Service

Among the many alternative career paths that will open up to workers in mid- and late career could be the option of performing social service. There are over 140,000 business–public school partnerships in the United States at present, and more and more companies are forming community partnerships with community groups and nonprofits. Elderly Americans have a strong proclivity toward volunteerism and contribute in great numbers in communities across the nation (Freedman, 1994). Businesses that involve themselves in education and community partnerships do so for many reasons, some strategic, some more in the spirit of goodwill. A new reason is the benefits to people's personal and career development (Mirvis and Hall, 1994). Evidence shows that those involved in community service feel better about themselves and, in the case of corporate-sponsored volunteerism, about their companies. We also believe that community service could be a substantial contributor to lifelong learning. If, over the course of a career, people have chances to, say, teach in public schools, work on community projects, get involved in environmental clean-ups, and so on, they will be tackling complex problems, meeting a variety of people with different interests and outlooks, and having to learn how to operate in new settings. All of this would give a boost to their adaptability. In turn, work in this arena would also expand their self-images and introduce them to new aspects of who they are and might become. Beyond personal gains, the benefits of this for civic life and civility in the nation cannot be overstated.

The Case for Continuous Employability

Our overall feeling is that the combination of market forces and demographic trends means that the business sector and our society as a whole will have no choice but to employ and develop older workers more in the future. We simply cannot afford to support a growing number of retired people with a shrinking base of employed people. Furthermore, as the definition of *older* keeps drifting downward, the nation will eventually reach a point of realizing that we need to keep everyone adaptable throughout their careers and in charge of their own futures.

Some of the ideas advanced here may seem far off and far fetched: continuous corporate restructuring; multiple skills for workers; career paths among the three leaves of the adaptable company;

the notion that people will move from job to job and even from employer to employer with the assistance of government, schools, nonprofits, and consortia of corporations themselves. However, many ideas seemed just as far out and far fetched twenty years ago: for example, participatory management, flexible hours, work-family initiatives, corporate-sponsored personal development programs, private-public partnerships in education, health maintenance organizations, joint ventures between businesses, and even total quality management and employee ownership.

We began by saying corporations have not treated their older workers kindly. We might just as well have said that they have treated them stupidly. Make no mistake: there is economic rationale behind the continued development of an aging workforce. Evidence is mounting that today's short-term, stop-gap measures, such as early retirement programs and targeted layoffs of older workers, have been quite costly (Hirschorn and Hoyer, 1992). Indeed, they are rapidly being abandoned by wised-up American firms. Furthermore, a series of studies documents how continuing to develop and even hire more older workers yields gains for economically rational organizations (McNaught and Barth, 1992). In fact, we would go so far as to suggest that global competitiveness will to some extent hinge on whether or not U.S. firms prove to be more (or less) strategically adaptive in this area than firms in Japan and Europe, who must also contend with dramatically aging populations.

Finally, we close on the civic and civil benefits of responding to the needs of aging workers. There are those who predict cross-generational warfare between younger and older Americans over health care and social security costs in the not too distant future. Stereotypes about "greedy geezers" are in fashion and are every bit as insidious as those about older people's inflexibility and inability to learn. Over the last thirty or so years, however, we have witnessed profound change in people's attitudes about women and minorities—and in women's and minorities' access to opportunities and contribution to the nation's economy. Most would agree that America is the better for this change. We expect just as dramatic a change in regard to aging American workers in the years ahead.

References

American Association of Retired Persons. (1989). *Business and older workers: Current perceptions and new directions for the 1990's.* Washington, DC: Author.

American Association of Retired Persons. (1993). *The older workforce: Recruitment and retention.* Washington, DC: Author.

American Management Association. (1994). *Responsible reductions in force: An AMA research report on downsizings and outplacement.* New York: American Medical Association Briefings and Surveys.

Anand, V. (1992, January 29). Older workers bear brunt of corporate cutbacks. *Investors Business Daily,* p. 10.

Barth, M. C., & McNaught, W. (1991). The impact of future demographic shifts on the employment of older workers. *Human Resource Management, 30*(1), 420–434.

Barth, M. C., McNaught, W., & Rizzi, P. (1993). Corporations and the aging workforce. In P. H. Mirvis (Ed.), *Building the competitive workforce.* New York: Wiley, 156–200.

Branco, K. J., & Williamson, J. B. (1982). Stereotyping and the life cycle: Views of aging and the aged. In A. G. Miller (Ed.), *In the eye of the beholder: Contemporary issues in stereotyping.* New York: Praeger.

Carnevale, A. P., & Carnevale, E. S. (1994, May). Growth patterns in workplace training. *Training & Development,* 22–29.

Cascio, W. (1994). *Documenting training effectiveness in terms of worker performance and adaptability.* Philadelphia: National Center on the Educational Quality of the Workforce.

Cox, T., Lobel, S., & McLeod, P. (1991). Effects of ethnic group cultural differences on cooperative and competitive behavior on a group task. *Academy of Management Journal, 34*(4), 827–847.

Davis, S., & Botkin, J. (1994). *The monster under the bed: How business is mastering the opportunity of knowledge for profit.* New York: Simon & Schuster.

Freedman, M. (1994). *Seniors in national and community service.* New York: Commonwealth Fund, Americans Over 55 at Work Program.

Gist, M., Rosen, B., & Schwoerer, C. (1988). The influence of training method and trainee age on the acquisition of computer skills. *Personnel Psychology, 41,* 255–265.

Gordon, J. (1988, October). Who's being trained to do what? *Training,* 51–60.

Hall, D. T. (1976). *Careers in organizations.* Glenview, IL: Scott, Foresman.

Hall, D. T., & Mirvis, P. H. (1994). The new workplace and older workers.

In J. A. Auerbach & J. C. Welsh (Eds.), *Aging and competition: Rebuilding the U.S. workforce.* Washington, DC: National Council on the Aging/National Planning Association.

Handy, C. (1989). *The age of unreason.* Boston: Harvard Business School Press.

Harris, L., & Associates. (1989). *Older Americans: The untapped labor source* (Study No. 884030). New York: Author.

Harris, L., & Associates. (1991). *Productive aging: A survey of Americans age 55 and over* (Study No. 902061). New York: Author.

Hirschorn, B., & Hoyer, D. (1992). *Private sector employment of retirees: The organizational experience.* Detroit, MI: Institute of Gerontology, Wayne State University.

Hogarth, T., & Barth, M. C. (1991). Costs and benefits of hiring older workers: A case study of B&Q. *International Journal of Manpower, 12*(8), 5–17.

Lillard, L. A., & Tan, H. W. (1992). Private sector training: Who gets it and what are the effects? *Research in Labor Economics, 13,* 1–62.

Maccoby, M. (1988). *Why work.* New York: Simon & Schuster.

McLeod, P., & Lobel, S. (1992). The effects of ethnic diversity on idea generation in small groups. *Academy of Management Proceedings,* 227–231.

McNaught, W., & Barth, M. C. (1992). Are older workers "good buys"? A case study of Days Inn of America. *Sloan Management Review, 33,* 53–63.

Mirvis, P. H. (Ed.). (1993). *Building a competitive workforce: Investing in human capital for corporate success.* New York: Wiley.

Mirvis, P. H., & Hall, D. T. (1994). Psychological success and the boundaryless career. *Journal of Organizational Behavior, 15,* 365–380.

Mirvis, P. H., & Kanter, D. L. (1992). Beyond demographics: A psychographic profile of the workforce. *Human Resource Management, 30*(1), 45–68.

Rix, S. E. (1995). Investing in the future: What role for older worker training? In W. Crown (Ed.), *Handbook on the older worker.* Westport, CT: Greenwood Press.

Sterns, H. L., & McDaniel, M. A. (1994). Job performance and the older worker. In S. E. Rix (Ed.), *Older workers: How do they measure up?* Washington, DC: American Association of Retired Persons.

Yankelovich Partners. (1994). *Yesterday, today, and tomorrow: How have generations changed?* New York: Author.

Chapter Thirteen

Finding Sanctuary in Post-Modern Life

Jane L. Hodgetts
William H. Hodgetts

Eight women sit around a boardroom table over lunch in a Boston public accounting firm. These are the busiest of women, in middle- and senior-level positions from inside the accounting firm and from a mix of nonprofit organizations and large corporations. All of them are mothers with young children. They juggle the demands of their work, children, and homes. Some of the women travel on a regular basis in the United States and overseas, yet they all make time to attend most of Jane's biweekly lunchtime Perspective, Renewal, and Balance (PRB) meetings.

At a comfortable moment, Jane welcomes the group, passes out a Dilbert cartoon, and points out some common themes from the prior session: the sense of life moving too fast and the imbalances in work and home life. She then asks the women to go around the circle and describe a concern, issue, or question that has come up since the last meeting. Within minutes, there are nods of recognition, occasional laughter, helpful suggestions. One of the rules for this group is to listen and not interrupt. This may be the only time in the week for some of these women to stop and receive this special treatment.

Kathy, pregnant with her second child, shares with the group her struggle over cutting back on her job. She is a director for a high tech company, the only woman at her level. What will happen to her career if she reduces her involvement? If she can manage to work a four-day week, as some of the other women in the group do, will she end up doing household chores on her one day at home? How can she deal with her husband's emerging expectation that she stop traveling and cut back on her career?

Some of the other women in the group have made the shift from full time to part time and offer their perspective. Mary agrees that it is easy on that one day at home to slip into doing errands and housework, but she says that if one makes plans, this doesn't have to happen. Diane is less encouraging. She warns Kathy that reducing her work schedule will most likely have a negative effect on her career and that new inequities will appear on the home front. Everyone wants to help Kathy, and although she cannot easily resolve her dilemma, her face visibly relaxes. She feels armed to return to her macho work culture and to talk with her husband about her needs and ideas.

The group runs fifteen minutes over. These women who rushed in to the meeting are now reluctant to return to the high-speed race. Jane thanks them for their participation, distributes a handout on ways to stay better connected with one's partner on a daily basis, and reads an inspirational quote to provide some closure for the session. These women have visited a lunchtime oasis in an office skyscraper.

It is 9:30 A.M., and six women sit around Sara's kitchen table. June offers to be the timekeeper. "Well, there are six of us here, so we each can have around twenty minutes." This amount of undivided attention seems luxurious to each of these busy professionals. They are all self-employed in a variety of consulting and training businesses and have been meeting now for more than two years.

Originally they had planned to form a business together. At their first meetings, Jane would become frustrated because at least an hour of the group's time would be spent on chitchat and personal topics. Where was the agenda, she wondered? In time the women realized that developing a joint business was not really where their career energy was, but rather coming together to share both the personal and professional aspects of their lives on a monthly basis made their time together truly valuable.

Today each member has something to bring up: a personal matter around family or health, the stress of doing too much this month, and specific career and business issues. By noon, it is time to pull out date books, schedule the next meeting, and find a host for the session. No one wants to leave. These colleagues have had a morning of connection, sharing, and sometimes intense dialogue.

Both groups are examples of what we are calling *developmental sanctuaries* or *developmental support groups*. They are "holding environments"—"psychosocial environments which hold us (with which we are fused) and which let go of us (from which we are differentiated)" (Kegan, 1982, p. 116)—for people with very demanding and often fragmented lives. In today's post-modern world, where we race to keep up with the increasingly rapid processing speeds of computers, where we feel uncertain about our identity or longevity in turbulent and reengineered organizations, where many of us by choice or by default find ourselves making a living outside of corporations, and where we may have no way of easily integrating our multiple and often separate life dimensions, there is a tremendous need for reflecting and sharing with others in similar situations.

These developmental support groups offer a kind of "sanctuary" for their members—a place to belong, a space for one's whole self, a rest from the results-driven work world, and an opportunity to pay attention to personal thoughts and feelings in the company of others who understand. They provide normalization and a healing context just by bringing together people who are in similar life structures and who share common dilemmas and struggles. Developmental sanctuaries can provide a container for dealing with the anxiety and fear that are an inevitable part of making career and life transitions and offer the opportunity to articulate and get feedback on new ideas that one might be considering during a transition period. Although each of the groups we are describing in this chapter serve different populations, they share some common elements that we believe are replicable and applicable to people at all levels within an organization and also those making a living outside the corporation. We suspect such groups occur with greater frequency outside of large organizations, but we are finding increasing evidence of them within corporate life as well.

Five men and five women executives, participating in a two-day meeting of a corporate internal consulting group, are finishing dinner around a table in an executive conference center dining room. Bob, hearing much laughter emanating from the table, approaches and asks if he can join the discussion. He is told that the price of admission is to share an embarrassing story. He thinks for a moment, then decides to go ahead and share an embarrassing moment he experienced on his first date with his wife. He tells how, when he first brought her back to his college dorm room, he broke out in hives. The group roars with laughter, and each individual in turn shares an embarrassing personal story, even the group's manager. The group has ceased to be a mere collection of co-workers who have gathered at this off-site to discuss work-related issues; it has become a small community of individuals who have begun to reveal themselves beyond their narrowly defined work roles. As the stories continue, no one wants to leave.

Benefits and Outcomes of Developmental Sanctuaries

Developmental support groups can yield a variety of benefits for their members: a sense of personal renewal, perspective, self-learning, and self-reflection; a kind of holding place for transitions; and a holistic sense of how one's work and other life areas fit. Although it is often difficult for the participants to describe specifically how these groups help them, their commitment to finding an hour and a half in severely overcrowded schedules speaks to the value of this time.

During her year and a half of leading PRB groups, Jane has observed some specific changes in participants' behavior, both at home and in the office. For example, Mary, a senior consultant in the management consulting arm of the public accounting firm, was offered a job opportunity in the Hong Kong office. She shared with her group her concerns about giving up the flexibility that she had created in the Boston office. The group encouraged her to ask for what she wanted without apologies and to be prepared to walk away from this assignment unless her conditions were met, thereby conveying confidence and gaining respect. The sense of empowerment and the opportunity to test out new ideas in the group enabled Mary to take a risk, and she successfully negotiated a four-day week in the Moscow office. Several other women in the group were thus inspired to approach their managers in this confident, unapologetic fashion and to ask for schedules that would work better with their lives.

The internal consulting group off-site was energizing for John, who had recently joined the company and the group. Initially, John had been unsure whether he truly fit in this company and its fast-paced culture. After the two-day meeting, he was still unsure about these things but now he felt he had peers with whom he could actually discuss difficult client situations—a rare occurrence in corporate life these days.

In the self-employment group, June spent her turn in one meeting talking about a particularly difficult consulting assignment. By looking at her situation from different perspectives and thinking and feeling out loud with this group, she came to the conclusion that, hard as it would be, she needed to walk away from this project. Her growing sense of self-confidence was reinforced by the group, and now she trusts that she will attract enough projects congruent with her skills and interests.

Common Elements of Developmental Support Groups

Although developmental support groups may differ greatly in their particulars, all share a number of common elements: the use of rituals, an expected level of commitment from members, a relatively small size, a comfortable setting (preferably nonbusiness), a participant mix that balances diversity and homogeneity, and a mission that blends task and social functions.

Rituals

In particular, three kinds of rituals seemed important to all groups we studied: rituals of nourishment, of transition, and of disclosure.

Nourishment: All groups we observed provide *food,* perhaps symbolic of a deeper psychological nourishment. Without the informality of eating together, these sessions might feel more like regular business meetings. On a day when participants might not get a chance to eat with family, shared meals become a special source of sustenance.

Transition: Each group has evolved *ways of marking the beginnings and endings of the time together.* In the PRB group, Jane always starts with a cartoon and a threading together of the prior week's themes and ends with a quote to inspire these busy women, thus creating boundaries between the normal workday and group time. In the self-employed group, the session officially begins when one person offers to be a timekeeper and tells the group how much time each one will have to talk. The meetings end with opened date books and agreements on time and place for the next get-together. There is room for catching up and lighter conversation among individuals before the meetings officially begin and at the end. With our rushed and often interrupted day-to-day existence, creating a clearly defined space with beginnings and endings becomes increasingly important.

Disclosure: Many groups have developed ways of encouraging a kind of self-disclosure that leads beyond narrowly defined work roles. At the internal consulting group's off-site meeting, for example, participants wrote down something about themselves that they thought no one would ever guess. All these items were then printed on one page, and participants were asked to guess which personal fact belonged to which person. One group member, it turned out, had been made an honorary Sioux Indian; another was a scuba diver; still another had hosted a radio call-in show in Tuscon, Arizona. In addition to being fun, this activity encouraged everyone to both self-disclose and to learn about other aspects of peers and colleagues' lives.

Commitment

In order for participants to have a sense of continuity, consistency, and safety, it is essential that members agree to attend regular meetings. In the PRB groups, members agree to attend eight to ten one-and-a-half-hour sessions over a two- to four-month period.

Often these groups continue beyond the initial time commitment, with some members meeting for more than a year bi-weekly. In the self-employed group, members agree to attend most of the monthly, full morning meetings. The corporate internal consulting group meets for two consecutive days each quarter. Given the multiple demands of participants in all of these groups, it is inevitable that some people will miss sessions, and this is accepted, but the expectation is one of fairly regular attendance. When participants know that they will see the others next time, they generally feel more comfortable sharing personal experiences. A regular group whose members are on similar journeys creates a safety zone in which to reveal private details. Trust and a sense of community can develop among reliable partners.

Storytelling and Active Listening

In our technologically driven culture of sound bites and interruptions by cellular phones, beepers, and fax machines, it is a luxury to sit and tell a personal story with the full, quiet attention of a group. This kind of sharing is reminiscent of nights around the campfire when we were all younger and less preoccupied and of the Native American tradition of sitting before a fire, passing the peace pipe—and the invitation to tell a story—to the next person in the circle.

In the PRB group, the women have heard humorous and challenging stories about combining motherhood with demanding careers. Deidre described the time her fifteen-month-old son decided to make an omelet on the floor moments before she had to get him out the door to the day care center; Amy related how she made her family eat breakfast in the dining room instead of the kitchen because the regular table was set with balance sheets instead of place mats. In the self-employed group, participants have listened to accounts of successful new ventures and less than stellar training seminars. Group members can identify with the particulars and generalize to their own experience. This kind of learning from others who are in similar work-life situations is often far more powerful than sitting in a training classroom or reading a book on the subject. Each story has a lesson or lessons. For the audience, it is sometimes a relief to "just be and not do" and to be helpful to a peer by truly listening. For the storyteller, the undivided attention of the group is an antidote to the constant demands and interruptions from people and technology. At one recent corporate consulting group off-site meeting, Jill, an internal consultant, found tears rolling down her face as she admitted to the group that she could not keep up with all the demands and requests being made of her. Rather than immediately trying to "fix" her problem, the group patiently gave her space to share her frustration. Jill later remarked that this was healing for her.

Elka, a mother of two young children and a self-employed work and family consultant, summed it up when she proclaimed, "You mean I am going to be listened to for fifteen minutes, and no one is going to ask me to do anything?" Sharing stories with an interested audience helps the storyteller understand things that might not have been apparent otherwise. When Diane told how angry she got with her husband when he objected to her attending a concert with a friend on the weekend instead of being with him and the children, she realized that she herself was ambivalent about this choice. For both the storyteller and the listener, time seems to slow down during storytelling, a welcome relief in our time-pressed culture. Storytelling is deeply relational, and participants often leave with these stories permanently stored in their memory banks, ready to be retrieved when needed.

For groups rooted within an organizational context, there can often be a carryover effect that continues when participants return to their regular roles and duties. During a recent internal consulting group off-site meeting, the facilitator noted how difficult it seemed for members to publicly admit and discuss their own personal fears about their work. The following week, at a meeting prior to an extremely important senior executive training event, everyone shared their *dreams* from the night before. Each, it turned out, had had an anxiety dream related to the upcoming event. In sharing these dream stories, each person was indirectly admitting and sharing personal anxiety and fear about the coming day, thus making the anxiety and fear much more manageable.

Small Groups and Comfortable Settings

For participants to feel safe and comfortable, smaller groups seem to work better than larger ones. The self-employment group currently has six participants, with a cap of eight. The PRB groups are limited to twelve women, and the optimal size seems to be around eight or ten. While the corporate internal consulting group currently has more than eighteen members, it frequently subdivides into smaller units as a way to facilitate open communication. Periodically, the PRB group has had meetings with only four women, which although more intimate have often felt too close, even intrusive, and lacking in the kind of energy that comes from a slightly larger group.

It is important to see everyone's face and to maintain intimacy; therefore the table should be circular or oval and the room not too large or imposing.

A Balance Between Homogeneity and Diversity

There are common denominators that make each of the groups attractive to the participants. The PRB group for mothers in demanding careers is fairly homogeneous but has enough variety to provide alternative perspectives that enrich participants' learning. Although all are mothers in middle- and senior-level positions, their work hours vary. Some have nannies, others use family day care or daycare centers to provide child care. The age range of children is between newborn and eight years old, representing many developmental stages and age-specific issues. Some of the women aspire to be at the most senior level of an organization; others see that ambition as not congruent with their desires to be available for their children and their husbands. Some are line managers, others are in staff and consulting positions. The mothers in demanding careers find it helpful to meet with other well-educated and achievement-oriented women to share common issues and dilemmas but also to learn from women who have made different choices. There they belong and can talk freely about the pain of missing their child's school trip or the joy of receiving a promotion. For women whose work peers are primarily men, there is great freedom in joining with other mothers who really understand what it is like to put on makeup while dressing and feeding the children. As one woman put it, "In this group I feel normal, instead of weird like I feel with the stay-at-home moms in my neighborhood or with women at work who don't have kids and don't really understand what the pressures are like."

In the self-employment group, the common denominator is working on one's own, servicing individuals or companies or both. However, the work each member does is different, and they all have different types of clients. There are enough similarities for the women to feel as though the others understand their struggles—for example, when a client backs out of an agreement, the others know that this has major income and scheduling implications—but the variations in each of the women's businesses make the meetings richer and also allow for the sharing of contacts and resources with limited competition.

In the corporate internal consulting group, the general principal of balancing diversity with homogeneity also holds. Some internal consultants work directly for and represent their line organization business units, and others are part of corporate human resources. Some participants come from primarily a training background, some focus much more on organizational development. Some members hold doctorates and are academically inclined. Others are more hands-on and practice oriented. The group has an even mix of men and women. As in the other groups, there is enough difference among members to allow conflict and learning to occur and enough similarity to allow for a common identity to emerge.

Some Practical Dilemmas and Possible Action Steps

In thinking about starting a developmental sanctuary group, potential members and facilitators face a number of dilemmas and strategic choices. Here we discuss some of the more important ones.

Facilitators

One important initial choice involves whether or not to enlist the help of a trained facilitator or leader. On the plus side, an expert facilitator can help to create a sense of safety and trust in the beginning stages of a group, especially if there is likely to be significant conflict among members. A trained facilitator can also bring extra resources and knowledge to the group, as when Jane sometimes summarizes recent research on work-parenting issues for her PRB groups. He or she can create a sense of coherence and identity for a newly forming group, summarizing themes from recent sessions and weaving them into the current discussion. Facilitators provide a kind of stability and continuity—members may miss meetings from week to week, but the facilitator will always be present. A skillful facilitator can also help the group move to a *deeper* level of openness, trust, and honesty more quickly than might be true in a leaderless group, by making observations about the group's process and by asking probing questions of participants or by reflecting their comments back to them in a way that invites exploration of hidden assumptions and feelings.

Despite these benefits, though, expert facilitators are not always needed. If a high degree of trust already exists among participants and if there is common agreement about the purpose of the group and its norms, then a facilitator may not be necessary. In our experience, leaderless groups tend to work best when participants are highly committed to each other and their learning and when they already possess good interpersonal skills. Even when group members have these qualities, however, it is sometimes helpful to enlist the help of a trained facilitator. The corporate internal consulting group, for example, chose to use an outside facilitator despite the fact that group members were highly committed to each other and interpersonally quite skillful; they felt they needed to step outside of their own professional "facilitator" roles in order to be free to fully participate in the group as members.

Content Versus Process

Effective and successful groups, we found, focus on a specific task (improving consulting work, sharing marketing ideas, and so on) *as well as* on social and process issues (for example, setting aside time to talk and be listened to). Both elements, in fact, seem necessary for the effective functioning of these groups. Striking the correct balance between them, however, often poses dilemmas for both leaderless and facilitated groups. How much time should be devoted to pure sharing? How much to a more task-focused discussion about business issues, marketing, and so forth? Should an outside speaker be invited in to discuss some specific topic? Members of leaderless groups must decide these issues for themselves. Facilitators often struggle with similar questions and may also wonder how best to balance their roles as "expert/teacher" and "process facilitator." In her PRB groups, for example, Jane used to spend the first ten to fifteen minutes of each meeting giving a "minilecture" on some important work-family balance topic. In doing this, she was acting more in the role of expert/teacher than as a pure process facilitator. There are no simple rules here about how to best strike this balance. Are there important participant needs that seem to be going unmet? If so, then perhaps it is time to renegotiate this balance.

Balancing Heterogeneity and Homogeneity

As noted earlier, effective developmental support groups also balance diversity and sameness. Members must be similar enough to create a sense of identification with each other, yet different enough to allow significant learning and conflict to occur. If members differ on some important dimension (as in Jane's PRB group, in which some members are committed to working full-time, others part-time), the facilitator or organizer should try to find some other quality or aspect that all members share that can serve as a unifying basis for the group. Although initial mistakes in member selection may be inevitable, these tend to sort themselves out in time. In groups with too much diversity, members who feel different may choose to leave the group eventually. In groups with too much "sameness," a sense of boredom may signal the need for more diversity. Jane found that in one PRB group with a preponderance of part-time professionals, two full-time professional women in very demanding careers felt judged by the part-time professionals in the group and unsupported in their life and career choices. These two women might have left the group had Jane not chosen to discuss this issue openly, thus turning this conflict into a unique learning opportunity for all PRB group members to examine their underlying assumptions and values about work-family balance. This leads to another point: the more skillful a facilitator is in surfacing and dealing openly with conflict or the more skilled and competent group members are at listening nonjudgmentally and dealing constructively with conflict, the more diversity the group will be able to tolerate. In our experience, heterogeneous groups generate more profound learning among members.

Violations of Rules and Norms

Another dilemma for both facilitators and group members is what to do when someone violates group norms by, for example, monopolizing the group's time or rushing in with unwanted "helpful" suggestions. In our experience, these kinds of norm violations are most damaging to the group when left unacknowledged. For example, John was genuinely unaware that others perceived him as committing just such violations. The group came to secretly resent John, contributing to John's vague sense of feeling judgment and disapproval from them. John thought seriously about leaving the group; had this occurred, an opportunity for learning would have been lost. However, with the help of the facilitator, John was instead able to surface his feelings of being "different." This led to a good discussion of the implicit norms of the group, which others felt he often ignored. In the ensuing discussion, John examined this situation, and the group realized that John had been genuinely unaware of what he was doing. In fact, the group decided to make some important explicit revisions in its norms.

Dealing with Conflict

Conflict can exist among group members or between the facilitator and the group. In one PRB group, for example, a woman told how, upon arriving home from work at 10 P.M., she woke her daughter and read her a bedtime story so that they would have time together. To Jane, this action clearly did not seem in the best interest of the six-year-old girl. Jane wondered whether to remain in her role as "neutral facilitator" or to be more explicit about her own values and her negative reaction to this story. She ultimately chose not to share her reactions, fearing that to do so at that moment would have broken trust and caused the mother to feel judged and less part of the group. At a later point in the group's development, however, when trust had been more firmly established, such a nonneutral or out-of-role response might have been more appropriate, especially if the facilitator publicly noted it as such.

Other Questions About Developmental Support Groups

Although our experience with developmental support groups has been mostly positive, there are some potential negative aspects of these groups, as the following questions suggest:

Is the time taken for these meetings always worth it?

There may be times in a busy person's work life when attending a developmental support group creates more stress than it alleviates, especially if work demands have become temporarily so high that taking any time away from work could result in failure to meet some critical goals. At those times, it may be best to postpone attending such a group and to "attend" instead to completing whatever tasks are required at work. If such a situation becomes chronic, however, as may be increasingly true in downsized organizations that seem to require ever more of their employees, then membership in such a developmental support group is *strongly* advised, for several reasons. First, the group can provide a kind of support and nourishment that can be of enormous benefit in surviving and thriving in continually chaotic, stressful environments. Second, in this kind of harried corporate world, the group can provide a *scheduled* structure for self-reflection and space to reflect on whether one wants to maintain or alter this life structure. Otherwise, one can become so busy that there is never time to reflect on one's busyness and to potentially break the pattern.

Are these support groups elitist or appropriate for all employee populations?

While our group facilitation experience has been primarily with professionals and managers, we see no reason why this model should only be useful for "privileged" populations. One of our colleagues has been leading a successful lunchtime support group for about a year in a "Big Six" accounting firm in New York for mothers who are secretaries and staff assistants. Her group focuses on parenting and child-care issues. In her opinion, the major difference between this group and another one she leads for professionals and managers is that the secretaries have less control over their schedules and need to put more effort into negotiating with their bosses for time off for group meetings. As with the other developmental support groups described, the benefits participants derive are very similar: increase in personal control, enhanced connection, normalization of one's life situation, empowerment, and reduction of stress. The company continues to fund our colleague's work, apparently finding the investment in time and money well worth it from the corporate perspective. (The question of whether most companies would actually fund these kinds of groups for lower-level employees is a separate issue, however.)

Do participants ever feel too much pressure to conform to norms of the group?

Whether such pressure exists will depend in large part on the kind of environment established by the facilitator and/or group members. There is little danger of these groups becoming overly oppressive or infringing on personal freedom, in our view, because members are always free to leave if they do not feel that they are getting what they need and because the level of commitment required of members, although significant, is bounded.

When is it time for an individual to leave a group or for a group to end?

Individuals generally join developmental support groups to help themselves with some life transition—however clearly or vaguely defined—with which they are currently struggling. It is entirely appropriate, in our view, for participants to leave a group when they have finished this work and completed their transition-in-progress. Sometimes individuals also leave groups because they feel misunderstood, judged, or "different." In some situations, such choices may be appropriate. However, we would caution against prematurely exiting for any of these reasons without first surfacing and discussing one's concerns with the group, as we have discussed earlier. Often these discussions will help *change* the dynamics of the group in such a way that leaving is no longer necessary. If someone is considering leaving a group because of such feelings of alienation, a good first step would be to discuss the intention with the facilitator (if the group has one) or with several key members. It might also be helpful to discuss one's experience with someone outside the group as a kind of reality check.

Groups can also end when their members have collectively completed the work that brought them to the group initially. More often, however, individual members will come and go, but the group will continue. If the mix of participants is not working well, for any number of reasons, then it also may be necessary to end the group or reorganize it with other members that will provide more balance or whatever other qualities are missing.

Do developmental support groups foster unhealthy dependency?

Some believe that individuals should be able to work out career dilemmas and life issues on their own. However, we believe that although doing so is certainly possible, it can be stressful and often does not yield the best solutions to one's problems. This is not to confuse mutual support with personal responsibility, of course. But we see no inherent conflict between taking full personal responsibility for one's actions and participating in mutual support groups. Furthermore, developmental support groups, in our experience, rarely if ever lead to the kind of unhealthy dependency sometimes found in more intensive therapeutic or cult-like groups. Developmental support groups are voluntary; they tend to be democratic and not authoritarian in nature, with egalitarian leaders or no leaders at all; they encourage members to work out their own solutions and choices to problems rather than handing them pat solutions. If anything, the kind of developmental support groups we are describing, by functioning as developmental holding environments for their members, actually help to foster psychological maturity, individuation, and growth.

Getting Started

Here are some guidelines to help career development professionals set up the types of groups we have been discussing.

- Determine what needs you are serving, and target the population that would benefit from a developmental support group.
- Sell internally as a low-cost alternative to reducing stress and increasing organizational commitment, empowerment, and self-direction.
- Contract for an outside facilitator unless an appropriate internal resource exists, considering issues of confidentiality and special expertise that would be beneficial for this group.
- Invite prospective participants via letter or E-mail with phone call follow-up.
- Monitor the group by communicating regularly with the group facilitator as well as with some of the participants.

- Evaluate the effectiveness of the group on a regular basis and provide feedback to the facilitator, suggesting appropriate adjustments on content, structure, size, or mix of group.

Conclusion

Although certainly not a panacea, developmental support groups can and do contribute significantly to both the personal growth and career development of their members. These groups may be increasingly helpful and important in a post-modern work world characterized by constant change, little security, and a diminishing sense of community. They offer a kind of badly needed sanctuary in which the hard developmental work of continuing to grow as adults can occur, even flourish. In this new, turbulent environment, the kind of mutual support offered by these groups is vitally needed.

Chapter Fourteen

Implications
The New Role of the Career Practitioner
Douglas T. Hall

Now that the preceding chapters have reviewed the major contemporary influences on individual career development, what does all of this mean for the work of the career development professional? If you are a career consultant, a counselor, an outplacement specialist, a human resource professional, or a manager who wants to do a better job of helping your subordinates grow, how do you begin to translate these good ideas into action? In fact, this question has already been partially answered within each of the previous chapters, but there is more to be said.

In our opinion, the most important single activity an organization can pursue is communicating openly with employees about the current psychological career contract. We will start here. Then we will look at more specific issues, such as career self-development, succession planning, assignment management, reflection and learning from experience, technology, diversity, and work-life activities. We will conclude by showing how organizations can tap employees' energy and excitement through having and communicating a clear and valued corporate purpose—to provide the environment for the employee to pursue the path with a heart.

Owning Up to the New Psychological Career Contract

Lost in all of the talk about the loss of the old career contract is an important fact: the new career contract is already here (Mirvis and

Hall, 1994). It has not been established universally, but in organizations that went through restructuring several years ago, the new contract is "up and running," as we have said in Chapters One and Two. Yet our research indicates that there is a perceptual lag in the awareness of the new contract because no one wants to see it! But let us start with what the new contract is and how it has emerged.

Chapter Three described in detail the implications of the new contract on the new workplace and the worker: self-designed jobs, self-development, continuous learning, and flexibility. But it takes a long time for employees to really comprehend this.

In research that Jonathan Moss and I have been conducting on employee adjustment to the new contract (Hall and Moss, 1995), we have found a significant time lag between top management's seeing this new career environment, on the one hand, and employees' awareness and acceptance of the "new deal," on the other. To see how the adjustment took place, we looked at companies that had been hit by the changed environment at different times. So, for example, we first looked at companies such as AT&T and NYNEX, which were pulled apart by the divestiture decree of 1984, and Xerox, which was severely challenged by competition from Japanese copiers in the early 1980s. We also looked at firms such as IBM and Digital Equipment Corporation, where the world changed drastically in the late 1980s or early 1990s.

What we discovered was that we were hearing quite different perceptions of the old and new contract, depending upon how long ago the change had occurred. We also found that after a certain period of time, the organization and its employees did seem to come to an acceptance of the new contract and a sense of equilibrium about it. This is not to say that the earlier state of equilibrium or relative stability was restored: far from it. It is clear that the old "business as usual" with a relatively low-pressure pace of work will never be seen again. The adjustment to the new contract takes the form of an adaptation to a state of permanent uncertainty, change, and learning. As we have said in earlier chapters, the new status quo is continuous learning and feeling continuously on the edge, off balance. For the individual employee, the adjustment takes the form of learning through personal experience that it is in fact possible to adapt quickly and survive various crises. The employee also learns to value this resilience and personal mastery as well as the increased personal freedom and power provided by the new work environment.

We were surprised, however, that in most cases it took about seven years before employees came to accept the new contract. Much of this was a matter of internal organizational communication coupled with a growing willingness to face up to the change and acknowledge it.

We also saw a lag between the organization's (that is, top management's) awareness of the new contract and the workforce's awareness. Invariably, senior management would read the signals from the environment (tougher competition, faster product and technology changes, more customer demand for quality, global competition) and try to communicate them to the rest of the organization. In time, most employees might realize the reality of the environmental changes, but it was difficult to know fully what they meant as long as little had changed inside the firm. Then at some point, drastic organizational changes would have to be made—perhaps a takeover, perhaps major losses leading to downsizing, perhaps divestiture of large parts of the firm—involving the separation of large parts of the workforce. Only when that happened would most employees truly believe that the world had changed.

Thus in such firms as IBM and Apple, where the changes are recent, the view of the old contract was primarily positive, expressed in terms of some form of employment guarantee (which had been violated), and the view of the new contract was negative, focusing on the actions of the organization (layoffs, restructuring, and leanness.)

For firms where the contract changed earlier, where there is more clarity and acceptance of the new contract, ironically, the old contract is viewed in more negative terms and the new contract is seen more positively. The old contract is described here with words such as *paternalism* and *dependency*. In discussing the new contract, employees use terms such as *training, growing, individual responsibility, empowerment, performing,* and *working hard.* Clearly, where the new contract has taken hold, employees see their personal responsibility for maintaining their own learning and development and for their own career moves. The career is no longer to be entrusted to the organization; it is managed by the employee, and employees value this new personal control they have over their lives.

Career consultant Cliff Hakim (1994) describes the new contract as one in which employees have to adopt a new mind-set: that of being self-employed. Hakim (1994) describes this new relationship with the organization as follows: "[N]ow you no longer work *for*, you work *with* a company. . . . *With* implies equality, dignity, and the ability to respond to challenges *as well as* to respect others. . . . *With* makes a statement about your interdependence. . . . *With* is also a statement about your independence. . . . *With* is a link to the team, project, or organization; it is also a safety net—parachute— and path toward other opportunities. *With* is your new reality. It is a mistake for people to think that they truly work *for* anyone" (pp. 86–87).

With the new contract, the employee no longer has the "luxury" of being moved around by the company to meet the company's needs and then having the company say "Trust us" when the employee questions or objects to the move. Now the employee must trust her- or himself.

In fact, I would even question how well the old contract worked in years past. In the best cases, the firm lived up to its end of the implied "Trust us" bargain by delivering some career reward later in time (perhaps a key promotion, a move back to the family's preferred location). In many cases, however, the employee ended up feeling betrayed upon hitting a career plateau or some other kind of setback. Perhaps what was really most different about the recent changes in the contract was that it happened publicly and across the board, affecting the whole workforce at the same time.

Ten Steps to Becoming a Better Career Practitioner

In much the same way as careers are profoundly different today from twenty or fifty years ago, so necessarily must be the practice of facilitating employees' career development. A logical question might arise for a thoughtful practitioner after reviewing the complex career issues in the preceding chapters: if the new contract is with the self and not with the organization, and if organizational life is so chaotic and the need for continuous learning so strong, is conscious planning for career growth even feasible?

In my opinion, an organization should not be in the business of promoting career planning. Assuming that you, the career professional, are based in an organization, here are some proposals for practice, which also apply to independent career consultants.

1.   *Start with the recognition that the individual "owns" the career.*
In the past, lip service was often paid to the idea that the career was the employee's responsibility. However, this tended to cover up the fact that the company was doing little or nothing to provide career assistance for lower-level employees. For them, the statement was in fact true but in a more negative sense: they were being left to fend for themselves. Also, in the case of managerial, executive, and key professional employees, the policy was overridden whenever the organization had a pressing need to place the person in a certain assignment. Under those conditions, the career was in fact the company's property under the guise of a succession planning or human resource planning process.

As the chapters in this volume have indicated, now organizations cannot—even if they want to—do meaningful planning for a person's career, not even for managers and key executives. Instead, development takes place "closer to the customer" in the form of coaching, feedback from various sources, mentoring, job demands, and other relational and work experiences, as Chapter Five has shown. Many of these are spontaneous, everyday activities that are difficult to control in an integrated program (although some organizations manage to do it).

Even a formal career program such as succession planning is usually a "paper process," where much effort goes into assessing the potential of management candidates for higher positions and where sometimes those assessments are shared with the candidate in a developmental way. But rarely do those assessments and developmental plans get translated into later action. Management staffing needs are usually very immediate, the available internal pool is often very thin, and increasingly companies are engaging external recruiters to fill key positions.

So much for organizational career planning. What can the organization and the individual do to promote career growth?

2.   *Create information and support for the individual's own efforts at development.*
Although the career professional and the organization cannot do much directly to develop a person's career, they can do a great

deal to provide the necessary empowering resources for career development. The two most important resources are information about opportunities throughout the organization and support in obtaining information and in taking developmental action.

With information technology, it is becoming increasingly possible to enable employees to learn about the strategic direction of the business, about work opportunities in different areas, about specific position openings, and about upcoming training and development programs. Electronic résumé systems make it possible for a person to be considered for a position without even knowing about it. There is a vast array of career software (Career Architect, CareerSearch, SIGI, Discover, and others) that helps individuals engage in self-assessment and obtain information about career opportunities outside their own organization. Many of these information resources are provided by educational institutions for their graduates and by professional associations and community organizations. There is a vast network of career self-help organizations and resources (books, computer software, mentoring programs, seminars, and so forth). An organization could do an excellent job of promoting career development simply by encouraging employees to take advantage of the full range of career-enhancing information resources available inside and outside the organization, at career resource centers and libraries. Organizational career development as a practice is shifting from being a direct provider of career services to being a career resource and referral agent. Let us look at this point in more detail.

3. *Recognize that career development is a relational process in which the career practitioner plays a "broker" role.*

Within an organization, the role of the career practitioner has shifted from the creator of career programs to the broker of career-enhancing experiences. Fletcher's research (Chapter Four) suggests finding ways to bring people together to redesign their work to make it more growth enhancing and more livable. It might mean advocating for new performance appraisal criteria, which would reward the relational work that Fletcher finds is now rendered invisible in many work settings.

Being a broker could also mean facilitating mentoring and other forms of developmental relationships as described in Chapter Four. It could mean helping people, especially managers and supervisors, learn to create "secure base" relationships to support the development of colleagues, as advocated by Kahn in Chapter Six. It could mean helping work teams and individuals find ways to create "safe havens" for reflection or for dealing with stressful situations, as recommended by Louis and Seibert in Chapters Nine and Ten respectively. In a similar vein, the career practitioner could help people create groups for promoting development, "developmental sanctuaries," as described in Chapter Thirteen.

Another kind of relational structure that the career practitioner could help broker is the dialogue group to help people do the personal development that Barbara Walker (Chapter Eleven) shows us lies at the heart of diversity work. A dialogue group is a type of developmental sanctuary, but whereas some sanctuaries may be made up of similar people dealing with similar issues, a dialogue group is generally made up of members who are different from each other and who can help each other learn how to deal with difference.

4.   *Become an expert on career information and assessment technology.*

In the past, with more corporate resources devoted to human resources, there were some professionals who specialized in career information and assessment technology and others who focused on counseling or organization development. Now, with fewer career professionals, they must be both specialists *and* generalists. They must be certified on the latest assessment and development instruments, familiar with the most recent computer software, *and* know how to work with line management to create experience-based career development processes. Thus career professionals must be at least as proactive regarding their own growth and cultivation of new skills as they are advocating for clients. Personal networking, developing alliances and partnerships, regular participation in professional conferences, attending certification programs for new technology, and professional reading are all "must-do's."

5.   *Become a professional communicator about your services and the new career contract.*

Being a broker and a recognized expert can also mean communicating the information about the specific nature of the new career contract to the employee and the employer. This is a role that external career consultants are often better positioned to play because they are independent of the issues and politics in any particular organization.

Some of the more innovative independent career consultants now publish career newsletters, which are good ways to communicate these new career expectations. For example, Boston-based consultant Priscilla H. Claman publishes *Career Notes* (see Exhibit 14.1), and in the September 1995 issue we see articles such as "A Revolution in the World of Work," "Rose Sells Her Strengths," and "Tom Finds Balance" in addition to information about upcoming local career development seminars and talks. Other examples of career professionals and firms with widely distributed newsletters, as well as track records of coverage in national media (for example, the *Wall Street Journal*), are the late Zandy Leibowitz's Career Strategies and Larry Stybel and Maryanne Peabody's Stybel, Peabody & Associates, Inc. Of course, internal career professionals can do the same with in-house newsletters from their career center, resource library, or professional development division (or whatever the career development unit is called).

6.   *Promote work planning, not career planning.*

As we have said, the key task for the individual in a complex, changing environment is finding a good fit with work that is needed in the world. This implies that the career practitioner should be encouraging people to think about areas of work and projects they would like to pursue over a time period of, say, three to five years. It is not realistic for most people to make plans beyond that time frame, and it is far less daunting to think about "my work for the next few years" than it is to "plan out my career."

Nevertheless, it is not as easy as it sounds. Although the time frame is intermediate, this still involves having a longer-term sense of personal direction, finding or knowing one's own path. It means being in touch with one's own identity and values, which may be expressed in different ways at different points in life through different kinds of work. But over time, even though the work activities might change dramatically, if the person is following his or her "path with a heart," which we discussed in the Introduction to this volume, there will probably be clear threads or themes underlying those work activities—and it is these threads or themes that form the career.

Exhibit 14.1. Career Notes.

The Newsletter of CAREER STRATEGIES Incorporated   Vol. 7 No. 3 September 1995

Priscilla H. Claman
President, Career Strategies

A Revolution in the World of Work

"We are all going through a revolution so immense, it may be even bigger than the Industrial Revolution!" My friend was standing there in front of my office on Beacon Street in Boston, gesturing wildly to make sure I understood the importance of what he was saying.

He is right, of course. We *are* going through a revolution in the way we work and in the relationship of people to their employers. William Bridges in his article "The End of the Job" argues that the "job" is merely a social artifact developed during the Industrial Revolution to package the work in the growing factories. We are in the process of dramatic change as "jobs" and the organizational bureaucracies built to sustain them crumble. The global

economy, reengineering, outsourcing, the quality and team movements have all affected the way we work. The "job" as we've come to know it is rapidly disappearing. The employer-employee "mutual loyalty contract" has vanished.

At Career Strategies, both our individual clients and our corporate clients are coming up with new bases for productive relationships now that lifetime employment is no longer a given.

For employers, it means hiring, promoting, training for and rewarding the skills and competencies needed to be competitive in today's marketplace. Companies are beginning to identify those competencies and actively put in place systems that reinforce them.

continued on back

continued on back

Rose Sells Her Strengths

After graduating from college, Rose used a personal connection to secure a position at a company that offered a good salary, a generous benefits package and presumably, the potential for advancement. "I suspected going in that the job itself wasn't a perfect match for my skills. But I thought if I could serve my time in that job, eventually I could move into something I liked better."

Try as she did, Rose just didn't have the skill set to sustain her in the position. "I'm more a big-picture, creative type. Details are a struggle for me." Less than a year later Rose found herself in a job search.

Before embarking on her search, she recognized the need to clearly identify her skills. "I never really took time to do this before. I majored in Business Administration in college because everyone said I could always find a job in business. I've

continued on back

continued on back

Tom Finds Balance

In Tom's retail business long hours were common. "I ran the entire operation. I was *always* on-call, seven days a week. That was the down side of the job. But there were many factors of the job that seemed to help balance those pressures." Tom thrived on the diverse nature of his work, the entrepreneurial flair, and his customer interaction. Then one day an opportunity presented itself. Sold on the 9 to 5 work hours, Tom left his retail position and moved into a single-focused sales position. "The money was right and the work hours sounded refreshing." But after just four months, Tom realized he had made a mistake. Working 40 hours a week compared to his previous 70-75, he and his family were thoroughly enjoying their newly found togetherness. "At first it seemed as though the better work/family balance would be strong enough to support my move." Then •

Success Stories
In the following accounts some facts have been changed to maintain confidentiality

---

For the career professional, this means putting more stress on the employee's or the client's self-assessment than on the specific jobs or career fields in any given organization.

7. *Promote learning through relationships and work.*

The silver lining in the current cloud of shrinking resources in most organizations is the increasing supply of two of the key resources for career learning (Hall, 1993): work challenge and relationships. In the restructured, delayered organization, the people who remain are left with far more challenging jobs and more team-based work. Organizations that are adapting successfully by becoming learning organizations are encouraging employees to help each other learn the new skills and competencies needed in their more demanding jobs. Although some of this learning comes from formal training programs (often delivered in a "just-in-time" format), we would argue that most real training comes from peer-assisted, self-directed learning through such vehicles as project teams, task forces, electronic relationships (the Internet and E-mail), personal networks, support groups, customer relationships, and boss or subordinate relationships.

For this peer-based, on-the-job learning to be successful, the organization needs to provide supervisory and technological support as well as a culture that promotes learning and risk taking. According to Leonard Wynn, quality director at AT&T's Baldrige Award–winning North Andover, Massachusetts, plant, this means a move away from pressure to "get it right the first time" to a stress on "prizing" the detection of defects and learning from them.

8. *Be an organizational interventionist.*

To truly help people learn through relationships and work, you have to be able to influence the kind of work they do and the kind of people with whom they come into contact. This means playing an active role in organizational practices, such as how job and other work (task forces, projects) assignments are made. If you have responsibility for staffing or succession planning, this is already part of your authority; if not, it means being proactive and positioning yourself so that you can have influence over work.

Being proactive could mean any of the following things:

Being assigned to the implementation task force for a major corporate restructuring

Enlisting the help of the boss (or the boss's boss) to get on the divisional personnel committee or to be part of that new task force on the development of high potentials

Volunteering to be on the firm's diversity committee and then pushing that committee to take on the task of increasing access to job opportunities

Developing informal relationships with key executives who are supportive of career development and perhaps pushing for the creation of a career development task force made up of key executives to promote better utilization and retention of talent

9. *Promote mobility and the value of the "learner identity."*

If major sources of career learning are challenging work and helpful co-workers, this implies that continuous learning should be promoted by continuous mobility. A key indicator of career growth in today's environment is job movement, so the career professional should promote the view of turnover as a positive, not a negative. Our criterion of success in a selection decision should not be how long a person has stayed in a position; rather, success should be defined as the person's ability to move easily from job to job. We need to promote a culture in which it is just as highly valued to be a learner as to be a peak performer.

This raises a complication in the area of the move to skill-based pay and performance-based compensation. Although skill-based pay is definitely consistent with what we are saying is needed for career growth, if there is too much emphasis on pay for high performance levels in a given position, it could create a disincentive for moving to a new job that requires starting over as a learner. This problem can be solved by large enough learning bonuses and premiums for mastering new skills.

The point is to put less stress on mastery per se (as an end point) and more emphasis on learning and improvement. As in total quality, there is no "finish line" in the race for continuous career learning. The career practitioner can promote several approaches, including moving through the "shamrock" described in Chapter One (that is, giving contingent workers the opportunity to become regular employees if they wish) and forming networks to provide information and support for job mobility.

10.   *Develop the mind-set of using "natural resources for development."*
Organizations today are seeing that several naturally occurring
resources use the everyday work environment as a development
tool. The role of the practitioner is to help the individual recognize such resources and find ways to utilize them. Elements in the
natural work environment that can be used to aid career development include assignments (jobs, teams, task forces, committees);
feedback (360-degree, performance review); developmental relations (such as mentoring); and coaching (skill-building, not just
remedial).

In the *organization,* certain resources are critical: corporate purpose (human meaning) and values (for example, for personal identification); support for development; commitment to diversity
(through dialogue groups or self-reflection processes); freedom of
movement (cross-functional, cross-business); easy access to career
information (such as on-line information); and value for balance,
for developing the whole person.

Finally, individuals need self-assessment resources (360-degree
feedback, PC-based instruments, and so on); the skills for reflection (journals, peer-reflection methods) and exploration (networks, openness); and the ability to ask for help (from peers, boss,
friends), adapt (go for novelty, learn new skills), make life plans
(with family, partner), develop action plans (which might be linked
to performance review), and take action (risk, move, take nontraditional assignments).

Linking Careers to Organizational Values and Purpose

While all of these activities are important in helping people pursue their career direction, the positive effects are multiplied if the
career professional can communicate compellingly the critical
need for the organization to be worthy of the person's respect.
Throughout this book, we have been talking about the current
need to find meaning, connection, and community in life and in
work. We would argue that if the workplace is the only source of
this larger purpose, then one's life is out of balance, but there is
evidence that the more meaning can be found in work, the more
fulfilled a person can be. In fact, it appears that the more this
meaning is found at work, the more likely this positive experience

is to spill over into the person's private life (Evans and Bartolome, 1980; Harmon and Hormann, 1990).

There is much attention in the popular press these days to this quest for meaning and spirituality in our turbulent environment, as Joseph Boyce points out in "Leaps of Faith: More People Join Clergy After First Pursuing a Career in Business" (1995). After decades of looking outside for a larger purpose, whether it was the Cold War and international threats, military service and economic achievement, or the corporate battleground and the huge financial rewards it offered in the 1980s, people are finding that the real challenge today is internal; it has to do with the way we think about our work and how we make sense of the ultimate value of that work.

A few decades ago, my colleague Benjamin Schneider and I looked into the question of what leads a person to identify with an organization and its mission. We looked at three quite different sorts of organizations, but they were all organizations with a high proportion of professional employees, where the motivation and psychological involvement of the individual employees had a direct impact on the overall success of the organization: priests in the U.S. Roman Catholic Church, foresters in the U.S. Forest Service, and engineers and scientists in a number of research and development firms (Hall and Schneider, 1973; Hall, Schneider, and Nygren, 1970; Schneider and Hall, 1972).

We found that where the values of the organization were shared and respected by the employees, the level of employee identification with the organization was the highest. The more the employee identified with the organization, the more the employee experienced psychological success and job satisfaction. Most important, the highest levels of identification were felt by employees who had a clear vision of the core mission and purpose of the organization and who placed a strong personal value on that mission. For example, the central purpose of the U.S. Forest Service is public service (and the management of public land to serve the maximum number of people with multiple uses). Those foresters who felt the greatest identification and personal meaning in their work were those who attached a high level of personal value to public service. Similarly, in the Roman Catholic Church, those priests who placed the greatest personal value on the theological values behind the church's mission had the highest levels of organizational identification and psychological success. (They were also the priests who were least likely to leave the priesthood.)

What this means today is that organizational leaders should stop using organizational jargon (words such as *strategy, reengineering, redeployment*), which not only are very abstract to the average employee but have also come to be seen as "antiemployee" because they are usually linked with downsizing and layoffs. Instead, leaders should communicate clearly the central purpose or mission of the organization in very human terms that show how the work of the organization adds value to the world. This applies to all types of organizations: for-profit, nonprofit, public, educational, health care, and all the rest. To tap the maximum potential energy from employees (and to help them see the larger meaning of their work), leaders must be able to show employees the organization's reason for being.

Corporations That Have Created Meaning

Let us turn to some corporate examples to make this talk of values and purpose more concrete.

Komatsu Corporation

For more than twenty years, the strategic intent of the Komatsu Corporation, as stated by Ryoichi Kawai when he succeeded his father as president, was to "catch up with and surpass Caterpillar" (Bartlett and Ghoshal, 1994, p. 83). Based on this strategy, each year a specific operating priority would be chosen (reducing costs, increasing exports) and translated into a detailed action plan, using Komatsu's tightly controlled "PDCA" (plan, do, check, act) management system.

However, by 1989, when the worldwide demand for construction equipment was down, competition had increased, and Komatsu's profits were dropping, the new president, Tetsuya Katada, saw that the firm's top management had become so obsessed with catching Caterpillar that the managers had stopped thinking in terms of broader options and questioning what business they were in. For example, their product development was focused on creating competition for Cat's high-end bulldozers rather than going after the smaller, more flexible equipment that the market needed.

Therefore, Katada challenged his managers to "go out and see the needs and opportunities and operate in a creative and innovative way, always encouraging initiative from below" (Bartlett and Ghoshal, 1994, p. 83). In a series of management meetings and discussions, a new definition of the company emerged—"total technology enterprise"—with opportunities to utilize its expertise in electronics, robotics, and plastics. The new banner was "Growth, Global, Groupwide." As Katada said, "Compared with our old objective, the Three Gs slogan may seem abstract, but it was this abstract nature that stimulated people to ask what they could do and respond creatively" (p. 83). In the first three years under the Three Gs mission, after steady declines since 1982, sales have picked up, spurred by a 40 percent increase in Komatsu's non-construction equipment business.

AT&T

Bartlett and Ghoshal (1994) also cite the example of CEO Bob Allen's statement of purpose at AT&T. Frustrated by an organization that felt like a regulated utility to many employees, Allen decided to communicate the firm's new purpose—"loading more traffic onto the existing telecommunications network and developing products to meet the needs of an emerging infocom business" (p. 82)—in different, more human terms: "bringing people together—giving them easy access to each other and to the information and services they want and need—anytime, anywhere" (p. 82). This was language anyone could understand, and the purpose was one that most employees could relate to personally and take pride in. In addition, Allen challenged his entire organization to interpret and operationalize this "anytime, anywhere" statement for themselves, and he created mechanisms such as a strategy forum, in which the firm's top sixty executives hold two- or three-day meetings five times a year to discuss and refine AT&T's overall direction.

Starbucks Coffee

On a smaller scale, consider the fast-growing Starbucks Coffee organization, run by entrepreneur Howard Schultz, who purchased the Seattle business in 1987. He envisioned an empire of stores "based on the notion that even though the term 'coffee break' is part of the vernacular, there's traditionally been no place to enjoy one, 'an extension of people's front porch,' as he puts it" (Witchel, 1994, p. C8). The firm is now the largest coffee-bar chain in the United States, with 470 stores, eight million employees, two million customers served each week, and net sales of $285 million in 1994, up from $176 the previous year. Starbucks also operates a large mail-order and wholesale business.

To implement his strategy of having Starbucks stores become "an extension of people's front porch," Schultz takes care of employees first, so that they will in turn take care of customers. "The customer does not come first, the employee does. It's sort of the corporate version of 'I'm O.K., you're O.K.'" (Witchel, 1994, p. C8). Starbucks was the first company in the United States to grant full health care benefits and stock options to its part-time workers (who make up 65 percent of its workforce). As Schultz describes his mission, "I always saw myself wanting to be deemed successful and good at the same time. . . . Service is a lost art in America. I think people want to do a good job, but if they are treated poorly they get beaten down. It's not viewed as a professional job in America to work behind a counter. We don't believe that. We want to provide our people with dignity and self-esteem, and we can't do that with lip service. So we offer tangible benefits. The attrition rate in retail fast food is between 200 and 400 percent a year. At Starbucks, it's 60 percent" (Witchel, 1994, p. C8).

Schultz describes the origin of his management philosophy in very personal terms: "My father didn't finish high school, and what I remember most was the way he was treated in his adult life, which beat him down. He didn't have the self-esteem to feel worthy of a good job. So, I try to give people hope and self-esteem through a company that respects them. Dad never had that opportunity. The culture and esprit de corps of the company is where I and others in Starbucks have come from. Every one of our actions have to be compatible with the quality of our coffee. It never lets you down" (Witchel, 1994, p. C8).

When asked about the secret of his success, Schultz looked a bit embarrassed and reflected, "Maybe I wasn't jaded. I always wanted to do something to make a difference. Maybe people gravitated to that" (Witchel, 1994, p. C8). Starbucks's performance seems to be an example of the notion that in business "you can do well by doing good."

Practical Steps in Creating Meaning

For instilling organizational values, Bartlett and Ghoshal (1994) recommend three actions. First, build on core values. This means that contemporary values cannot exist totally separated from the firm's traditions and culture. For example, when Jamie Houghton of Corning was trying to instill values of quality and corporate leadership in the early 1980s, he overlaid these on the firm's traditional beliefs of respect for the individual and commitment to integrity.

Second, corporate leaders must spread the message. (Career professionals can encourage them to do so.) Houghton sets himself the goal of visiting ten different Corning facilities each quarter to "talk, listen, and feel the atmosphere." He also made sure that business units whose strategies did not fit with the corporate values were either redirected or were divested or spun off.

The third step in communicating values is to measure progress. To ensure that the hard measures of financial performance will not drive out these softer objectives related to larger purpose, tangible forms of measurement must be found. For example, in the 1980s, Houghton set the objective that by the mid 1990s Corning would be listed as among the world's most respected companies—for example, by being listed in *Fortune*'s annual poll of "America's most admired corporations." This measure combines financial performance with leadership in quality, innovation, and corporate responsibility. This is certainly a measure with which employees can identify and take pride (Bartlett and Ghoshal, 1994).

Giving Meaning to Employees' Work

To bring these organizational activities down to the level of the individual employee, Bartlett and Ghoshal (1994) again boil it down to three simple steps. First, recognize individual accomplishments. Although this may sound obvious, everyday life in most corporations is full of incidents of employees' performing significant acts of accomplishment—that go unnoticed. Thus concrete actions by leaders to provide recognition can be extremely powerful in energizing human effort. For example, consider Ingvar Kamprad, founder of IKEA, the world's largest manufacturer and retailer of home furnishings. With fifty thousand employees in twenty countries, Kamprad still tried to visit each of the firm's seventy-five outlets and meet every employee. On a visit, he would often invite employees to stay for dinner after closing (with sales associates going through the dinner line first, then managers, then Kamprad), and he would circulate among employees, offering praise, encouragement, and advice.

Next, the firm must commit to developing employees. In the aftermath of downsizing and reengineering, many firms have abandoned the idea of employee or career development—and thus even employees who survived still feel abandoned. Yet top management is asking, "How can we rebuild the psychological contract?"

A simple part of the answer is that the firm must devote efforts to developing employees, even if it cannot promise long-term employment. This training should focus on general "employability" skills, such as learning how to learn and personal development. As Anita Roddick, founder and CEO of The Body Shop, said on establishing an education center that focused not just on company products but also on AIDS, sociology, aging, and urban survival: "You can train dogs. We wanted to *educate* our people and help them realize their full potential" (Bartlett and Ghoshal, 1994, p. 87). Corning's Houghton is committed to an objective of increasing education and development to 5 percent of every employee's total working hours. Andersen Consulting sees the development of its employees as a strategic objective in and of itself because intellectual capital is the basis of Andersen's service. The company makes no proprietary claims to the skills and knowledge it provides to employees and promotes this investment as a form of career security. According to its recruiting information, "after training with us, you could work for anyone anywhere—or you could work for yourself." The result: "an exceptionally well-trained and extremely loyal group of associates" (Bartlett and Ghoshal, 1994, p. 87).

Empowering Yourself and Helping Others To Do So

A critical part of development is empowering employees for continuous learning. The key competencies in most kinds of work now are not know-how but learn-how. Employees must learn how to be both independent and integrated with colleagues in doing the learning that is required now for successful performance. A bit part of this empowerment for self-development consists of learning how to operate effectively as a "middle" in work relationships, either in a middle-level position in an organization or in between a customer and someone else (a supplier, a boss, another customer). Barry Oshry (1992, 1995) offers two strategies and five tactics for "empowering yourself in the middle" (organization-based career professionals, take note):

Strategy I: Do not slide into the middle of other people's issues and conflicts and make them your own. Be clear when an issue is *their* issue, not yours. Do what you can to empower them to resolve their own issues.

Strategy II: Do not lose your mind. Being in the middle is an easy place to lose your own independent perspective on what is going on and what needs to happen. Seek out your own information and formulate your own perspective to operate independently.

Tactic 1: Be "Top" when you can, and take the responsibility of being Top. Utilize the areas of autonomy that you have. Assume authority and responsibility. Do not ask for permission if permission is not necessary.

Tactic 2: Be "Bottom" when you should. Rather than just acting like a "sewer pipe, passing garbage down from the top to the bottom," explain to the Tops when garbage is garbage. "Don't be a mindless funnel. Work it out with Tops. The buck stops at the Top; the garbage stops in the middle" (Oshry, 1992, p. 13).

Tactic 3: Be coach. When others bring their problems to middles, middles often assume it is their job to resolve the problem and feel guilty if they cannot. But do not let them shift the monkey from their back to yours. Instead, listen, understand, offer to support them in finding solutions. Result: you not only empower the individuals but you also create a more powerful organization with more independent resources to solve problems.

Tactic 4: Facilitate. Do not act as the go-between among various parties, although others would be happy to put you in that role. Instead, bring together people who need to work together to solve a problem and facilitate their interactions in whatever ways are necessary to be effective. The more productive connections you create among a network of people, the stronger the system becomes.

IMPLICATIONS 333

Tactic 5: Integrate with one another. An "occupational hazard" of being a middle is that middles tend to become alienated from one another because they are often placed in competition with one another (for example, department heads, heads of business units). Middles who can see this system process and can overcome it by integrating as a team become a great source of power. Learning to form alliances is a potent form of self-development.

You might be asking at this point, what do these strategies and tactics have to do with careers? Surely these are ways to develop the organization, not individuals. Not so: since relationships and work challenges are so central to the development process, these practical ideas for self-development for people in middle positions (a space where most of us live most of the time) provide rich resources for continuous learning. Furthermore, as we know, continuous learning is the "coin of the realm" in the new career environment. Also, for the career professional, these strategies and tactics can be useful bases of career coaching in work with clients, both individuals and organization.

Now that we have considered some of the practical implications of this new relationship between employer and employee, let us consider some important issues and challenges that future research might help us understand.

What the Career Practitioner Needs from Career Research

A major implication of these ideas for research is that the study of careers has to get messier to help us understand current career realities. Like the old careers they studied, the neat, orderly studies predicting career outcomes, studies of career progression, and the like have become irrelevant in the shifting ground of today's organizations. The nature of the research will have to reflect the nature of its subject: rapidly changing, fast learning, and complex.

What this means is that we will need more short-term longitudinal studies that capture the complex processes of career learning. Knowing that work challenge and relationships are key inputs to learning, we need to study exactly how people learn from work experience. Is learning how to learn a characteristic of the individual that is relatively fixed, or can it be developed? If people can learn how to learn, learn to be adaptable and to be comfortable with change, what experiences and programs can promote this "meta-learning"? If this is a fairly stable personal characteristic, how can we best assess it?

If learning how to learn cannot be developed, what are the ways in which people who are low in this ability can be successful? A Center for Creative Learning–type study of low-adaptability people who have succeeded and those who have not would be fascinating. Is it possible to select types of work or industries or organizations where change is less rapid and in which highly developed, long-used skills are at a premium?

A key element in learning from experience that needs more research is the process of reflection on experience. It appears that reflection is a luxury in a fast-paced environment, and people who are most adaptive and quick in their responses may be disinclined to engage in reflection. But people who are able to learn from experience do have ways to look at themselves, to seek feedback from others, and to consciously plan personal change (see Chapter Ten, this volume; McCall, Lombardo, and Morrison, 1988). How does this sort of self-reflection occur? How might it be promoted by an organization?

A natural opportunity in which to study these career learning processes is during a work transition. When a person is leaving one position and moving to something else, known or unknown, this is often a period of great self- and task exploration. A transition represents a microcosm of larger career dynamics. The great "wealth" of corporate changes occurring today offers us an equally rich set of research opportunities.

One of the complications about doing this kind of research, however, is that when individuals and organizations are undergoing such fundamental change, participating in a research study is not generally a high-priority activity. As a result, it has to be clear to the organizations and individuals involved that the research will add value for them. In the more stable past, people often participated in research to contribute to knowledge or for the intrinsic interest of being part of a research study. By now, many people have been "surveyed to death" (as we have often heard), and contributing to knowledge is seen as far less critical than spending that time contributing to one's own survival. Thus the burden is on us as researchers to be customer focused in our research. This means collaborative planning with participants, using data-collection methods that will provide useful data to the participants as well as to the researchers, and providing useful "products" of the research to participants as well as to the academic community. Such an approach should be especially feasible in an area such as careers because the issue is so important to so many people today.

Conclusion

Because careers have changed, so too must the role of the career professional. Just as employees have become more self-directed and empowered in their work, so too are they becoming more autonomous as agents of their own career development. With this change, the role of the career professional shifts to that of a coach, enabler, and broker. For those practitioners in organizational settings, this shift means being a more active interventionist, creating the conditions favorable to development.

In this chapter we have detailed the specific implications of these changes in the role of the career professional. We are not saying these ideas represent accurately the *present* role of the career practitioner, however. But this is the direction in which the role must necessarily move in the years ahead.

References

Bartlett, C., & Ghoshal, S. (1994, November-December). Changing the role of top management: Beyond strategy to purpose. *Harvard Business Review,* 79–88.

Boyce, J. N. (1995, August 9). Leaps of faith: More people join clergy after first pursuing a career in business. *Wall Street Journal,* p. B1.

Evans, P.A.L., & Bartolome, F. (1980). *Must success cost so much?* New York: Basic Books.

Hakim, C. (1994). *We are all self-employed.* San Francisco: Berrett-Koehler.

Hall, D. T. (1993). Managing yourself: Building a career. In A. R. Cohen (Ed.), *The portable MBA in management* (pp. 190–206). New York: Wiley.

Hall, D. T., & Moss, J. E. (1995). *The new psychological career contract.* Executive Development Roundtable, School of Management, Boston University.

Hall, D. T., & Schneider, B. (1973). *Organizational climates and careers: The work lives of priests*. New York: Academic Press.

Hall, D. T., Schneider, B., & Nygren, H. T. (1970). Personal factors in organizational identification. *Administrative Science Quarterly, 17*, 176–190.

Harmon, W., & Hormann, J. (1990). *Creative work*. Indianapolis: Knowledge Systems.

McCall, M. W., Jr., Lombardo, M. M., & Morrison, A. M. (1988). *The lessons of experience: How successful executives develop on the job*. Lexington, MA: Lexington Books.

Mirvis, P. H., & Hall, D. T. (1994). Psychological success and the boundaryless career. *Journal of Organizational Behavior, 15*, 365–380.

Oshry, B. (1992). *Converting middle powerlessness to middle power: A systems approach*. Boston: Power & Systems Training.

Oshry, B. (1995). *Seeing systems: Unlocking the mysteries of organization life*. San Francisco: Berrett-Koehler.

Schneider, B., & Hall, D. T. (1972). Toward specifying the concept of work climate: A study of Roman Catholic diocesan priests. *Journal of Applied Psychology, 56*, 447–455.

Witchel, A. (1994, December 14). By way of Canarsie, one large hot cup of business strategy. *New York Times*, p. C1, C8.

Long Live the Career!

Douglas T. Hall

Cal Ripken, Jr., who broke Lou Gehrig's consecutive-game streak of 2,130, loves baseball. "It's been my whole life, my dad's whole life." Ripken played shortstop alongside his brother, Billy, for five and a half years and wore the same Baltimore Orioles uniform as his father, Cal, Sr., who coached and managed the team.

But ironically, even though Ripken cherished the times in the dugout with his dad, living with a baseball dad also often meant life at home without him. "It wasn't my dad who took me to my games [when I was a kid]. It wasn't my dad who practiced with me out back. It wasn't my dad who put his arm around me when I had a bad day. The little pat on the back when it did come was all my mom."

So now a midlife Ripken is faced with a career dilemma: what to do when he stops playing—become a coach and manager or do something that would keep him closer to home. "As a son, I saw baseball take my father away a lot. . . . So I'd like to figure out a way, if possible, that I'd be able to have dinner at home at five o'clock every night. I don't know if I can do that, being a manager or whatever else. . . . The other side says you spent all this time developing your knowledge of baseball, your expertise, and you want to be able to apply that someplace. I don't know the answers to those things right now" (Smith, 1995, p. 33).

In this volume, we have attempted to provide an array of concepts and resources that would help equip a career professional to assist someone like Cal Ripken in making a good decision about finding and pursuing his own path with a heart. It is clear that he is entering a new learning cycle in his career, and he is wrestling with issues of identity and adaptability. He may not have the answers yet, but he is asking himself good questions.

We hope that now you have a deeper understanding of career and life issues such as Ripken's and of the new ways you might provide help. Although finances are tight everywhere, there has never been a greater range of resources available to individuals to help them map out their own career futures—and many of these resources are relational, as the preceding chapters have attempted to show.

Reflections

In Part One, we saw just how fundamentally the career landscape has changed. We are now beyond the point of asking what the new contract is. As Phil Mirvis and I discussed in Chapter One, and Barbara Altman and Jim Post showed in Chapter Two, it is certainly clear to managers and to many lower-level employees what the new deal is—and it looks protean. As we said at the end of Part One, it is now the responsibility of the individual to be a continuous learner and to adapt quickly as well as to change identities over the course of the career.

The good news in all of this turbulence is that once a person learns to be adaptable and protean, to expect the unexpected, he or she is less likely to be traumatized by sudden change and in a sense has made friends with change.

A nagging question in all of this flexibility is, to what can the individual become committed? Is there anything that is dependable or stable? This is a problem for individuals looking for meaning and purpose as well as for organizations that are trying to rebuild a committed workforce in the wake of restructuring. For Cal Ripken, his anchors appear to be family and baseball, which would seem to provide a pretty solid foundation.

In Part Two, we see some answers developing to this question. One thing that is dependable is the incredible capacity of human beings for growth and development. Another is the power that one human being can have in helping others go through that growth process. In fact, the relational model of development, as described by Joyce Fletcher in Chapter Four, informs us of a new source of growth that we did not see in our texts on development before the mid 1980s. Our main challenge in tapping this relational source of growth is to recognize it when it occurs, value it, and of course stop "disappearing" it. A creative career professional should be able to identify countless sources of relational help for a person such as Ripken, with the rich network that he has developed.

We also need to be more explicit about how relational influences operate in work and organizational settings. In Chapter Five, Kathy Kram lays that out for us very clearly; her model of how the process works, along with her diagnostic questions for the career practitioner, provide us with some powerful tools.

Chapter Six by Bill Kahn and Chapter Seven by Vicky Parker describe more specifically how individuals can help one another. Kahn looks at secure base relationships and shows how they provide the necessary holding environment for growth. But he ends with a warning: when we need them most, we are often too overwhelmed and anxious to reach out and create meaningful attachments. Career practitioners need to find forums to bring people together for development in today's stressful work environments.

One group that may not have easy access to relational sources of development is single adults without dependent children, as described by Mary Young in Chapter Eight. This group is at risk of being exploited at work because co-workers often see them as having more flexibility in their personal lives. Thus they may be asked to put in overtime, to work on holidays, or to take a travel assignment that coupled employees or parents find difficult to do. Also, the potential for overinvolvement in work can deprive SAWDCs of what Young calls the "nonwork aha!"—the wake-up call to development, often provided by some experience involving one's children or spouse. The career practitioner can be helpful by creating conditions for dialogue and other kinds of encounters between SAWDCs and other people that involve self-reflection and discussion of work-life issues, with a healthy dose of questioning the value of such high involvement in work.

In Part Three, we moved to an examination of specific vehicles for promoting development. Meryl Louis (Chapter Nine) and Kent Seibert (Chapter Ten) described the ways growth is promoted by reflection processes and by safe havens in which they can occur. As Seibert has found, people engage in reflection far more than we might imagine in this busy world, and there are specific steps we can take to be more effective in our learning from reflection. (It sounds as if Ripken is already using reflection to some extent.) In addition to individual reflection, we can reflect in dialogue with other people, especially people whom we see as different in some way. Barbara Walker (Chapter Eleven) tells us how we can adapt the skills used in learning about diversity to the more general skills needed for career learning and personal development.

There are special challenges of development for older workers, many of which exist only in the minds of younger people. In such cases, relational influences may tend to work *against* development. Although many of the forms of flexibility described in other chapters could fit the needs of the older worker perfectly, many employers are reluctant to hire people at this stage in their careers. Phil Mirvis and I review some of these issues and consider some rather bleak possibilities, such as two classes of workers, those with futures, benefits, and learning opportunities and those without. (Guess where many older workers are.) As this demographic group continues to swell, there is much opportunity here for good development work by the creative career practitioner.

In Chapter Thirteen, Jane and Bill Hodgetts describe in detail how support groups specifically designed to be away from the action of everyday work life can serve as developmental sanctuaries—and what pitfalls to look out for. Many of the concepts of relational learning are integrated and applied here. Again, what is striking is how practical—timewise and moneywise—these groups are and how much lasting benefit results from these short meetings. Look for these developmental sanctuaries to grow as people learn their value for self-development. (In fact, for professional athletes such as Ripken, group-based career self-assessment and planning workshops are already being used.)

What the work of the Hodgetts shows is how fundamentally the work of the career development practitioner has evolved since my last book on careers (Hall and Associates, 1986). That brings us to Chapter Fourteen, which applies the ideas in this book to offer guidelines for the new role of the career professional. Not only has the role changed but we also see many more varieties of career practitioner in different settings; it is unlikely that any one person would do all of the things that this chapter recommends. If corporate restructuring has done nothing else, it has greatly enhanced career opportunities for career development professionals.

The Protean Career: The New Relational Contract

An ongoing theme from chapter to chapter has been the concept of "relational," so let us reflect a bit on what that means and how it connects to the new career contract.

The Spirit of the Relational Force

In this book, we have been viewing the career in the context of the person's total life (a holistic approach), with the focus on helping individuals take charge of their careers. To understand development, we can look at the role of other people and work activities. For example, as Bill Kahn and Vicky Parker have suggested earlier, the family can be a good holding environment for growth as can family-like relationships, such as with mentors and old friends.

Consider a case in point: golfer Tom Weiskopf in relation to his wife and his senior colleague, Jack Nicklaus, and their role in his victory in the 1995 U.S. Senior Open golf tournament. Weiskopf described 1995 as a stressful year for him, with his wife's battle with breast cancer and a difficult stretch on golf's pro tour. He declared that the 1995 U.S. Senior Open was dedicated to his wife. In the concluding round, he wore a small pink ribbon, symbolic of a season-long fund-raising project for breast cancer research sponsored by players on the senior tour. "I could see it occasionally, in my shadow, or I'd touch it," he said of the ribbon. "I'm a sentimental guy. It was just a reminder that this one was for her" ("Weiskopf Wins First Major Title," 1995, p. 31). Weiskopf, who had never won a U.S. major tournament, played inspired golf, winning the tournament by four shots.

Weiskopf was also influenced by his relationship with his friend Jack Nicklaus, whom he has always looked up to but rarely beaten. Nicklaus observed, "His talent has been enormous all his life. And sometimes he just hasn't been able to get there, but today he played fantastic. I've been a shot better than Tom in a lot of golf tournaments. This week he was four shots better than me, and I think that's wonderful for Tom." Weiskopf responded, "That means a lot, because you don't beat that guy very often" (p. 31).

Weiskopf described the special way he was playing on that final day: "I actually could feel the spin on the ball coming off of the club head. I was hitting it so crisp, I actually had that sensation. Everything was in slow-motion. Maybe the golf gods have a way of allowing some people to have this feeling. Really, it's just tremendous" (p. 31).

From Transactional to Deeper Relational Contracts

One lesson of Tom Weiskopf's psychological success is that people can be deeply affected by influences beyond the boundaries of the career work. To understand the full meaning of a person's career experience (especially peak experiences such as Weiskopf's inspired play in the Open), we need to widen our lens, to see the whole person as part of a family, part of a community of friends and colleagues. We do not define *relational* merely as *interpersonal* or as *transactional* but also as *interactive with the person's entire social environment.*

In the spirit of the Cal Ripken and Tom Weiskopf examples, I would like to revisit the issue of the nature of the new psychological contract at work. As we said in Part One, the traditional or older model was called *relational* by MacNeill (1980). After going through the writings in this volume on relational development theory, it appears that MacNeil's use of the term was rather narrow, describing the one-to-one link between person and organization. The objective at that time was to have a long-term, secure relationship with the organization.

Although the trend in most organizations has been described in the early 1990s as a move from a relational to a transactional psychological contract, we question whether the transactional model is valid for the future. We see employees and employers now going beyond this transactional connection, wanting more than merely a series of negotiated exchanges as well as wanting more integration between work and home life. As the chapters in this book have shown, people now need meaning, purpose, and connection (at work and in private life) for career development—and they need psychologically satisfying work as well. Also, organizations need employees' full minds and hearts, creativity and commitment, to meet the tough demands of the competitive market. The more whole and integrated people can be at work and in their personal lives, the more psychological success they will experience.

Accordingly, we have argued that the new protean career is moving back to a deeper form of a relational contract. This new contract is more with oneself, in connection to other people, and with one's work, and less with the organization. We see the protean career as defining a new relational contract because it is based on the self in relation to these other entities. Also, while the time horizon may be shorter (not lifelong employment), it entails an expanding depth of present experience, and it is rooted in a sense of mutual commitment. Even though all parties recognize that there are no long-term guarantees (of either employment or retention), at the same time there is a sense of hope that the relationship might turn out to be a long-lived one. But if it does last many years, it is different from the old contract in that it is a mature adult-to-adult connection, not a parent-child, security-based bond.

Accordingly, many boundaries are shifting: temporal boundaries, psychological boundaries, role boundaries, and physical boundaries. A person's work and career may span several boundaries as well as several organizations. As Kathy Kram says in Chapter Five, we are looking more at individually based careers than at organizationally based careers. This idea is expanded in Cliff Hakim's popular book, *We Are All Self-Employed* (1994). Whether Cliff intends this or not, we can read *self* in two ways: (1) we work for ourselves; (2) our work includes working on the self and there is much of the self in our work.

In this vein, in the authors' early discussions we wondered whether the subtitle of this book should be "Taking Charge of Your Career." However, as we talked, we realized that the best way to empower employees in pursuing their career work is through the support of developmental relationships—hence the subtitle, "A Relational Approach to Careers."

The Dark Side of the Protean Career

In our meetings, Phil Mirvis reminded his fellow authors about the "dark side" issues related to contemporary careers. Many people are in dead-end, no-hope jobs. Many people lack the skills and experience to get—or hold—jobs. We talked much of the sausage plant worker; what do we have to say to her or him? We need to keep that in mind. Many people are scared. Many have given up.

Phil and I hear a lot of questions and concerns about this "dark side" when we present our research on older workers to different groups working on expanding employment opportunities for older workers. There are many strong and negative reactions when we present our rosy view of psychological success and protean careers for older, postretirement workers who could pursue second careers. We have heard of older people eating dog food, older people without health care; these people are working for survival, not psychological success.

How can we career professionals help people who may be just a few years older than we are? With the baby boomers now solidly in midlife (turning fifty) and moving quickly toward "older worker" status (fifty-five), how will *we* provide for ourselves?

What does all this imply for the dual role that a career professional plays, serving the organization and helping the individual with career issues? The work of Kathy Kram and Bill Kahn suggests that the new role of human resources regarding careers and mentoring is not just to help the new person assimilate in the organization but also to help bring the whole person to work.

But how exactly do you help people be whole at work (and at home)? How do people have careers when they are barely staying afloat in white water? How do you help them make sense of work when the world seems to have gone awry?

The Answer

We think the answer is in the white water. The current chaos provides the two prime ingredients for career growth: challenging work and relationships. Other people and seemingly impossible tasks provide rich ground for learning. Furthermore, this learning must take place in the context of work (or an organization) to whose overall purpose the individual can commit her- or himself with pride.

Kent Seibert found in his research that people do not learn from experience alone; they learn from the *meaning* they find in experience. Thus we return to relational influences: meaning is created through dialogue with other people.

In these chapters, we have shown ways that relational growth can be fostered at work. As career professionals, we must use these resources to help individuals pursue their own diverse callings. We do, in fact, know how to help workers and their employers in this strange new world. Once we help people and organizations clarify their direction and purpose, life seems less strange—and more meaningful.

In the first century A.D., the great Jewish teacher Hillel the Elder said, "If I am not for myself, who will be for me? If I am only for myself, who am I? If not now, when?"

References

Hakim, C. (1994). *We are all self-employed.* San Francisco: Berrett-Koehler.

Hall, D. T., & Associates. (1986). *Career development in organizations.* San Francisco: Jossey-Bass.

MacNeill, I. R. (1980). *The new social contract.* New Haven, CT: Yale University Press.

Smith, C. (1995, September 4). On baseball: Ripken learned a lot from everyday people. *New York Times,* p. 33.

Weiskopf wins first major title in U.S. (1995, July 3). *New York Times,* p. 31.

Name Index

Subject Index